Enjoy!

Arne Waldstein

WATER RUNS DOWNHILL

A Journey Through A Time Gone By

by

Arne Waldstein

Cover photo by Fredric Waldstein

Publisher: Arne Waldstein, 1009 Ridgewood Blvd., Waverly, IA 50677 • 319-483-1873

E-mail: AFMEWALD@AOL.com

Printed by:

McMillen Publishing.

A Sigler Company

ISBN: 1-888223-43-X

www.mcmillenbooks.com

All the opinions expressed herein are solely those of the author or subjects and do not necessarily reflect those of McMillen Publishing.

Waldstein, Arne, 1925–
    Water Runs Downhill: A Journey Through Time Gone By/
    by Arne Waldstein
    [Iowa] printed by McMillen Publishing, 2003
    247 p.: ill; 23m
    1. Farmlife - Iowa   2. Depression, 1929 - Iowa   3. Tractors
    4. Iowa - Farm Life   5. Buena Vista County (Iowa) - Biography

DEDICATION

This book is dedicated to my immigrant parents and their descendants. In a broader sense, it is dedicated to all immigrants who saw hope and believed in the opportunities of this land called America and to all their descendants who learned to cherish, value, honor, and defend those freedoms that have made these United States of America a refuge for freedom-yearning people from even the remotest parts of the globe.

About the Book's Title

The title, "Water Runs Downhill", originates from a commonplace happening told in Chapter Two of the book. However there are other connotations that the title implies:

In making it through the great Depression, farm families had to "go with the flow." This meant accepting the hard times as a circumstance beyond their control but making the best of it.

It also personifies another trait usually found in a farmer, a lot of "common sense." Of course water runs downhill!

ACKNOWLEDGEMENTS

I'm indebted to my parents and siblings who indelibly stamped my growing-up experiences. I owe special thanks to my sister and only surviving sibling, Mrs. Lois Hubley, for her confidence in me and her encouraging me to write this book. As the stories in this book are largely drawn from memory, it was satisfying when Lois and my niece, Donna Graham Baker, were pleased with the genuineness of the stories. Other family members, Cindy Graham Stewart and nephew, James Hubley, (both college teachers) didn't show mercy in reading and editing my early drafts! Thanks to son, Arne Paul Waldstein, for timely suggestions about style, and to daughter, Elizabeth Hart, and sons, Fredric and Mark, who all encouraged me to bring my experiences "to life."

Many conversations with journalists and knowledgeable friends have been most helpful in keeping me focused on the work. I thank them, but it is not possible to list them all here individually.

Thanks to John Anderson, former publisher and editor of the Storm Lake *Pilot Tribune* newspaper, who gave me helpful guidance for submitting public issue articles as well as reports on Iowa Senate activities. Dana Larson, the current and capable editor of the *Pilot Tribune* demonstrated his dictum that "Writers have to write" by challenging me to write a monthly "Philosophies" column for his editorial pages for five years. Barb Doyen of Newell, Iowa, literary guru, gave me candid advice and encouragement to write the book.

Thanks to Loren Kruse, a friend and editor of *Successful Farming* magazine for his urging, early on, that the history of the Great Depression era should be told and preserved.

Thanks to Suzette Qualey, Iowa Department of Agriculture statistician, for helping to uncover census data that reported farm production during the early part of the twentieth century.

Special thanks to my niece, Ulla Ekener, Karlstad, Sweden, for invaluable information about my mother's youth and family. Thanks, also, to my great-nephew, Claes Waldstein (Lil Edet, Sweden), for information about my dad's family.

While most photos are from our family albums, friends and others have been helpful in providing a few period photos. Where appropriate, we have cited credits.

Thanks to Carl Dillon, retired English teacher, for his diligence in copyediting the manuscript draft before it went to the publisher's. To Robert Gremmels, Professor Emeritus of Journalism, Wartburg College, for his constructive critique and comments.

Carole Lackey provided computer expertise and formatting knowledge. Her urging helped to keep the project moving.

Finally, I must thank and acknowledge my wife, Marianne, for her critique of my story drafts and continued support of my bringing the manuscript to completion. She also kept the coffee pot on!

TABLE OF CONTENTS

Forward

Preface

Part One
The Family Farm: The Farm Family

Poem: Settler and Prairie

Part Two
Plants: The Wealth of Man Starts with Food Produced from the Soil

Poem: Morning on the Farm

Part Three
Animals Empower Man: Draft for Heavy Loads—Food for Energy

Part Four
The Mechanization of Farming

Poem: Oiling the Windmill

Part Five
The Aftermath: Heirs of the Great Depression Inherit a War

Part Six
Epilogue

Why write it? This book is written to share and preserve the history of a unique place and time in American agriculture. While reflective of all rural America, it focuses on the western Corn Belt and converges on a family farm in northwest Iowa where I was born (1925) and raised. The time encompasses the two most cataclysmic events of the twentieth century: the Great Depression (1930–1940), and on its heels World War II (1941–1945). The first steeled farm people to face hardship, and the second manifested what a recent author called America's "Greatest Generation."

Why now? Writing it now, at the end of one millennium and the beginning of another, is motivated by another reason. When my generation of farm boys, born in the decade of the 1920s, is gone there will be no one left who experienced it, to tell the story.

This story is about growing up, family life, working, playing, entertainment, and other family undertakings. Despite the two overwhelming historical events, the real stories are about the daily lives of individuals: what we did, the personal involvement in growing crops and raising livestock, and how that shaped our lives. These stories bring out the joys of farm family life and some of the frustrations, the humor—even hilarity—sadness, tragedy, the profitable endeavors, and some severe setbacks.

Growing up on a family farm in the western Corn Belt from 1925 to 1940, and participating in the ensuing consequences of World War II was a unique American experience.

I hope you will enjoy a slice of that time.

Arne Waldstein

Figure 0.1: From the late 1800s through the 1920s, thousands of grain elevators such as this one became landmarks at railheads when railroad tracks snaked their way west across the Corn Belt and out over the Great Plains wheat lands.

One of my early memories was hearing farmers say, "You better know the lay of the land." It had many connotations beyond its obvious meaning. It had to do with knowing who you were and where you came from. It had something to do with history and a lot to do with common sense as a way to cope with uncertain but inevitable change.

Western Corn Belt agriculture was getting underway by the middle of the nineteenth century, but didn't really set course until after the Civil War. By then railroad tracks were networking through most Midwestern states. Lumber yards, farm supply stores, grain elevators, and livestock slaughterhouses soon appeared at outlying railheads. These created dependable markets for farmers. By the decade of the 1870s, hay and small grain acreage was giving way to the more hardy and profitable row crop: corn.

From the earliest settlers through the 1920s, farming was powered almost entirely by animal power: some oxen at first, then predominantly horses, a few mules and—not the least—brute human strength. This began to change during the 1920s when farmers shifted to improved "standard tread" farm tractors for plowing and heavier tillage operations. Tractors provided belt power to run grain threshers, corn shellers, grinders, and other basic processing machines.

In the latter 1920s, unwieldy row-crop "tricycle" tractors came on the market to accommodate corn and other "row crop" cultivation. When the worst of the devastating Great Depression hit in 1931–32, farmers couldn't buy new tractors or even gasoline for the ones they already had!

As the Depression dragged through the 1930s, farmers still couldn't afford to buy the more improved row crop tractors, even at moderate prices. This extended the time in which farmers had to rely on horses as the main power source. By 1934, President Roosevelt's Agricultural Adjustment Act (AAA or "triple A") and other government programs began to improve grain prices and put money in farmer's pockets. The farmers began buying newer "general purpose" tractors that were geared toward row crop production and for both heavier tillage and lighter cultivation.

The change from horses to tractors was hastened by an outbreak of sleeping sickness (equine encephalitis) across the Midwest in 1936, which killed and disabled many farmers' best draft horses. The disease disabled one of our best geldings.

This rapid mechanization was the most important, even revolutionary, transition period in U.S. farming:

- Horsepower to tractor power
- Kerosene lamps to electricity
- Muscular biceps to hydraulic cylinders
- Ineffective grease cups to pressure-powered grease guns
- Steel-lugged wheels to rubber tires
- Open pollinated corn to hybrids

These advances, in only six or seven years (1935–1941), came when we were under siege of the Great Depression!

The momentum for mechanical power was irreversible by the beginning of World War II, caused in part by the military drain on farm labor and the push to produce "food for peace" as a part of the war effort. With more powerful and adaptable tractors, farm size began to increase and there has been no turning back—to this day. Farm size in Iowa averaged 150 acres in 1935 and grew to 170 by 1950.

Visible during this period is "the beginning of the end" of the family farm era as it had dominated the farming landscape for a century, from 1870 to 1970. At that time, large-scale commercial farms began to appear. As an agriculturist, I witnessed and—without realizing it—participated in the demise of the "family farm" as we knew it then. Now, at the end of the twentieth century, it is gone.

As the post-war recovery years affected the lives of these same Great Depression farm kids, that experience, too, is told in this book's epilogue.

Those times, both exciting and tragic, are gone but the deeply rooted nostalgia remains.

From 1995 to 1999, I wrote a monthly column, "Philosophies," for our local daily newspaper, the *Pilot Tribune* (Storm Lake, Iowa). A few of those published articles that relate directly to the subject matter are included and noted in this book.

Part
One

The Family Farm: The Farm Family

Settler and Prairie

Arne Waldstein

Came homesteaders with impatient ardor
Pursuing virgin bounty
Strong, weak, rich, rabble
To find fortune or failure

Fertile earth offered up her treasure
As a bride's innocence to please
Man unwittingly ravaged his espoused
Prostituting God's given measure

In hope and trust
They met in mutual embrace
Sought refuge, and wealth
To flourish from her breast

Prairie wedding veil, blackened
Redressed in mourning pall
No rosary for her wake
No sacred burial ground

Forgive Man, God, for his incest
With vigorous passion, strove his caress
Her beauty scarred
Her mantle laid to rest

Settler, his dominion proclaimed
Erringly subdued his mistress
Whose purity
Can never be reclaimed.

The "Settler and Prairie" poem, written at the Centennial (1973) celebration of Storm Lake, Iowa, reveals the original stage and reflects the emotions that evolved in the earliest pioneer days. Storm Lake, its beginning and history, typifies farm communities throughout the western Corn Belt.

CHAPTER 1
IMMIGRANTS: FROM SWEDEN TO IOWA

My parents were born and raised in Sweden. They came to America in the early 1900s. Their immigration, finding a new home, learning a new language, securing a new occupation and raising a family was repeated thousands of times across this new land. Their lives, hardships and rewards were a part of the gigantic fabric portraying the fertile Midwest.

Dad and Mom (Arthur and Anna Waldstein) never told their children very much about their young lives, courtship or personal experiences. The Americanization process continually erased interest or concern about their Swedish upbringing. Being the youngest of eight kids left little meaningful conversation or documentation for me. Later in life I came to regret not knowing or inquiring about their lives.

My mother's family lived in the southern seashore city of Trelleborg and was influenced by shipping and the seafaring life. Her two brothers "went to sea." Anna (later my mother) apparently completed required public education. As was customary, she hired out for domestic work as a young teenager and worked some years in Malmo, twenty-five miles up the west coast from Trelleborg. My mother and Dad carried on a courtship prior to Arthur's immigration to America in November 1908. Subsequent events and correspondence resulted in Anna and their son Nels following Arthur to Marcus, Iowa, U.S.A., in June of 1910, where Anna and Arthur were married. Mom spoke of unease because the ship was so crowded, but the immigrants soon fell into informal support groups. After the scramble of Ellis Island and New York City, she was grateful to get on the train for the journey to Iowa. On the train, a bond of camaraderie soon developed among the "new Americans."

Mother's brother, Uncle Charley, spent his life as a merchant seaman and after retirement lived in Rio Grande, on the southern tip of New Jersey. In 1924, a year before I was born, he traveled to Iowa to visit the Waldstein family on the farm. Uncle Charley was the only relative we ever knew, until fifty years later. Then, through the efforts of Swedish relatives, we discovered paternal great nephews in 1974, and maternal relatives in 1978.

My Dad was raised in Halmstad on the west coast of Sweden. He completed ten years of schooling and worked for a fish merchant. Arthur's mother's family name was Pehrsdotter, and it appears he did not know his father. In their youth, Arthur and his brother Bror carried the name Persson. It is not clear how or when they took the name Waldstein. The name change is most likely connected to their obligatory year's service in the Swedish military when, at conscription, name changing was common. When telling about it, Dad seemed to take pride in his service with the Swedish cavalry.

America Beckons

Because of the grandiose opportunities in America, and probably with some urging by his good friends and later shipmates John Bartling and Dan Zackau, my Dad departed Sweden with them and arrived in New York on November 28, 1908. I remember Dad telling of his emotion when the Statue of Liberty came into sight, then

Figure 1.1 and 1.2: Mom and Dad as young adults in Sweden. (circa 1907)

of his apprehension about immigrating through Ellis Island. What a contrast the hustle and bustle of New York City was to his home. Because Bartling was already settled near Marcus, Iowa, Dad went there. His first job was to help area farmers complete corn harvest by handpicking. From his later comments, I learned Dad wasn't enthralled with corn picking as a way of realizing American riches!

Benefited by his recent military service in Sweden, Dad was hired as the Marcus night marshal in January 1909, a job he held for about a year and a half. I remember Dad telling us kids, when I was about five, that part of his job was to check that all stores were securely locked. He occasionally had to keep late-night rowdies in line also.

Probably relating to his storekeeper experience in Sweden, Dad became a drayman (freight hauler) in Marcus. All freight and merchandise were transported in by the Illinois Central Railroad that ran between Chicago and Sioux City, Iowa. As drayman, Dad hauled all the freight from the depot to local establishments, including store merchants, repair shops, and private homes. His business required a good team of draft horses and a heavily built freight wagon. Dad told of hauling a two-ton steam boiler from the depot to the new Holy Name Catholic Church under construction in Marcus. When pulling off the graveled street and onto the church lawn, his wagon sunk a foot into the soft ground. Though straining vigorously, his team couldn't budge the wagon any further. The boiler was skidded off the freight wagon and then rolled on logs to the church. There was plenty of dray work and ample opportunity to build a business, at which Dad was apparently quite successful.

Figure 1.3: Now prospering in America, the family takes a drive in their Model T Ford touring car. (circa 1918)

Becoming A Farmer

During Dad's three years as drayman, a German landowner named Frank Ruppert noted his ambition and offered to rent him a 320-acre farm just northeast of Marcus, although Dad knew very little about farming. My parents, like many immigrants in America, had to learn a new trade—whatever opportunity became available. By this time my parents had two additional children: Astrid and Kenneth. Ironically, because of his Swedish accent, Dad never could pronounce his own son's name the "American" way. He was always "Kennet." In 1912, my parents launched their farming career, which they pursued until their deaths: Mom in the spring of 1950, and Dad a year later in 1951.

After farming only six years, four near Marcus and two near Gaza in O'Brien County (where daughter Lois and son Howard were born), my parents realized the "American dream" and bought a 240-acre farm northwest of Rembrandt in Buena Vista County, Iowa. Ominously, the World War I economic boom had driven land prices to new highs. They paid $385 per acre, a near high at that time. Neighbors assured him he had made a good buy!

Moving the family thirty miles from Gaza to Rembrandt epitomized the physical hurdles that early American families took in stride. Household goods, machinery, and livestock were moved from Gaza to Linn Grove by railroad. Then, livestock was driven across country six miles to the new farm. Teams and wagons hauled all other possessions.

Things were going well. The farm proved to have good soil and the farmstead had a well built, two-story house and a good set of outbuildings. My parents joined the Little Sioux Valley Lutheran Church, only a quarter-mile east of the farm, where they were lifelong members. Two more children were born on the Rembrandt farm: daughter Dorothy on May 26, 1921, and son Art on December 31, 1922. At a few weeks of age, baby Art's severed umbilical cord (navel) had not healed well and became festered with infection. Dr. Berger, the family doctor from Linn Grove, was asked to stop and check the situation. They laid Art on the dining room table, a makeshift operating table, where Dr. Berger lanced the fester, stitched it closed, and swabbed it with iodine. In a couple of weeks Art was fine. Another successful—and sometimes impromptu—procedure by a country doctor.

Crash: Years Of Struggle

Compared to the Great Depression of the 1930s, little has been written or noted about the sharp economic crash in 1921 and 1922 following WWI. The severity of the Depression hit farmers hardest because of a sharp drop in grain and livestock prices. Manufacturers, busy filling the wartime backlog of orders for autos, machinery, and other material, never felt the Depression. As a result, my folks' rapid climb to wealth came crashing down around their heads. They couldn't meet the mortgage payments and lost their farm!

In the spring of 1923 they moved five miles west to a 240-acre farm, rented from the L.C. Christianson Estate, where they lived for the next seventeen years. I was born there on January 17, 1925, the youngest of their thriving "brood" of eight.

All through the Roaring Twenties our family struggled to get out of the financial hole. The farm economy improved but my folks had eight kids to raise and debts to pay. As if they were not challenged enough, the stock market crashed in October 1929; thus beginning the ten-year-long Great Depression. It was nationwide, even worldwide, but few were more devastated than American farmers. I remember glancing uneasily through the large bank window and seeing my Dad in a long discussion with bank President H.T. "Pinkie" Haroldson. They were probably talking about Dad's ability to make payment on a bank loan coming due. Years later, I heard these sessions referred to as the "sweat box." Some economic recovery became apparent by the late 1930s, but it took the WWII economic surge to really end the Great Depression.

Unexpectedly the Family Grows

Life's sometimes peculiar way of compounding hardship occurred, when my oldest brother Nels got married and lost his wife Lurline, at the birth of a second daughter in January 1932. There were no welfare programs, just the County Poor Farm and a few orphanages. As Nels was not able to care for the girls they had no place to go.

Despite struggling to raise their own eight children, my parents—especially Mom—would have it no other way but to take the two girls in, newborn Maxine (Mickey) and two-year-old Donna Jean. To take them in was no small commitment because it was during the very depths of the Great Depression. It was one of the few times I saw conflict and disagreement between my parents. Dad, scared of hanging on financially, feared taking on more responsibility. The girls were fully accepted as "sisters" by us, their aunts and uncles. Only five years older than Donna Jean, I called her my sister until an older sibling advised me, "No, they are really your nieces." We encouraged Donna to pronounce her younger sister's name: "Say Maxine plainer." For several days she walked about calling to "Maxine Plainer"! But then she called a pencil a "goalie-go" and me "Wa Wa," plus a few other odd expressions. The girls added a lot to our family life, had a good upbringing, and came to be helpful and appreciated by my parents in their older years.

Figure 1.4: Because their mother died in childbirth, January 1932, nieces Donna Jean, age two and Maxine, a newborn, joined our family. (circa 1934)

To say times were tough during the Great Depression is an understatement. They were devastating. Hundreds of farmers lost land purchased in the Roaring Twenties. They were forced off the farm and into one of Roosevelt's many New Deal economic recovery programs. One was the Works Progress Administration (WPA)—a program to provide work for the head of the family, usually repairing or rebuilding public property such as roads, buildings, and parks. The Civilian Conservation Corps (CCC) enrolled hundreds of unemployed young men, many from farms, for whom no jobs existed. In a somewhat military lifestyle, living in tent camps, they worked on conservation projects, controlling soil erosion, grading waterways, building dams to heal gullies, and planting wildlife habitat and shelterbelts to contain the dust bowl. Following the mid 1930s, when the drought magnified the dust bowl in the western Great Plains, these projects enjoyed public support. Though unintended, the CCC camps provided some regimental experience to many young men who where conscripted into the WWII military within a half-dozen years.

Interestingly, we never complained about our lot in life. Who was there to complain to? Who was better off than we were? In the Depression years, we were all in the same boat. We had no choice but to dig in and make the best of what we had. Each family member did his or her part to save on expenses and each pitched in to produce as much as possible from the family farm.

An Afterthought

My folks, like most immigrants, made a special effort to speak, read, and write in English, the language of their adopted country. They did not ask for nor receive any special help from the local schools. They were self-taught.

After years of listening to debate about immigration policy in the U.S., hearing arguments about language conformity (English only), and witnessing prejudice surface in American society, I am reminded how much my Dad enjoyed speaking in his native tongue. In his later years, a trip to town on some errand could give Dad a chance to speak Swedish to an old acquaintance, probably over a glass of beer. He always came home in good humor and enjoyed telling about his visit.

Prejudice against speaking their native tongue surfaced in WWI with resentment and conflict toward German-speaking people; this feeling was often directed toward Scandinavian immigrants also because the languages sounded similar. In 1917, Iowa governor Harding issued a proclamation prohibiting the speaking of German in public gatherings. The vast majority of these immigrants turned into loyal, patriotic Americans. Many who joined the U.S. Armed Forces fought against kinfolk in Europe during WWI, and their sons again fought forebears in WWII!

As a result of this intolerance many people, including my parents, quit talking Swedish in the home, in church sermons, and in the community. To me, it is somewhat sad that they were forced to give up a part of their heritage and we children missed a great opportunity to learn a second language, something public schools are now struggling to teach.

As a "senior citizen" looking back, I have no doubt the Great Depression steeled us to face the oncoming WWII—and win it! That edge continued to serve us all well in our careers, our family, and community lives.

Figure 1.5: Arthur and Anna's American family in 1948: (Front row, seated) Nels, Mom (Anna), Dad (Arthur), Lois. (Back row, standing) Astrid, Kenneth, Art, Arne (me), Howard, and Dorothy

CHAPTER 2
THE FARM AND FARMSTEAD: DEFINING A FAMILY FARM

The Big Picture

For decades we have heard and read about the family farm. Politicians rant about saving it. Editorial writers lionize the beleaguered family farmer. But what does "family farm" really mean? Generally, it means the place where a farm family lives. Often it is much more: a place where families become emotionally attached—"the old home place." For the latter, memories and nostalgia endure for the rest of their lives, even though many move to distant parts of the U.S. Technically, a family farm is a geographical portion of the earth's land surface. The U.S., except for the Atlantic Border States which were described by metes and bounds survey, is legally and accurately described by the rectangular survey system. It is a permanent, definable piece of property (real estate). Though we say the family farm casually, it is supported by both Federal and State statutes, is laid out by a unique yet systematic surveying system, and is defined by a simple yet accurate legal description. How the rectangular survey system works, and its physical and economic influence on all pioneer land settlements, rural and urban, is discussed in the epilogue of this book (chapter 32).

In the western Corn Belt, original land titles (or patents) were granted by the federal government, starting around 1840. To encourage settlement and expansion to the western frontier, the Federal Homestead Act was passed in 1862. It granted homesteaders title to a quarter section (160 acres) if they agreed to live on it for five years and "improve it." Because of the Homestead Act, 160 acres became the most typical family farm size from the later half of the nineteenth century up through WWII. This period and the twenty years following WWII can appropriately be called the "family farm" era. Thereafter, due to mechanization and economies of scale, farm size progressively increased and commercial farming began to dominate. This shift to larger farms is apparent from the decreasing number of farms in Iowa, which translates readily into more acreage per farm. Iowa reached its highest number of farms, 223,000, in 1934. In a half-century the number of farms dropped 53 percent to 105,180 in 1987.

The extent of changes over the fifty-two-year period, 1935 to 1987, is reflected in Iowa Department of Agriculture statistics. The number of farms referred to as "Eighties" (80 acres plus or minus) dropped from 16 percent in 1935 to 11 percent in 1987. In contrast to 1935, by 1987 eighty-acre farms were operated mostly by part-time or hobby farmers. In this same period "quarters," 160 acres, dropped from 59 percent to 30 percent. "Half sections," 320 acres, increased from 24 percent to 37 percent. "Large farms" (500 to 1,000 acres) increased from 1 percent to 18 percent, and farms of over 1,000 acres increased from .01 percent to 4 percent in 1987.

These statistics become more significant when one considers that the above figures show the number of farms only. With more acres in the larger farm categories, the actual number of acres shifting to larger farms is more dramatic. However, the prairie was not all homesteaded. From 1860 to 1880, wealthy eastern investors were buying a few very large land holdings across the Corn Belt. Examples in the western Corn Belt were the 7,000-acre Adams Ranch near Odebolt in Sac County, Iowa, the Close Land Company's extensive holdings in Plymouth and Harrison Counties in western Iowa, and several large group settlements such as the Amana Colonies in southeastern Iowa. Other Corn Belt states had similar land ownership patterns such as the 4500-acre Coburn Estate in Murray County, southwest Minnesota, where, years later, I had extensive management responsibilities.

Our family lived on a typical western Corn Belt farm of 240 acres for seventeen years, from 1923 until 1940. I was born there in January 1925 and grew up during the Great Depression years. The farm was located in Buena Vista County, northwest Iowa. Our family considered this the "home place," as we developed a love and nostalgia for it that we held well into adulthood.

My Dad rented it, as did most farm operators (tenants) of that time. We leased under typical fifty-fifty crop share terms, meaning the landlord and tenant each got half the crop. Cash rent was paid for pasture and hay land. Basically, the landlord furnished the land and buildings and the tenant provided his daily management, machinery, and labor. When renting their farm, landlords took note of the tenant's family size: husky boys translated into ample labor to get farm work done on time.

Moving Day

Because of spring planting, farms were leased for a year from March 1 to February 28. The fast turnover of tenants on some farms was troublesome. For example, the eighty-acre farm bordering us on the north had seven different resident tenants from 1931 to 1940. Such rapid turnover was usually caused by one of two reasons: a poor farm or an unrealistic landlord. The number of movers each March 1 resulted in a rather disorganized shuffle of farm tenants and a disruption to the family and farming operation. Moving heating and cooking stoves had to be reasonably orchestrated: cooling them down, loading them, hauling them five to fifteen or more miles, and setting and firing them up to heat the new home. The household: furniture, bedding, clothing, cooking utensils, and food, all had to be moved on March first, by wagon or truck. Livestock were driven or hauled. Farm machinery and tools were loaded on wagons and pulled by horses. The prior tenant had to get out and make room for the family moving in. A chain of switchovers, all in one day! When we moved in 1940, I drove a team pulling, in tandem, a loaded hayrack and a wagon fourteen miles. I was barely fifteen years old.

After moving in, the neighbors usually held a house-warming party so everyone got acquainted. It was a nice gesture and a good way to meet new neighbors. The children had to enroll in the new school. This meant new classmates and teachers, and often a different curriculum. In 1940, I had completed three-quarters of my freshman algebra at Highview Consolidated, then discovered it wasn't being taught at my new school, Lincoln Lee Consolidated. Superintendent Knudtson offered to instruct me individually to finish the course. With no structured classroom teaching or classroom discussion, I didn't learn that much—though I got credit for the course.

Moving day on the farm was a disrupting process, but people coped with it.

Early Signs of Change

Farm people in 1930 could not have known they were on the brink of a long, gradual period of unrelenting change. The primary inertia behind this change was economic: larger, more efficient farms. This change was amplified by mechanization (tractors) whereby one family could farm much more land.

In the first half of the Great Depression (early 1930s), smaller farmers could not generate ample income because of low acreage and devastating grain and livestock prices. They couldn't hold on financially and were the first to be driven off the land.

Persistence of this long-term, but steady, trend is confirmed by the preceding farm size discussion. At the end of the twentieth century this trend still continues.

Dogs

Every farmer kept one dog, hopefully a good one. Having more than one was avoided. We kids were occasionally offered a pup from a neighbor's newborn litter. That temptation was squelched when Dad explained that one disciplined dog was much better then two "playmates." The first dog I remember was Scot, half Airedale and half Shepherd. Fairly large, he probably weighed sixty pounds. Scot was a great dog. More than just a constant companion around the farm, he was a working dog. Most farm families became very attached to their family dog.

Farmers looked for several desirable traits but seldom found them all in one dog. The most important traits were a loud, sustained bark whenever a visitor entered the farmstead, and a menacing growl that would keep a stranger at bay until the dog was commanded to back off.

A few farmers kept pretty vicious watchdogs. Many had a sign "Beware of Dog" at the farm entry lane. At about age ten, I walked over to visit neighbor and friend John Hurless. When I crawled over the driveway gate, my feet no more than hit the ground when their eighty-pound black Labrador knocked me down and held me with his massive jaws astraddle my waist! I was paralyzed by his hot breath. From a distance, Mr. Hurless calmly said "Here, Tolivar," as if I wasn't near death! Tolivar released me, and my friend Johnny said, "He was just playing." Oh, yeah!

A good dog was protective of family members, especially children. There have been many cases of a farm dog attacking a bull to save someone's life or holding a mad sow at bay when she was protecting her litter. When a young bull turned on my older brother, our dog, Scot, charged the bull, diverting him long enough for Howard to scramble over the fence.

Farmers liked a dog that would kill or drive off varmints. The smaller Rat or Fox Terriers were good for killing despised rats. Livestock farmers preferred a shepherd or Collie for driving livestock. A few would go to the pasture by themselves and bring in the cow herd at milking time. Scot was good at all of the above except he lacked the instinct to go "get the cows."

Even though he was getting old, we kids sobbed many tears when my brother Kenneth found Scot in a neighbor's pasture, caught in a steel animal trap with his leg broken. It was hard for Kenneth to come home and report the sad news. Dad refused to let us sobbing kids go to the pasture and see what happened or witness the gunshot when Scot had to be destroyed.

After that we got a Fox Terrier, black with white spots. We named him Spot. He barked lustily at strangers and was a good ratter and driver of livestock. Against Mom's inclination, but at our urging, Spot was allowed in the house. We taught him tricks. One was standing, walking, and hopping on his hind legs for a full half minute! One time when we kids were playing in the yard a car came by slowly. Spot was immediately up on his hind legs barking. The driver stopped and hollered to us kids, "That's quite a dog you've got there!" Only then did we realize the uniqueness of Spot's talent and how odd it looked to strangers.

Cats

My parents liked to have one or two good "mother" cats around the farmstead, mostly to help control the mouse and rat population. We regularly fed the cats milk in the barn at milking time and table scraps near the house . The happy outcome, usually twice a year, was a litter of newborn kittens. Observing the mother cat, we soon knew she had given birth. With a little detective work, we discovered where she had hidden the cute little kittens. For reasons we could never understand, the promiscuous tomcat (sire) would return and kill the little kittens unless the mother cat could drive him off. When we spotted the marauding assassin, all hell broke loose! Sling shots, clubs, pitchforks and sometimes the .22 rifle came out. We were going to save those kittens, and often did. But sometimes, much to our sorrow, the tomcat was able to commit his treachery.

We kids were mystified by the cruelty of the tomcat returning to kill the kittens, but learned it was not uncommon in the cat family. Though it confounds survival theories, it may bear out the male's sex drive: When the nursing kittens are killed and nursing stops, the mother cat will come into estrous (heat), ready to mate with the tomcat again.

We soon learned the only real safe haven for the kittens was placing them with the mother in a bushel basket and keeping them in the house until the threat had passed, after a couple of weeks. By then, the kittens all had names, designated "owners," and hours of playful antics. Once a month old, they were returned to the barn. Later they would range and hunt around the farmstead like the mother cat.

More Domestic Animals

In addition to the ever-present and essential chicken flock, many farmers kept ducks and geese. Rarer were flocks of turkeys or guineas. These birds scavenged for feed around the farmstead. In return, they offered variety to the dinner table menu! A drake and two hen ducks produced ten or more ducklings, which when grown made not only a delicious roast duck dinner, but down (feathers) for making pillows. Our gander and two female geese would hatch fifteen or more goslings. Geese were more intrusive than ducks. While brooding her nest of eight or more eggs, the goose was very possessive. More than once we kids had to make a hasty retreat when the goose charged hissing, with wings whipping to protect her nest. After hatching, the goose strutted around the yard proudly displaying her brood of cute, fuzzy little goslings. The half-grown goslings irritated Mom when they hung around the house, making a mess with their manure droppings. However, they made many delicious Thanksgiving, Christmas, and Sunday roast goose dinners!

A peculiar trait of the geese flock was very annoying. Working around the farmstead often required us to call out to one another: "Bring the hammer" or "Shut the gate." Whenever this happened, the geese flock instinctively let out a storm of loud cackling, drowning out our conversation. It was as if they were responding to—or worse—mocking us!

Figure 2.1: Those early telephones were crude wooden boxes containing wiring, batteries, transmitter, receiver, and two bells that rang to signal an incoming call.

Many times man and animal had to tolerate each other!

Telephones

Early 1900s farms and farmsteads had only the bare essentials of what we later called "utilities." Very few had electrical service. By 1930, however, most families in our neighborhood had telephones. These were wall-mounted wooden boxes with a hand-crank on the side. A few turns of the crank, with "shorts" and "longs" in combination, rang up the intended neighbor on the party line. One long crank got "central" (the operator), who was always a woman. The operator would connect us for long distance calls, provide the time of day, or report on community happenings. She was a friendly lady who knew all of the telephone line members by their voices. In an emergency, such as a fire, the operator would give a "general ring," four long cranks, whereupon all party line members would hurry to the phone for the announcement! To make a call on the party line, we had to "listen in" to be sure no one was using the line. If neighbors were talking it might lead to "rubbering," which meant listening in to hear some of the latest news or gossip! Oftentimes Mom would recognize the voices on the phone and chime in for a three-way conversation: a forerunner of high-tech, up-scale conference calls "invented" fifty years later. If someone on the party line needed the phone for an emergency, the talking parties would nearly always give up the line.

We made long distance calls only in an emergency, and then often couldn't hear well because of line noise or a bad connection. The few times my Dad talked to my sister, Astrid, at nurse's training in Sioux City, he hollered as if his voice had to carry the eighty miles!

Some social calls got a little involved and lengthy. I remember, as a pre-schooler, looking up at Mom and persistently begging for a cookie while she was talking on the phone. Preoccupied with getting the latest neighborhood news, she often ignored my pleading. I got a crick in my neck! I guess none the worse for wear—but no cookie!

Figure 2.2: Dirt roads were a challenge for cars.

Town people, with neighbors next door and stores two or three blocks away, considered the farm a pretty isolated place. Geographically we were more isolated, but farm people often had a more interdependent relationship with their neighbors. Farm families relied on each other in exchanging help, such as the threshing run. This resulted in being aware of one another's well-being in the neighborhood. Quite a few town people shared a phone with their next door neighbor or a relative. Farmers, usually living a quarter-mile or more apart, needed their own telephones—even if it was through a party line. The party line helped connect people socially.

Roads Leading to Someplace

Township roads leading to each farm were necessary and right-of-way was provided in the rectangular survey system by section line mile markers. The early roads were built by horse-drawn graders mounding a crest of dirt at the center and leaving a shallow ditch on each side for rainwater to drain. As soon as gravel pits were discovered along nearby creek or river floodplains, gravel would be hauled and spread on the dirt road to provide an "all weather" road. Well, not entirely all weather—drifting snow could rapidly close them. While dusty when dry, the roads turned into muddy quagmires during the spring thaw and heavy summer rains. Poor roads often delayed travel and hindered hauling grain, livestock, and produce to market.

During the Great Depression, government WPA programs provided jobs for the unemployed, often through road maintenance work. Farmers brought their own teams of horses to pull road drags or dirt scrapers. With no money, poll taxes were "worked off " by doing road repair to pay the taxes. Laws prohibiting people from voting unless poll taxes were paid was declared unconstitutional in 1964.

By the mid 1930s, most gravel was hauled by small trucks. Local farmers hired out to the county, using their own trucks to haul gravel. Their more "daredevil" sons usually drove the trucks. As they were paid by the cubic yards hauled, there was competition to haul as much as possible. This led to a half-dozen or more drivers

Figure 2.3: Farmers with horses and grader.

racing up and down the dusty country roads—much to the consternation of neighboring farmers.

Before graveling, it wasn't at all uncommon for a traveler to come walking up our lane and ask us to bring a team to pull his car out of the mud! Usually no payment was offered or demanded, though the stranded driver occasionally made a token payment.

Rural Free Delivery, Parcel Post, and the Mailman

Improved rural roads led to another indispensable service to the rural family: rural free delivery, known as RFD. Started by the U.S. Postal Service in 1896, RFD offered mail delivery to rural homes. The RFD mailman, a respected post office employee, was our reliable link to the outside world. We could buy stamps (three cents!), send letters, and receive letters, newspapers, magazines, and catalogs in the mailbox right at the end of our farmstead lane. I clearly remember our family keeping a daily lookout for the mailman. Any letters with news from relatives in Sweden caused excitement, as did letters from other family members, and friends. In the mid-1930s, when a check for the government Price Support payment was crucial income, the mailman was awaited with special anticipation.

Daily newspapers, such as *The Des Moines Register* or the *Sioux City Journal,* were awaited and read thoroughly. They kept us informed about area, state, national, and world news. My Dad studied the editorial pages to keep abreast of political and economic news. He would occasionally express his agreement or disgust: "Those eastern writers don't understand farming." We all enjoyed Ding Darling's adroit front-page cartoons. A staunch supporter of farmers and land conservation, Ding enjoyed wide popularity in the Midwest farming community.

Looking back, I admire my Mom's tenacity. Despite her Swedish vocabulary, she worked, daily, through the crossword puzzles; never giving up, my parents accomplished self-education in America.

We kids absorbed the comics or "funny papers" and some sports highlights. Regular farm magazines such as *Wallace's Farmer, Successful Farming, Farm Journal,* and others kept us abreast of government agricultural policy and new research developments. The advertising pages whetted our appetite for the latest ideas, machines, and gadgets.

In 1913, Parcel Post was inaugurated to deliver packaged shipments to postal RFD customers. This made Montgomery Ward, Sears Roebuck, and other mail-order catalog business possible. Through Parcel Post, the mailman delivered all sorts of packages ordered from catalogs or boxes sent by family members. If the package was too bulky for the mailbox, or appeared fragile, the friendly mailman would obligingly drive up the farm lane and deliver it to the door. The rural mail carrier was indispensable to the farm family. Parcel Post opened up new shopping opportunities for farmers.

We poured over each year's new catalogs, "wish books," from Ward, Sears and others. We boys read all about guns and gadgets. Dad and older brothers studied over the latest tools. With catalogs laid out on the dining room table, Mom and my sisters would drool over the latest fashions in clothing and hundreds of household needs. Though it seldom happened, there was real excitement when an order was finally filled out!

You could even buy a Shetland pony through the Sears Roebuck catalog.

The mail-order business exposed us to modern marketing techniques and advertising. Nothing was ever priced for even money, but 29¢ or $2.98. Still is! In 1937, Sears' new bicycles featured balloon tires to replace the narrow, harder ones. Under every one of the dozen bicycle pictures in the catalog a caption dutifully stated, "float over bumps."

When RFD brought letters and Parcel Post brought packages to our mailbox we were "country hicks" no more. We didn't have to take the backseat to "city slickers!" It changed rural America.

Meanwhile Back on the Farm

While the farmstead was usually divided into a house lot and barn lot, the entire farm was sub-divided into fields. This accommodated crop rotation and livestock grazing. In addition, permanent pastureland, usually lighter or poorly drained land, was fenced for the ever-present milk cow herd.

Cattle and hog lot fencing at the farmstead was a priority and, built with woven wire, was "hog-tight." Often, only three strands of barbed wire were used for the cow pastures. Farmers were anxious to have the boundaries of the farm fenced "hog-tight" so livestock could range, grazing all fields after fall harvest was done. Dad took pride in having good fence. Setting the corner and brace posts, then stretching the wire and stapling all had to be done *just so.* Harking back to Robert Frost's line, "Good fences make good neighbors," it seems we boys were either building or repairing fences every spring and fall.

Fortunately, Corn Belt custom and legal rulings allowed for a single fence built on the property line to suffice as a boundary fence. This practice was known as "the right hand rule," whereby standing near the center of the boundary line and facing the neighbor's farm, each farmer had to build fence on the half to his right. This avoided fence line disputes and was the most practical way to preserve boundaries. I came to appreciate this years later while working in the state of Georgia where I saw farm boundaries with two parallel fences resulting in a three-foot "no man's land" in between.

Every farm was bordered—in part—by a public road, along which the three- to four-acre farmstead was located. The farmstead was home for the farm family and headquarters for the farm business.

Water

"You don't appreciate the water, "'til the well goes dry." Indeed, a water supply was critical to any farmstead. In some areas, obtaining an adequate water supply was difficult even in normal conditions. During dry spells, such as 1934 and 1936, wells often went dry, causing a crisis—or at least a hardship—as we struggled to meet family and livestock water needs. During these times water would be used sparingly, as it had to be hauled from a neighbor's well or, if available, from a nearby creek or river to be used for livestock.

The need for water often created a flourish of interest in water "witching," or "dousing" for underground water. Witching had believers and skeptics, and still does! "Witchers" were considered by many to have some mystical powers. Generally, the witcher carried a metal bar or a freshly cut, small willow branch and walked in a straight line across the farmyard. The bar or twig would supposedly dip when an underground water vein was crossed. The most common device was a "Y"-shaped willow branch, similar but lighter than the crotch we boys used to make slingshots. Some witchers even claimed to be able to tell how deep the well would have to be dug. If the witcher happened to find a good water supply, word spread rapidly and failures were passed off with a knowing shrug!

Admittedly, I was a skeptic—having observed a little "show business" in the performance! Once, at a neighbor's farm, my brother Art and I watched a witcher in action. Gripping one branch of a crotched willow in each hand, holding his breath (until red faced!), he walked in a straight line across the farmyard. Suddenly, it appeared the branch was forcibly pulled down. To prove how strong the pull was, the witcher showed how the green bark had twisted off while held tightly in his grip! Art and I experimented by holding a similar willow "Y," slingshot crotch and were able to peel the bark off by intentionally turning our gripped fists inward, and causing the willow stick to turn down—it didn't matter where we stood. Years later, I was urged to try locating field drainage tile by witching. The results fortified my skepticism.

Farms had bored (augured) farm wells before drilled wells were widely used on farms. Our main well was sixty feet deep with thirty-six-inch diameter concrete curbing at the top, that reduced to thirty inches about ten feet down, then to twenty-four inches at twenty-five feet. The windmill located over the well pumped water faithfully. During extended calm weather, our one-cylinder John Deere gasoline

Figure 2.4: This large, elaborate barn with dormer windows on the gambrel roof implied status of the owner. Photo taken in 1996, some sixty years after the barns "heyday."

engine was belted to a pump jack. The engine gave off an aromatic exhaust as it went *pop! pop! huh! huh!* for an hour or more until the livestock watering tanks were full.

Another shallower well, with a hand pump, was located nearer the house. It provided water for cooking and drinking. Mom's call for "Water!" got prompt response. We grabbed the water pail, ran to the well, hung the pail on the pump spout, fifteen to twenty strokes of the pump handle filled the pail that was hurriedly carried to the house.

A jug-shaped, underground cistern by the house collected "soft" rainwater from the house eave troughs.

Windmills remind me of family camaraderie and finding humor in an incident that was stressful to a young boy. Our windmill was located about 300 feet from the house, down a narrow lane bordered by the large grove—at night it was filled with odd noises and spooks! Occasionally, always after dark and approaching bedtime, Dad would remember we hadn't shut off the windmill. We stiffened with fright at being chosen to go shut it off. Invariably, a sibling would offer to go along, maybe only halfway—to ward off any nighttime attackers! Pulling down hard on a spring-loaded, two-foot, wooden lever and securing it with a wire loop turned the windmill fan on. To shut it off, the lever was released; thereby it would snap up in a split second, stopping the fan. Back at the house we laughed at ourselves when Dad or Mom commented, "See, that didn't take so long." Then an older sibling would knowingly chide, "They were back in the house before the lever was up!"

Figure 2.5: Smaller barns like this one were more typical.

Big Barns

The barn was often the centerpiece of the farmstead. Its large size amounted to a success symbol. When traveling in the area, we boys were always on the lookout for the biggest barns. Nearly all buildings were of wood-frame construction. Barns were usually painted red and trimmed decoratively in white. Our barn had nine stanchions for milk cows, and a small feed bin. Across a three-foot feeding alleyway were four stalls for eight horses. Young cattle were confined in adjoining pens. The overhead haymow was filled with hay in summer, for feed in winter. With no electricity, winter chores were done by kerosene lantern light. Every pail, basket, or wagon box of stored feed required hand labor and every fork of hay and shovel full of resulting manure had to be carried out. How did the labor-intensive family farm survive? The family provided the labor! No wonder big families with five to eight kids were common.

Part of Saturday's winter chores was bedding cattle sheds with straw, which meant more manure to haul in the spring—more family hand labor. When the first tractor-mounted mechanical loaders were built in the late 1930s, we agreed it was the best invention ever! I learned a valuable lesson: there is a difference between drudgery (to be avoided) and work (a necessity).

The large haymow was a haven for pigeons. To reduce their number we boys would, on the sly, close their escape routes (doors and windows). We used slingshots to bag a dozen or more of the trapped birds. As Mom wasn't excited about butchering the small birds, we were "invited" to do it. But when dressed and fried like chicken, they made a tasty meal.

The hog house with pens on each side of a three-foot center alleyway was used for farrowing newborn pigs in early spring or fall. We boys took turns helping Dad save as many newborn pigs as possible during farrowing. Being a part of this, we readily understood something about animal sexual reproduction.

The hog house, having a wooden floor, was a haven for rats. After dark, using a flashlight or lantern and a .22 rifle, we boys eradicated many of the varmints. It was one of the few "hunting" activities Dad encouraged.

The double corncrib had an eight-foot-wide crib (bin) on each side of an eight-foot-wide center alleyway. An outside elevator reached to the roof-peak, from which corn was spouted to the cribs. In a good year we would fill the alleyway and occasionally some temporary round wire rings in the farmyard. It was exciting when the neighbor brought a tractor and corn sheller to shell the ear corn from the cribs. Shelled corn was sold for cash income or stored for livestock feed. Corncobs provided welcome fuel for heating the house and for cooking. In 1935, wood shingles on the crib roof needed replacing. Wanting to keep the cost down, there was no hesitation when the landlord said he would buy the shingles if Dad would put them on. Under Dad's supervision, two older brothers and I (age ten), each with a hammer and a pocket full of shingle nails, were positioned on the roof. Carefully laying each course of shingles, we moved up the roof rapidly. It was another example of everyone gladly pitching in to finish the job—in less than a day.

Attesting to the sparseness of the Depression years we always saved and straightened old used nails when we did any carpentry repair or reconstruction. When, years later, my brother unthinkingly continued the practice it brought some droll kidding. Adapting to the throw-away culture came hard for the Great Depression generation!

The granary was filled with oats at threshing time. The elevator was used to fill the granary but, whether carried in pails to feed livestock or loaded on a truck for hauling to market, it had to be emptied with a scoop shovel!

The chicken or hen house was used to confine the laying flock. It was equipped with horizontal roosting poles, nests for egg laying, feeders, and waterers.

The double garage was used for the family car and a Model T Ford truck. The truck was not used during the worst of the Depression years because there was no money for license plates or gasoline. A workbench at the front of the garage was used to fix harnesses and for other repair work. We kids built slingshots, rubber guns, sleds, other gadgets and a few "inventions." We drove many imaginary miles, making the "irrr, irrr, putt, putt," motor sound, while sitting in the truck cab.

A gasoline shed was separate from the garage for fire safety. Three, fifty-gallon, steel barrels lay horizontally on a low wooden bench. When the tank wagon (gas man) delivered gasoline, five-gallon cans (pails) were filled from the tank wagon (truck) and transferred to the barrels. A dial and ratchet gadget attached to the truck was used to count the number of cans poured into the barrels. Yup, pretty crude compared to the electric-metered pumps in use by 1940! One barrel was for gasoline, two held distillate for the tractor, and a smaller barrel held kerosene for house lamps, chore lanterns, and to start a fire in heating stoves.

The smokehouse was used in fall and spring to cure hams and bacon for the family table. Though used seasonally, the pungent, charred, smoky smell inside persisted the year around.

In the wash house, a turmoil of activity took place every Monday (washday). Not the least of buildings was the "two-holer" outhouse that attended to the family toilet needs.

Grove or Windbreak

One of the first things early settlers and homesteaders did was to lay out and plant trees on the north side of the farmstead. In a few short years, a large grove protected nearly every farmstead from bone chilling, northwest winter winds. The trees were mostly maple, box elder, ash, mulberry, and cottonwood. I never realized how much protection the grove provided until I had to go out in an open field on a cold, windy, winter day to drive in livestock. The grove also provided firewood. In conjunction with and adjoining the windbreak, we had a fruit orchard with apple, cherry, mulberry, and other fruit plantings. The orchard produced much needed food for the family.

In addition to the planted orchards, many native fruits and berries grew along creeks, rivers, and wooded areas. A few grew in the open prairie. Our family gathered wild plums, mulberries, black walnuts, hazelnuts, wild grapes, gooseberries, and asparagus.

The Land

Though we tended daily to farmstead matters (grain and feed storage, livestock, family provisions, and shelter) we didn't overlook the land. Planting, cultivating, weed control, and harvesting all continued throughout the growing season. Beyond this, we were looking for ways to improve the land. The glacial drift soils covered much of the northern expanse of the Corn Belt. These heavy, low-lying soils and prairie potholes benefited from tile drainage. Tile consisted of one-foot-long by six-inch diameter tubular clay sections. When laid end to end three feet below ground, they formed a conduit to gather and carry away surplus ground water. The loess (wind blown) soils of western and southern Iowa needed conservation practices. Terraces, contour tillage, and seeded grass waterways, all helped reduce soil erosion. Farmers improved the land as improved conservation methods and money became available.

Our cow pasture was a different universe. It remained the same year after year. It was left to permanent pasture for two reasons: a small creek ran through it, and we needed a place for the cows to graze. During dry spells in August, the creek shrunk to a bare trickle. Lying in the loess soils, our farm had no stones or boulders as found in the glacial till soils only a mile to the east. Oddly, a large, four-foot-diameter boulder lodged in the creek channel—a vagrant that escaped the icy grasp at the perimeter of the receding glacier 13,000 years earlier. The boulder, or island as we called it, dammed up the creek channel, forming a small pool. We kids were often attracted to it when playing or exploring in the pasture. There were a couple of buck brush patches from which we could usually spook a jackrabbit. Meadowlarks and killdeer enjoyed nesting in the peacefulness of the pasture. Numerous thirteen-striped gophers acted as if the pasture was their personal domain.

Following a very heavy rain, Art and I followed Dad out to observe that several acres of the pasture were flooded. Water flowed off bordering fields, followed the creek, and slowly mushroomed over the lower-lying land. Believing the pasture to lay quite level, I queried Dad about what caused the flooding. Glancing and waving toward the creek he drolly commented, "water runs downhill." More accurately, he enunciated, "Vel, vater runz downhill."

A few years later, I again walked out to another field with Dad to check drainage and flooding after a heavy rain. I got an interesting lesson in physics, or more accurately hydraulics. As we came up over a hill, we saw that thirty acres of low-lying land, planted to soybeans, was under six inches of water. A tile line main running through this area drained land lying higher on the above watershed. Excessive tile line water blew the grated lid off the intake and water was shooting four feet into the air—a regular gusher—adding to the flooding. The higher-lying feeder tile lines were forcing more water than the main line could handle, thus causing a "hydraulic head"—an artesian. Noting my amazement, Dad glanced at me curiously. I quickly responded: "That's right 'water runs downhill.'"

Farmers were grateful for the rich, tillable Corn Belt land and the bountiful crops it produced. The amount of "prime land" in each of the chief Corn Belt states—Ohio, Indiana, Illinois, and Iowa—exceeds 50 percent of their respective areas. It was believed, then, that in total it made up the largest and richest chunk of farmland in the world! But as it grew great crops, so did it also produce an abundance of weeds. Dozens of common weeds were a continuing plague to farmers. Years after the Great Depression, a professor at Iowa State College (now University) put it in perspective: "A weed is just a plant out of place." I thought of this when walking soybean fields to cut out pesky "volunteer corn plants."

Controlling weeds in field crops was a necessity, and in the 1930s we had no chemical herbicides. Field weeds were controlled pretty well with cultivation and with some hoeing and machete hand labor. At the farmstead it was all done by hand: corn knives (machete), scythes, hoes, and by pulling. Because we were so intent on producing traditional crops, we never gave much thought to how "weeds" could be used. For example, marihuana came to western Iowa in contaminated grass and legume seed that was needed to fulfill the 1930s government program (AAA) requirements. Marihuana was immediately damned as a weed. In five years time, however, it was grown in the western Corn Belt to furnish hemp for making rope—badly needed by the military in WWII. Common weeds that defiantly competed with us around the farmstead were ragweeds (its pollen blamed for hay fever), burdock, dog fennel, plantains, bull thistle, buffalo bur, curl dock, sour dock, buckhorn, milkweed, horseweed, and foxtail. Weeds found in most permanent pastures were ragweed, purple vervain, thistles, and buck brush.

Weeds are nature's way of keeping us humble!

Quaint

In the country on a still, foggy morning, sound carried unbelievably far. We could often hear the neighbors hollering a quarter-mile away. This is when I observed what our schoolteacher talked about in science class: while light traveled at 186,00 miles per second, sound was a slowpoke at 1,100 feet per second. On one foggy morning, my brothers were using an iron maul to drive steel fence posts almost a quarter-mile from the farmstead. As I was finishing chores, I could clearly see them swing the heavy maul and strike the top of the post, but it was several moments before I heard the *clang*! It confirmed what we learned in school.

In a way, the family farm was a microcosm of a self-sufficient, small village.

Figure 3.1: Homegrown "work force"—a 1938 photo of Dad with his five boys.

CHAPTER 3
THE FARM HOUSE: WHERE A FAMILY LIVED AND THRIVED

While the farmstead's outlying buildings were the center for livestock, grain storage, and machinery, it was the fenced-in house yard that was the center of family activity.

The day started for us when we were jarred out of bed by Dad's firm call "time!" From spring fieldwork until the end of corn picking, we were up and going by 6:00 A.M.—5:30 A.M. during peak planting and harvest times. During winter we enjoyed the warm bed until 7:00 A.M.—but there was no way to avoid the shock of bare feet touching the ice-cold linoleum-covered floor!

The House Yard

Our pleasant two-acre house yard had lilac, snowball, trumpet vine, and other ornamentals around the house and ample shade trees of elm, maple, and box elder around the yard. In the center, an open bluegrass lawn was well used for softball, foot races, and a variety of games. The house yard often served as a pasture for our pony, Dixie, and—at times—for young, milk-fed calves.

In small towns, and certainly on the farm, a family garden was considered a necessity. At the south end of the house yard we had a good-sized vegetable garden which each of us kids helped seed, weed, and harvest. From mid-June (first radishes and lettuce) to late fall, the garden provided tasty and healthy vegetables for the table. In midsummer and fall, Mom canned peas, green beans, and tomatoes while pickling beets and cucumbers. Carrots, onions, beets, cabbage, rutabagas, and potatoes were preserved in the cool cellar.

As winter approached, the outside house foundation was "banked" with straw to shut out the cold. The back porch screen door was replaced with a weather-tight storm door. We didn't have storm windows—and plastic covering wasn't invented yet!

A House is a Home

The farm house I was born and grew up in was similar to most others found in the plains of the western Corn Belt: two story, wood frame, five or six rooms set on a stone foundation.

Wood clapboard siding painted white and a cedar-shingled roof covered the exterior. Two brick chimneys extended above the roof. Inside the foundation a three-foot-wide earthen ledge formed the cellar walls. With the cellar dug four to five feet below the ledge, it barely left standing room from the dirt cellar floor to the overhead floor joists. The floors inside were pinewood, covered with linoleum. I looked in awe when, on a windy day, air forced up through the cracks in the wood floor caused the linoleum to rise up momentarily. Replacing linoleum got exciting when it came to choosing a new color and pattern. The walls were covered with wallpaper, and when re-papering Mom and my sisters turned creative. They chose bright, colorful patterns

Figure 3.2: House and front yard. Note wind charger projecting from tree at left of house. (circa 1935)

to enliven the usual drab surroundings. With no storm windows, a cracked glass-pane resulted in ice forming inside along the crack. We kids couldn't refrain from licking the ice!

In the summer months, the house had some unwelcome guests—more accurately pests. The worst were the houseflies. With animals and resulting manure piles, the farmstead was a prolific habitat for insects. Even with screened doors and windows it was impossible to keep them out of the house. It didn't help matters with us kids continually going in and out. We employed all kinds of measures to control the flies. Kerosene-based fly spray was ineffective, and its use was avoided inside the house. Scattered sheets of sticky flypaper trapped a few. Sticky fly ribbons hanging from the ceiling were much more effective. And the sure-fire weapon—a fly swatter—was always close at hand.

Other insects seemed to take their turn through the seasons: box elder bugs, ants, mosquitoes, wasps, gnats, "no-see-'em's" and spiders. We humans usually won out, but it was an ongoing battle! It was said that every creature had a purpose, but some days I wondered!

Back Porch

An enclosed back porch entry provided escape from the stinging cold winter winds. This was the most used entry and stopping point for muddy shoes, softball and bat, slingshots, ice skates, and other outdoor paraphernalia Mom didn't want cluttering up the house. Here lingered the antiseptic smell of the daily washed cream separator. In summer, the icebox filled with fresh food was on the back porch, which in winter was the place for overshoes, heavy overcoats, cold-stored foods, and firewood. I can still remember the smell from the small one-gallon, spouted kerosene can, kept handy for lighting stove fires and refilling house lamps and outdoor lanterns. I responded quickly to Mom's call when the kerosene can was empty. Hurrying to the fuel shed, removing the filler cap, I carefully filled the can from the spigot on the kerosene barrel. I replaced the cap and returned the can to the back porch—another ten day supply.

Kitchen

The porch led to the kitchen, the busiest room in the house, where three meals were prepared daily. The kitchen range miraculously produced room heat, hot stovetop cooking, and a baking oven from which came the aroma of fresh bread, pies, cookies, and hot dishes. A side reservoir stored warm water. Warming ovens above hurried bread dough to rise and assured warm dry mittens for winter chores. The range did all these things with no dials or fancy control knobs. Just my mother's magic sense of heat and timing!

The kitchen table, usually covered with a white and bright red checkerboard oilcloth, was used daily in preparing food. An iron, enameled sink mounted on metal wall brackets held a smaller washbasin. A small hand pump drew "soft" rainwater from the cistern filled by rain collected from the house roof. This sink was the washing-up, tooth brushing, hair-fixing, and shaving place for the entire family. A shelf next to the sink held the ever present "water pail" for drinking and cooking water. This water was hand pumped and carried from a well 200 feet from the house. We all drank from the same metal dipper!

My parents were regular coffee drinkers but once or twice a year they set the coffee pot aside and took a neat round, brown teapot down from a high shelf. The teapot lid had been broken in half for as long as I could remember, and the two pieces were bound together with a strand of wire. They seemed to relish tea for a change; however, I don't recall any of my older siblings developing a taste for it. I never did.

The kitchen reminds me of another practice: the disciplining of children. On a couple of hooks over the kitchen door our parents kept a thirty-inch-long, supple willow stick. When our behavior got unruly or out of hand, the willow stick came down and punishment was swift and painful. We knew the rules and the limits. I don't ever recall getting an undeserved whipping and, consequently, never suffered any long-time effects. Back then, hard-working parents with big families didn't have time for, nor were they knowledgeable of, the newfangled psychological methods. Now, fifty years later, spanking kids is not only discouraged but can even lead to charges against a parent. I practiced more restraint in spanking my own kids. However, because of the urgency to get work done during the Great Depression, there was no time for quibbling—discipline was swift. Those times produced many well-disciplined citizens.

The cream separator on the back porch reminds me of another disciplinary situation that years later brought laughter to the family. One rainy afternoon, Art and I had milked the cows and placed the milk on the back porch to be separated when Mom asked us to come in for supper. We could separate the milk afterward. After supper, Dad was reading the newspaper while Art and I got involved in horseplay on the front porch. I shoved Art against a window, breaking the glass. Knowing we were in for trouble, I jumped off the porch, ran around the house in stocking feet—through the muddy yard—to the back porch and started cranking the separator. By then, Dad was out on the porch reading Art the riot act and saying "Get out there and help your brother with the separating!" For years, Art never let me forget that he took the rap for our crime, letting me come off as the hero!

Pantry

The small pantry was a mysterious place with its variety of cooking, baking, canning utensils, and supplies. It also contained a "cabinet" with a tin-covered surface on which Mom used a rolling pin to prepare pie and cookie dough. Built-in above the metal working surface was a small storage cupboard with a "fancy" roll-down door and a metal flour bin from which Mom sifted flour for great apple pies, bread, cakes, cookies, and other favorites. In the pantry floor, a metal ring was used to open a door, where steep stairs led to the cellar. It was used only in severe winter weather when using the outside entry was difficult.

Dining Room

The dining room table seated eight family members and had extra leaves if more room was needed. An Aladdin brand lamp hung from the ceiling over the dining room table. It burned kerosene, and its asbestos mantel gave a bright white light. It caused some worry, as flames might unexpectedly shoot up through the glass chimney. With the ceiling covered with wallpaper, it presented a very real fire hazard. After lighting the lamp, it was observed for several minutes. If it flared up, the lamp wick was quickly adjusted. All other lighting was from kerosene lamps, moved around as needed or placed in wall brackets. The dining room table is where most family discussions, laughter at humorous incidents, and all school homework took place.

In the early part of the great Depression, after my oldest brother, Nels, and sister, Astrid, left home, there were usually eight of us at the dinner table. At age three, I sat at the end of the table in a highchair next to Mom. For a time, as soon as I finished eating I would lean over and go to sleep on Mom's soft warm arm. I recall being bemused and even puzzled—although it gave me a sense of assurance—when, in my sleep, I subconsciously heard family members laugh at my snug repose and agree it was bedtime for the "baby."

A buffet in the dining room held my mother's few nicer things such as linens, additional silverware, serving bowls, several small objects, and mementos my folks brought over from Sweden. Two top drawers held sewing supplies, writing paper, and other household necessities. An open library cabinet with five shelves stored our books.

The hand-cranked telephone was mounted on the wall in the corner of the dining room. The indispensable Singer sewing machine was usually kept handy in the dining room.

In winter, a cob-fired barrel heating stove in the dining room gave quick early-morning heat. It was a good place to gather and finish dressing on a cold winter morning. As the tin sides of the stove turned red hot in just a few minutes, we had to turn around like a rotisserie! I'm amazed at the fire hazard it posed. Indeed, fires destroying farm homes was not uncommon.

Living Room

The living room contained a sturdy, wood rocking chair, Mom's favorite reed rocker, a straight chair, and leather davenport (couch). Potted flowers sat on a small table or on a windowsill when in need of more sunlight. Ferns grew vigorously from a trough-like container standing on four legs. The ferns descended two feet to the floor. Fern leaves were often added to a pot of vegetable soup.

The plain, upright piano awaited high hopes for a potential musician. We had dubious expectations when circuit-riding piano teacher, Nellie Olson, drove her big four-door, 1928 Dodge into the yard. It was a bit of an understatement when Dad commented that spinster Nellie, "Wears too much red paint." We anticipated Dorothy or Lois's plinking on the piano keys would result in a rendition at the school Community Meeting program. Considering the meager musical results, the twenty-five-cent lesson fee proved no bargain.

There was quite a commotion and excitement each fall when three strong men carried the large, heavy, wood-burning, "parlor furnace" from the washhouse to the living room. It was quite ornamental, with "see-through" Isinglass in the doors to the fire chamber. We kids loved to sit and watch the flames. It was our job to keep the one-gallon iron tank, built into the top of the stove, filled with water to restore humidity in the house. Carrying firewood in and ashes out was a continuing winter chore.

Twice a year, when the heating stove was set up or taken down, my sisters were excited about rearranging the furniture. Although we boys pretended to have no interest, we were happy to see a change of scenery.

Downstairs Bedroom

There was a double bed and four-drawer dresser in the downstairs bedroom. Since it was convenient for Mom to look in on and care for us kids, it often served as the "sickroom" when we were confined to bed with measles, chicken pox, mumps, or other illnesses. Mounted wall mats with the Lord's Prayer and other verses written in Swedish were memorized, helping us gain some familiarity with our parents' mother tongue. Infrequent overnight company slept in this room.

Front Porch

On the south side of the house was a large, open, front porch: a favorite gathering place during long summer evenings. Hide and seek, tag, foot races, and other games were initiated from the porch.

A problem common to farm homes was invasion by colonizing honeybees. Finding the smallest opening, bees would set up residence (a beehive). The void space between the ceiling and roof of our front porch enticed a swarm of bees every spring and they were not easy to get rid of. When actively carrying out their natural role of producing honey, bees become aggressive. This made for many fast exits from the front porch—and a few bee stings!

Upstairs

Upstairs were three bedrooms and a much used walk-in closet. Two older boys shared one bedroom, two or three girls another. Mom and Dad slept in the largest one but shared it at times with a baby crib and—nearly always—a juvenile bed. My

brother Art and I shared the juvenile bed for several years from late 1920s to mid-1930s.

We kids sneaked into two small attic storerooms and played with my parents' keepsakes, Christmas decorations, and other seldom-used items. A fancy silver coffeepot, mounted in a cradle for easy pouring, fascinated us. I don't remember Mom ever using it, even for special company on Sunday.

Cellar

Entry to the cellar was through outside hatch-type doors and stairwell. Or, in winter, the pantry floor entry was available. We kids imagined the dank, earthen-smelling cellar to be a "spooky" place. While we never admitted to being scared—an unspoken code provided that we

Figure 3.3: Kids "goofing around" on the front porch. In summer, it was a gathering place. Art and I with nieces Donna and camera-shy Mickey.

accompany one another when going in to the cellar after dark. The cellar walls were lined with board shelving, stocked with jars of canned goods. There were several crocks with pickled foods, onions, and apples. A large bin was filled each fall with newly grown potatoes. A sturdy, ten-gallon wood keg with a wooden spigot lay on its side storing wine my parents made from wild grapes.

Wash House

Some forty feet from the back door of the dwelling was the washhouse. During extremely hot weather, the wash house was used as a summer kitchen to avoid heating up the house, which hindered sleeping at night.

Every Monday, Mom coaxed the temperamental Dexter double tub washing machine into doing the weekly laundry. Soft rainwater was carried from the cistern to an old kitchen range in the washhouse, where it was heated in an oblong eight-gallon copper boiler. From here, it was transferred to the washing machine tubs. Thin slices of homemade soap were added. Just a few steps out into the yard were two thirty-foot wire clotheslines where the wash was hung out to dry. In winter, even on a mild day, clothes would freeze-dry.

The Dexter washing machine had two wooden tubs and a clothes ringer. A belt from the washing machine pulley was driven from the rear wheel of the Model T Ford car. In 1934, a one-cylinder John Deere gasoline engine was used instead of the awkward Model T arrangement. In the late 1930s, we got a Maytag washer, equipped with a one-cylinder gasoline engine—quite an advancement! And even more so in 1940, when the gas engine was replaced by an electric motor.

Figure 3.4 and 3.5: Washboard (left) and sad irons (above)—washday accessories.

As a little pre-school boy, I hung around the washhouse with Mom who busied herself with tending the fire for hot water, sorting clothes, and—if need be—using a small hand washboard to scrub out grimy spots on clothing. Mom used a cut off broom handle to poke clothes, keeping them submerged in the washing machine tubs. Next she would run washed clothes through the ringer into the rinse tub and then again through the ringer into clothes baskets. Finally, she hung the clothes out on the line to dry. I liked to smell the fresh aroma of clean, sun bleached, air-dried clothes as they were gathered from the clotheslines. Mother never complained, though washing clothes for eight or more family members was an all day job.

Washday on Monday meant ironing on Tuesday. First, each article had to be "sprinkled," then rolled to up to get the proper dampness for ironing. A steady fire in the kitchen range heated three flat irons at a time. They were rotated to provide a continual hot iron as clothes were pressed. Mom or my sisters would clasp a handle onto a hot iron, lay clothing out on the ironing board, and within four or five minutes a starched and nicely pressed shirt was hung on a wire clothes hanger. Many a housewife spent the better part of the day doing this tedious and hard work—all to keep her family "spiffed up" so she could be proud of them. Some relief came in the mid-1930s when a gas-burning iron was developed and much more when electric irons came into common use by the late thirties.

Haircuts

Few farm kids (none in our family) went to the barbershop during the Great Depression. Most families had a hand-operated hair clipper, a pair of barber's scissors, and a large comb. Dad "couldn't cut hair for sour apples!" Mom was better, but had a multitude of other things to do. My older brother, Nels, and sister, Astrid, were pretty good—though reluctant—barbers. The joke about using a bowl to form the hairline was often a reality.

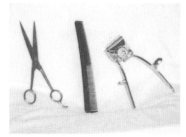

Figure 3.6: The "home barber's" tools: clipper, comb, and scissors.

For a few years, neighbor Bill Green assumed the role of barber; he said he "learned it in Canada." In the summer, we sat on a stool in the yard and the "barber" shuffled around. In winter it was done on the back porch. To reduce the number of haircuts, we were "sheared" close on the sides, which had two adverse effects: any protruding ears were magnified—and so were cold temperatures. We kids found it best not to make a fuss over our own hair or ever criticize anyone else's, not knowing who might be our next barber! I was a teenager before getting my first barbershop haircut. It cost twenty-five cents.

The Saturday Night Bath was for Real

The Saturday night bath prepared us for church on Sunday. No school on Saturday usually meant getting dirty from a day's work and that called for a Saturday night bath. Mom set out a two-foot-square galvanized tub in the middle of the kitchen floor, added warm water from the cook stove, a bar of soap, a wash cloth, and in we went! There wasn't any room for modesty, and our older sisters didn't help matters by finding some excuse to come into the kitchen—with appropriate giggles! We were cleaned up for another week!

Proving that farm boys are innovative and able to "make-do," in the summer we made a shower in the corncrib. A thirty-gallon barrel was mounted on the south outside wall of the crib: solar heat—ahead of its time! A short hose between the cribbing boards brought warm water inside. A spray nozzle, from the garden sprinkling can, was attached and a short rod controlled the faucet. We were set for a refreshing shower!

Earthly Matters: Toiletry

For the most part, toilet needs were relegated—summer or winter, rain or shine—to the "two-holer" outhouse some seventy-five feet from the house. A bedroom chamber pot was reserved for the sick, for emergencies, or for overnight visitors! For some reason, outhouses were always the "butt" of jokes and mischief, such as tipping them over on Halloween!

Nora Cleveland's Outhouse

Farm families, isolated somewhat from daily town activities, created their own social entertainment. We stretched those efforts at times, to milk the greatest amount of fun and humor from the situation.

Mom was a member of the neighborhood women's "stitch and chatter" club—the title conveys the purpose. The eight or so members met once a month, rotating between homes. Stitch meant sewing or crocheting and chatter meant that local gossip and rumors were thoroughly discussed. I remember Dad, who normally shunned gossip, would take a few minutes to let Mom fill him in on the "latest."

One time, when the club met at Mrs. Ole (Nora) Cleveland's home, Mabel Johnson had to use the outhouse. Upon returning to the house, Mabel kidded Nora about how neat her outhouse was: with wallpaper, doilies, and a cloth-covered seat. In fact, Mabel said, "it was so neat I hesitated to sit down!" That sparked a succession of witty responses that snowballed into a long interlude of comments and laughter. Trying to relate the situation to us, Mom could hardly tell what happened without breaking up! Just listening to her telling about it, we were so consumed by the humor of the scene, our whole family exploded into laughter.

The many jokes that persisted about outdoor toilets proved that people, possibly as an escape, would find humor in even the earthiest

Figure 3.7: Typical country outhouse (toilet).

necessities. There were constant jokes about the slick-papered Sears or Ward catalog pages used for toilet paper in the outhouse. Buffering a sheet between fists helped soften it. This was before soft, absorbent toilet tissue was available! Of course, by necessity, substitutes had to be used when working in the fields and under other circumstances.

A fresh, soft corncob has served the purpose quite well, as substantiated by a joke circulated years ago. The great Detroit baseball player, Ty Cobb, was known for the scorn he heaped on opposing players. At a gathering where rookies were introduced, Cobb chided one James Hicks: "I suppose you know what we do with hicks in Detroit?" Hicks responded, "No, but I know what we do with cobs in Missouri!"

The use of corncobs in the absence of modern "toilet tissue" is evident in many museum displays of an outhouse, which includes a small box inside containing a few corncobs.

It Was More Than Just Growing Up

In that home I unwittingly acquired many nuances about life. When Art and I looked cravenly at the last piece of apple pie, Mom—without hesitation—offered a most common sense solution to our dilemma. And taught us something about precision and a sense of fairness: "Okay, one of you can cut the piece of pie in half and the other one gets to choose first."

Our house and yard, with their many attributes, were similar to thousands on Midwestern farms, serving as home for a multitude of growing farm families. We learned that sharing was not only valuable, but necessary if a family was to thrive. With the extremes in weather and the adversity of economic times, it is amazing that we did it so well!

CHAPTER 4
A COLLECTION OF HAPPENINGS, HUMOR, CUSTOMS, AND MORES

"Hard Up"

The term "hard up" was descriptive of just how tough it was for people during the Great Depression. Simply put, people didn't have any money. Farmers bartered their milk and eggs for groceries and saw very little cash in the process. We were brought up to believe that honest people paid their debts, implying if you didn't—even couldn't—pay up, you were dishonest. Many years later, when working as an Equitable of Iowa farm loan fieldman, my boss, Everett Martin, put it this way: "In the Great Depression, honest people—good people—couldn't pay debts on time, but in no way were they dishonest." I fully accepted Everett's credo.

A farm neighbor, Sena Haahr (Mrs. Vic), told my folks about Red, a young man in the community from a good family. Red drove into her farmyard and, seeing no one, went to the chicken house and grabbed a hen. He was carrying the chicken back to his car when Sena stepped out onto the porch and asked Red where he was taking that chicken. Red said, "I was going to take it home for my mother to fix a meal." Sena turned away, as if to say "Oh well, take it." Red, embarrassed, dropped the chicken and drove off. It was the worst of times for all people.

One time, after butchering a hog, we stored the larger cuts overnight in the back porch. The next morning, my folks discovered three or four pieces of meat had been stolen during the night. They felt terrible about losing the much-needed food and even more so because they were quite sure who took it. It was a quandary, but I remember my folks finally saying, "Maybe they need the meat worse than we do!"

People held in grim financial circumstances are prone to grasp at any help, even scams. Early in the Depression there was a somewhat secretive promotion of the Drake Estate. Supposedly, anyone buying shares of stock in the Drake Estate would be richly rewarded when England was forced to release Sir Francis Drake's vast fortunes—accumulated from piracy of Spanish frigates and from raiding newly established American colonies. Somehow, Dad was very skeptical of the scheme and said so at a rural gasoline station and gathering place where the Drake Estate was touted. I remember Dad telling Mom that it got awful quiet lately when he stopped in for some gasoline. In a year or so, news stories exposed the Drake Estate as a hoax. I gathered that Dad's suspicions of the scam went back to his Scandinavian roots, where people knew the English colonizers to be shrewd businessmen—they made money and hung onto it.

Cockleburs, Crows, Pocket Gophers, and Bounty

We kids always had our eye out for a way to earn a few cents for some spending money to buy a treasured gadget. I yearned for the sixty-nine-cent jackknife I saw with my nose pressed against the glass on the counter showcase at Edwall & Rystad hardware store—it loomed a treasure. Carrying it in my bib-overalls side pocket would give me manly status! Sometime later I laughed at myself after reading statesman Ben Franklin's parody about craving a whistle displayed at the local store. After several weeks he saved up an extra nickel, dashed to the store, and bought the whistle. Out on the street he lustily blew his whistle, then again—and again. Then, he suddenly realized the whistle didn't mean that much to him. Thus, his *Poor Richard's Almanac* line, "Don't pay too much for your whistle!" I've observed it many times in my life: "If you want something very much, over a long time, you'll likely be disappointed if you get it!"

In 1936 at age eleven, I joined my older brothers walking a neighbor's cornfield all day cutting cockleburs, sunflowers, and other weeds. When we finished, my older brother Ken was handed a check to be divided up between us. On the way home I was doing mental arithmetic, figuring out my share—even though I didn't even know the amount of the check! It was pro-rated by age—fair enough because the oldest took a wider swath through the field. Being the youngest, I had some proportionate anxiety. When my share came out to be fifty cents, it made a large addition to my savings. I soon forgot about the long, hard day's work to earn it.

Another opportunity to make money was the bounty on crows and pocket gophers. Crows were condemned as varmints that damaged gardens and fields and spread disease from one farmer's feedlot to another. I had never observed a crow doing much crop damage. But they were at times a noisy, even brazen, nuisance. I sometimes wonder if our dislike for them didn't spring from crows being one of the smartest and craftiest pests around. But at ten cents for each pair of crow's feet, we gave little thought to justifying our deed. Crows were fair game.

Crows would steal any shred of cloth or string to add to their twig-framed nests built high in the maple trees of our grove. After laying two to four eggs, their brooding started in May, with eggs hatching in June. We began to listen for the young babies' noisy response to the daily feeding of insects or carrion by their parents, delivered in a silent, swooping glide to the nests. Timing was critical, as the young would take wing and leave the nest in three or four weeks. We made our move before that. Our "move" was for one of us to climb the tree and eject the young, which were retrieved by an accomplice on the ground. The parent crows and their gathered cohorts were menacingly aggressive, diving to within inches of our heads to defend their young. The "tree man" often found himself in a precarious situation!

The accomplice was armed with a .22 caliber rifle, not only to protect the nest robber but also to shoot the emboldened, attacking crows for their feet. It seems strange now in hindsight to see a couple of well-meaning farm boys cast in the role of bounty hunters.

We attempted to preserve the collected crow's feet in lime, and later brought the stinking, half-decomposed, crows feet to the county courthouse for our bounty payment. With a quick glance into the paper sack and a sniff of the rotting crow's feet, the auditor promptly took our word for the count and gladly paid us ten cents a pair!

We also were paid a bounty for pocket gopher's feet. Pocket gophers built troublesome eight-inch-high dirt mounds in the fields as they constructed their network of tunnels. They were named for cheek pouches (pockets) used to carry dirt from their tunnels to the surface. Pocket gophers were furtive, only emerging from

Figure 4.1: Dad with the team and wagon he had used when hurrying over to Grant's farm.

their tunnels in the evening, seldom in broad daylight. They never emitted a sound. Because of this, pursuit and trapping wasn't nearly as exciting or successful as the crow hunt!

The Great Depression Strikes Near Home

The stock market crash of October 1929 signaled the beginning of the Great Depression. People were stunned to read about financiers in New York and other large financial centers, having lost a fortune, committing suicide by jumping out of windows.

The harshness of deteriorating conditions on Midwestern farms was not as abrupt as the stock market crash. Financial ruin hit farmers hardest in 1932 and 1933, the depth of the Great Depression. Losing the farm drove people to despair, even suicide!

One morning in March 1933, Dad got a phone call: "Come over to a neighbor's farm. Something terrible has happened." The neighbor lived one mile west of our place. Grant, sixty-some years old, was thought of as a well-to-do gentleman farmer. He was tall, gray haired, and always carried a cane. Grant kept a hired man the year around so did very little manual labor himself. He stopped at our place quite often to visit with Dad. He drove an impressive Hupmobile car and was always accompanied by two black and white Boxer Terriers. We kids were impressed and, at the same time, curious about Grant.

Because the dirt road running between our farms was muddy, Dad had to drive a team and wagon, in response to the earlier phone call. On arriving at the farm, a family member and a nearby neighbor told Dad that Grant had taken a revolver to the barn haymow where he shot himself.

Though visibly unsettled by the tragedy, Dad described the tragic scene that evening at supper. Grant was lying on his back on the hay, his right hand still holding the revolver extended out from his body. There was no grimacing expression. He looked like he was asleep, with his mouth open. It was no easy task for Dad and two neighbors to carry the body down from the haymow.

Suicide was a seldom and an extreme occurrence in our community. The motive for Grant was clearly financial ruin. The tragedy left psychological scars on our neighborhood—another of many scars the Great Depression generation carried hidden in their psyches for the rest of their lives.

Mores: Accepted Codes of Behavior Endure in a Depression

Among our farmer neighbors there was an unwritten moral code about borrowing things: particularly a tool or piece of equipment. Borrowing itself was done with reluctance. An article of faith was to always return a borrowed item in as good or better shape than when you got it. If anyone broke the code it soon become known, and a cloud hung over that person's reputation for the rest of their life.

A neighbor named Carl, occasionally known as "Cool," lived under that cloud. One time while making hay, he asked Dad if he could borrow our side delivery rake. Though reluctant, Dad felt he shouldn't say no. Carl hitched his team to the rake and drove back to his field. The next day we noticed the rake had been returned, parked in its usual place at the perimeter of the farmyard. It was unusual for a neighbor not to mention returning something borrowed and at least express gratitude. When we went to use the rake several weeks later, we discovered it was severely damaged. The cast-iron frame of the main gear drive was broken. Dad was distraught. He felt we had been violated. I'm sure he was angry, but because of the time lapse (and probably to avoid a confrontation) he said nothing to Carl. Chris Olson, an ingenious blacksmith in nearby Alta, welded the cast pieces back together and the reassembled rake worked fine.

Carl broke the farmer's code and lived under the cloud of dishonesty because of it.

Who Ate the Walnuts?
The Dilemma of Being Falsely Accused

One of the great dilemmas in criminal justice is arriving at just verdicts when defendants deny guilt in the face of preponderant evidence. We have no way of measuring the veracity of denial. It has been accepted that an incorrigible criminal can lie convincingly and without emotion. I am reminded of this by an incident that occurred when I was about eight or nine years old.

In the farm kitchen, pantry and storage cellar, a considerable larder of food and cooking supplies were kept for all the family to share equally. It was our sustenance, and there was an unspoken code that it was to be saved and shared. It was ingrained that we should never individually help ourselves to food that was meant for all.

My mother was a genius at keeping an ongoing inventory in her head. Without a lot of record keeping, she always seemed to know what to put on her lengthy weekly grocery list. English walnut "meats" were one of several special ingredients that were scarce, costly, and used sparingly. One time, the limited supply of walnut meats seemed to have disappeared. An inquiry went out to us five or six kids: "Who ate the walnuts?"

My mother's question was not threatening, but at the same time was taken very seriously. I recall that as the question went around the table I, for some reason I cannot explain, giggled. That was the wrong thing to do! It seemed that all heads turned toward me, having as much as admitted guilt. My quandary grew more intense when I reacted with more giggles at accusing glances. Eventually when I saw my position deteriorating, I denied having taken the walnuts. I hadn't, but was not sure that my family believed me. That was a frightening experience and it bothered me for years.

Another aspect of the situation also troubled me. Had someone else around that table taken the walnuts? Was one of my brothers or sisters letting me take the rap for a crime I didn't commit? The only other explanation was that Mom's inventory might not have been infallible.

This incident has crossed my mind many times as I've seen and read about individuals convincingly declaring their innocence in the face of strong evidence of guilt. Apparently, our yearning and need for absolute truth caused the famous, or infamous, lie detector to be invented. I wonder how I would have done on the lie detector!

Food: Feeding a Growing Farm Family

My folks relished the taste of Swedish foods they grew up on. They had a particular longing for fish, rather than the constant Iowa diet of pork, beef, and chicken. Every fall Dad would buy the first of a few wooden buckets of pickled herring cutlets, most often with the skin left on. I learned to like them and still do.

In early winter Dad and Mom ordered a box of fresh frozen herring caught from Lake Superior. The two by three feet, one-foot-deep, box was made of plain pine boards. When our box arrived at the Rembrandt railroad depot, there was little delay in making the trip to town and bringing the treasured cuisine home. The box was stored outside to stay frozen, often in a snowdrift. With us kids in school during the winter, our big meal was supper. Mom would roll the fresh herring in cornmeal and fry it in lard, using her large cast-iron skillet. The fish was usually served with fried potatoes and a vegetable. Coming in from the cold after doing farm chores, we were elated by the aroma of fresh fried fish. It truly melted in my mouth!

During the Great Depression, we ate what was put on the table. There was little or no tolerance for being picky. We learned to like the many Swedish favorites of my folks: anchovies (fish), hardtack (rye bread), limburger (cheese), lefsa (bread), even lutefisk (fish)!

Eating whatever food was placed on the table was occasionally taught the hard way. Once, Mom made some perfectly good bean soup with pieces of ham added. For some reason, an older sister voiced her distaste for the bean soup. Like robots, we younger kids—without tasting it—decided we didn't like it either! My folks didn't say much, but in clearing the table each dish of soup was saved on a pantry shelf. The following day at supper, each bowl of soup was back on the table. Not a word was said. We all ate it. I relish a good bowl of bean and ham soup to this day!

Our large orchard produced abundant fresh fruit. We agile boys climbed high in the trees to get the nicest apples, and it wasn't unusual to hear of a youngster getting hurt by a fall from a tree. I remember a schoolmate being the center of attention when he came to school with his broken arm in a cast and sling. Sure enough, he had fallen out of a tree! Though cherries were picked for delicious pies, we managed to eat plenty during the picking process. As mulberry trees were plentiful on our farm, my brother Art and I practically lived in them at the peak of their fruit-bearing season. All these foods were eaten, both fresh and canned (for winter use). We had thirty black walnut trees along a field fence line. Gooseberries, watermelons, and cantelope added to our household larder as well as wild plums (made great jam) and wild grapes (made into jam except for those Dad made into wine).

In a large family, some common—yet peculiar—facets of human nature and the economic principle of scarcity came into play. This first occurred to me when I saw some families had disdain for the "heel," or crust, of a loaf of bread. Restaurants treat it as a waste product. Not so in our family: with eight or more at the table and only one crust on the sliced bread plate, everyone wanted the crust! It was the same with chicken gizzards.

Humor

Even in the darkest times of the Great Depression, most people tried to maintain a sense of humor. Homespun jokes were a welcome relief among the Scandinavians. Ole, a local character, met Sven who engaged in his usual needling:

"Ole, I see you lost a shoe."

Ole replied, " Noooah, I yust found vun!"

Swedish jokes and stories were low-keyed and whimsical and lightened the daily worries.

"Say, Sven, did you know Ole vent ice fishing?"

"No."

"Ya, he got forty pounds of ice."

A common remark about someone who had some up and down luck: "That Henry can't stand success!" Mr. Edwall, the local hardware man, gave it a poignant twist by adding—"especially someone else's." From these droll exchanges I learned that if you ever have any doubt about telling an off-color joke—don't tell it.

Clothing

The most common apparel worn by men and boys were blue denim bib-overalls, along with light blue chambray shirts. We would save a newer pair of overalls for dress-up and wore older ones that Mom had patched—sometimes over patches! In the fall with school approaching, Mom and Dad would buy us boys new overalls. We spent some time just enjoying the fresh smell of the new denim cloth and took special care to avoid laundering them to preserve that scent! Overalls were very practical. Besides the left and right side and rear pockets, there was a handy loop for carrying a claw hammer, and on the opposite leg there was a pliers pocket. Having a one-dollar Westclox pocket watch secured in the bib pocket with a braided leather chain was a "rite of passage" for every young boy.

In the wintertime, we usually wore two pair of overalls, layered for warmth. For reasons I still don't understand, we never liked to wear "long handles," or winter underwear—but we wore it during severely cold weather when our folks ordered us to do so. Undoubtedly, we were better off for it. In the summer we usually wore belted blue denim trousers called "cow punchers" and no shirt, resulting in a sunburn which turned brown after a couple of weeks and remained all summer.

Getting a new pair of leather high shoes was a proud and happy moment. The smell of the freshly tanned leather surpassed that of blue denim. I always envied the sixteen-inch leather high-cuts our older brothers wore in winter. Most of us farm kids went barefoot all summer long, then got a new pair of work shoes in the fall for school. Many farm boys never had dress shoes, but simply polished their work shoes.

Figure 4.2: Our "official" timekeeper sometimes overplayed his role.

I was somewhat perplexed by an incident that happened years later when in the Army Air Corps and temporarily stationed in snowy Portland, Oregon, in December 1944. With some anticipation and curiosity, I was ordered to pick up a pair of "arctics" (army nomenclature) from the supply room. Curious about what arctics were, I was startled when the supply room corporal threw me a pair of ordinary, four-buckle rubber overshoes, the same as I'd worn on the farm in Iowa for years! Ironically, at that same time, the army didn't have "ordinary overshoes" for GIs suffering badly from frozen feet during the Battle of the Bulge in Europe. But the army had plenty of "arctics" in Portland, Oregon!

Upon returning home from school each afternoon my sisters stayed inside to help Mom. Though they often hoped for a new dress from the catalog, they were not left wanting for clothing. When buying flour for baking or livestock feed Mom would select sacks according to the color and print on the sack, knowing those sacks would be sewn into very attractive dresses, aprons, and other articles of clothing. With her foot activating the treadle, Mom's Singer sewing machine hummed along "clickity click" hour after hour. Even at age four I empathized with her tedious work. I was pleased that I could help when she asked me to thread the sewing machine needle because of her declining eyesight. I remember how pleased my sisters were when they came home from school and saw an attractive new dress draped over the ironing board.

Up to the mid-1930s boys wore short, knee pants for dressing up. Then we boys wanted the more fashionable long pants, like men wore. Though many parents were hesitant to make the style change, we boys couldn't wait to get rid of those darned knee pants, which all of a sudden became "funny looking!" I think the girls felt the same way about having to wear full-length cotton stockings, held up with garters. Not so strangely, similar cotton stockings became a popular fad forty years later!

It seemed odd to me later how, even in those sparse times, as youngsters we were style conscious about clothes. In 1937 my sister, Astrid, not long out of nurses' training with meager earnings from her first nurse's job at Lutheran Hospital, had little spending money. Yet for Christmas, having access to big-city department stores (Sioux City), bought Art and me each a then unheard of "hooded sweat shirt," probably costing eighty-nine cents each. They were warm and very practical. However, the hood came to a peak. We envisioned ourselves looking like elves or worse—wearing dunce caps! Thus, we didn't put the hoods up when wearing them to school. Apparently we weren't entirely goofy because the hood style was soon cut round to fit the head and has been ever since.

In a large family like ours, hand-me-downs were a way of life. Being the youngest of five boys, it seemed like that is all I ever wore! And, I was happy to have them. I got my first dress-up suit in 1938 at age thirteen, for $6.50 at the J.C. Penny store. The suit was for my confirmation in the rural Little Sioux Valley Lutheran church.

Route Men and Peddlers

A network of route men, traveling salesmen, and peddlers developed during the Great Depression to serve farm families. Mostly it was a convenience and an appreciated service. However I recall Mom, with maybe a dollar to spend, becoming irritated by an overly pushy salesman.

Cream Man

The cream man came twice a week to pick up the fresh cream for delivery to the town cream station, a collection point for an area creamery company, where it was churned into butter for the retail market. A portion of the cream went to ice cream factories. The cream man's truck was rigged with an open rack on which both five- and ten-gallon metal cream cans were stacked. There was no refrigeration, and we wondered if, after several miles over rough country roads, the cream was churned to butter before it got to the creamery station!

Ice Man

Warm temperatures of early June caused problems in preserving food, even for two or three days. Milk—a mainstay of our diet—would sour, butter would melt, and meat would become tainted. Blue mold grew on bread and cheese. Pickling was useful in preserving vegetables and some meat. Canning fruits and vegetables extended their storage time.

However, all fresh foods were subject to spoilage in a short time. Of course the cool cellar was used, and many farms had caves or fruit cellars which often doubled as storm cellars ("fraidy holes") when tornadoes threatened. Many families used a rope and sling to lower food down the well, which always remained cool during the hottest summer days.

In the 1920s, ice delivered by horse and wagon was available to families living in town. By the early 1930s, motor trucks and rural roads had improved enough for delivery to farms. Ice was cut from rivers and lakes, in the dead of winter, and stored in large double walled sheds, packed in layers of sawdust. Starting in early June, the iceman laid out rural routes for delivery to farms.

Our iceman came twice a week from Linn Grove where ice had been harvested from the Little Sioux River. The solid wood-sided truck box was loaded with ice. Sawdust was packed between the sixteen-inch-thick, two-by-three-foot ice slabs. The iceman was careful to keep the ice covered with a heavy canvas to reduce thawing. Even then, there was a steady drip, drip from the truck box.

When the ice man came, we kids gathered around for some friendly chitchat. The iceman knew the size of the ice compartment of every icebox on his route. Ours was a typical double-walled wooden cabinet with sawdust and shredded paper insulation in the walls. Thick front doors opened to the ice and food storage compartments. Our icebox was located in the back porch.

Using ice tongs, the iceman quickly positioned a chunk of ice and "sized it up" to fit our icebox. He used a large-toothed crosscut hand saw to cut the approximate size, then an ice pick and a six-tined ice chisel to shave it to fit exactly. As ice was a novelty in summertime, we kids caught flying ice chips and popped the pleasantly cold pieces into our mouths. Occasionally, a piece would escape our grasp and fall on the ground. It was quickly picked up and washed off in the leaking trickle from the truck box—then popped into our mouth!

The ice was cut from the river, but we didn't worry about pollution then. I remember holding a piece up to the sun and clearly seeing foreign material. Dead vegetation? Or maybe some fish waste!

The iceman grabbed the ice block with tongs, slung it up to the hook on a spring scale mounted on the truck, then made note of the weight. He hurriedly carried the ice block to the back porch and slid it snugly into the ice box

Some days when he was in a good mood, he let us grab the scale hook and weigh ourselves. We proudly reported our weights to Mom who wrote them on the calendar. Big deal? You bet!

Grocery Man

There was always anticipation of an "all day" sucker when the "grocery man" or "rolling store" drove into the yard. The grocery man had it figured out: he maintained his route only during summer when the kids were home! The "store" was an enclosed box with side and rear doors mounted on a two-wheeled trailer. It was loaded with groceries and a few tempting goodies. Usually, it was pulled behind a car or occasionally mounted on a small truck or a converted sedan. Mom often bought some spices, a loaf of bread, or other small items. We kids hung around hoping for a penny to buy a small candy bar or a caramel (all day) sucker. I think Mom preferred to shop in town at Rystad grocery and dry goods store.

Three or four times a year, the Watkins and Raleigh men stopped at the farm. They had more specialty items: spices, salves, patent medicines, trinkets, or new kitchen gadgets such as a potato peeler. The Minnesota Woolen man stopped every fall with attractive woolen clothing. I was elated when I got a nice blue-plaid wool winter jacket that I wore until I grew out of it.

It was a complex and difficult time: farm wives had little or no money to spend, yet they wanted to help the route men survive.

Indians

I heard stories and lore about small bands of Indians that occasionally traveled through rural communities in the early 1900s. I recall seeing only one such band travel by our farm, probably in 1928. We could see four people: an older man, a woman, and two juveniles. They were traveling in a rickety wagon, partially covered with canvas. The team pulling it was clearly mismatched: a thin, gangly draft gelding and a pony. Our parents cautioned us to stay away and not say anything to them. We presumed they were traveling to the shelter of the trees, and possibly to fish along the Little Sioux River, a few miles to the north.

I probably romanticized the Indian hunters and warriors as brave and skillful heroes. No doubt I had a feeling of sorrow about the way the white man took over their land and hunting grounds. In many ways it was a tragic injustice of human history.

Gypsies

Often, during the Depression years, a gypsy family would stop in late spring with the pretense of wanting to buy some produce or sell some cheap, ornamental jewelry. With their dark skin, black hair, and flashing dark eyes, they were a curiosity to us light-complexioned Swedish kids. Gypsy family members had a discernable scent which Dad and Mom said was from strong perfume and eating garlic. Curiosity was transformed into suspicion and, unfortunately, planted seeds of racial prejudice. Dad and Mom told us to keep a sharp eye out, as gypsies were known to distract the farm family in order to steal a chicken for their next meal. Strangely, fifty-five years later, I witnessed a deep-seated prejudice toward gypsies while doing agricultural consulting work in the Slovak Republic in Eastern Europe.

Living in the Midst of Changing Times

These route men or salesmen built a commerce that filled a niche in bringing goods and services to previously isolated rural dwellers. It was an important phase and factor in farm life before good roads and better cars freed farm families to travel to larger county seat towns to shop at the big department stores.

Figure 4.3: Earthen crock jars for pickling food.

Figure 4.5: Hand-crank, strap-on grass seeder.

Figure 4.4: Meat grinder.

Figure 4.6: Coffee bean grinder.

Figure 4.7: Portable kerosene lantern.

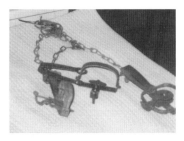

Figure 4.8: Animal traps.

A few, typical tools of the farmer's trade.

CHAPTER 5
THE TERRIBLE WEATHER OF 1936!

The Wind
by Arne Waldstein

The wind is nature's mood,
Energy expressed in subtle wisps
Or waving torrents.
Life's variety painted
In gusts,
Brushed on the landscape.
Free, beyond man's grasp
An unharnessed, vestige of escape
From his embrace and rape.

Feel the wind—
God's Braille touching the soul of man.

People in the upper Midwest must cope with more weather variation and extremes than most other regions in the nation. The 1930s farm homes were only one step beyond log cabins. They offered no more protection from the cold than those prairie abodes of pioneer days, except for better heating stoves. Arctic "nor-westers" swept down from Canada with a fury. I clearly recall having to leave the protection of our large grove to rescue a calf trapped behind a gate in the field. In a matter of minutes I was chilled to the bone! We wore layers of clothes but had no thickly insulated or down jackets. I hurried to the safety of the windbreak, to the barns warmed by animals, and finally to warm stoves in the house.

Below Zero in Hip-Deep Snow
The winter of 1936 had the coldest temperatures, heaviest snowfall, and severest winds. Overall it was considered the worst winter on record. It was a cruel blow to a land already suffering the misery of the Great Depression.

Farm homes were flimsy structures in the face of nature's challenges. The wood frame, clapboard-sided house did not have solid sheathing on either the sidewalls or roof. As there was no wall or attic insulation, we could feel cold air migrate through the walls. With no storm windows, curtains at each window would quiver from the northwest arctic blasts. Ice formed along the edges of each glass pane. It was a running battle: nature's fury versus wood-burning stoves.

From mid-January to mid-February in 1936, there were twenty consecutive days when temperatures fell below zero. Walking around the farmstead caring for livestock, we could feel and hear the snow crunch under four-buckle overshoes with

Figure 5.1: With six-foot drifts we spent most of the day caring for livestock and household needs such as cutting firewood.

each step. We were probably saved some alarm, as the radio weathermen hadn't yet invented the term "wind chill"!

Drifting snow closed roads and stopped car travel for days. Schools were closed for six weeks in January and February. Snow removal equipment, a flat wedge-shaped snow plow mounted on the front of a Caterpillar tractor, was slow and ineffective: the

Figure 5.2: With snow pushed up on the road shoulders, the distant snowplow isn't up to the challenge of clearing roads like this one: one more blizzard would block it.

Farmers Help Shovel Highways

*Figure 5.3: This photo of men scooping out the snowplow appeared
in the Storm Lake Pilot Tribune newspaper February 10, 1936.*

first pass through went pretty well, but as snow banks six feet and higher piled up on road shoulders, snow plows stalled. There was no place to push the snow—that is, until ten to twenty neighborhood farmers volunteered to scoop out the snowplow (often for several miles distance).

Neighbors joined together to drive a team and bobsled six miles to town for supplies. Though the load was supposed to be restricted to essentials, I recall my older brothers laughing about neighbor Bill Green sitting in the rear of the bobsled drinking a bottle of cold beer in bitter cold weather on the return trip.

We became short of food supplies on our farm. Though an unusual situation, we had to look to the livestock herd for relief. Dad selected a 900-pound roan steer from the feedlot for butchering. The butchered steer carcass hanging in the corncrib alleyway was amazingly large compared to that of a 200-pound hog. Killing the steer was a difficult decision, as income from the sale of that critter would help pay farm expenses or possibly a note at the bank. But with having six kids at home there was not much choice. I remember how we relished the meals of hamburgers, beefsteak, and roasts. Those calories helped fend off the severity of days on end of sub-zero weather.

Characteristically, miserable times can bring out people's sense of humor. In 1936, the following story was going around:

Upon finishing chores on one of the coldest nights of the winter, a farmer stepped out of the barn, held up his lantern, and raised the glass globe to blow out the flame. Much to his surprise, the flame was frozen. He broke the flame off with his fingers and tossed it aside, thinking nothing of it. As spring approached, warm temperatures melted the flame and burned the barn down!

104 Degrees Above and a Severe Drought

After the harshest winter on record, it was ironic when the summer of 1936 gave us our worst drought on record.

Compounding distress from the drought, in 1936 the western Cornbelt was inundated by the dust storms that for three years had plagued the Great Plains states from Texas to North Dakota. Large, dark dust clouds rolling in from the southwest that summer were frightening. The fine, black dust, sifted in through ill-fitting windows and doors and accumulated on windowsills, furniture, and elsewhere. Adding to our worries was reading about the "Okies" (Oklahomans) abandoning their farms and fleeing to California.

The drought hit our farm on the Fourth of July when family members had gathered to celebrate. Standing around the livestock-watering tank, we boys couldn't resist the temptation to mischievously splash water on one another. Intuitively Dad called out, "Boys, don't waste any water!" Hot, dry, hard winds blew out of the southwest all day as temperatures soared to 104 degrees. The corn crop curled and withered before our eyes. When we didn't get rain, the crop never recovered. As did many neighbors, we salvaged what feed value was left by cutting it for corn silage. Having no upright silo, we boys all pitched in using teams and dirt (slip) scrapers to dig a twelve by seventy-five-foot trench-silo over four feet deep, with earth banks built along each side. Making silage was something new, actually exciting!

I clearly remember the sweet aroma of the fresh-cut corn and the mildly rancid smell as it "ensiled," or cured, to curtail spoilage. The silage provided badly needed livestock feed for the next winter.

Storms Brought Disaster

Though winter weather was punishing, it was the extremes of summer storms that got scary! Many times while standing in our farmyard we watched low, boiling, gray and black clouds tumble out of the northwest, blowing up dust clouds when crossing fields. We prayed for much needed rain and for no hail. The lightening was spectacular and thunder seemed to shake the ground!

One Sunday in June 1936, my brother Art and I were visiting the Stanley kids a mile north of our place when an afternoon storm came up very fast. We raced our

Figure 5.4: Tornado damage to farm buildings in Buena Vista County, Iowa.

ponies to their barn, hoping to run for shelter in the house basement. I tied Dixie in a horse stall as fast as I could and headed for the open barn door. At that moment, the storm front hit and raised the north wall of the large barn a foot off the stone foundation! We leapt through the open door, bucking the gale force wind as sand from the yard stung our faces. It was so terrifying I didn't have time to get scared! We made it to the house. When the storm stopped suddenly, Mrs. Stanley (probably to relieve our fright) fried some nice thick hamburgers served with a full thick slice of onion. It tasted so good. Our parents were concerned and visibly relieved when Art and I rode into the yard. Their worry was punctuated by pointing to the neighbor's place, a quarter-mile south, and seeing that their nice, big eighty-foot-long, gambrel-roofed barn had blown down!

Cyclones (tornadoes) struck the western Corn Belt every year and were always feared during the summer cyclone season. I remember seeing only two distinct dark gray funnel clouds. One moved slowly, hovering 300 feet above the ground for several minutes—but, thankfully, never touching down. The other swept across an open field, riling up a swirling cloud of dirt and plant debris. It was scary to watch! Many other instances turned out differently as the tornadoes' paths wiped out farmsteads and caused heavy damage in small rural towns.

Hailstorms Can Wreck Your Day—Maybe Your Year

Hailstorms were, and still are, a constant threat during the growing season. This is true not just in the Corn Belt, but also in the Great Plains from Texas to North Dakota, where a wheat crop can be wiped out in a few minutes—sometimes only hours before harvest!

Similar to wheat, Corn Belt crops of oats and other small grain along with soybeans are severely damaged by an ordinary hailstorm. Corn, a larger and sturdier plant, can withstand and recover much better. The amount of damage is directly affected by the size of the hailstones, often varying from one-half- to three-quarters-

Figure 5.5: Severe hail damage to corn.

inch in diameter. However, there have been many reports of baseball-sized hail. Wind velocity is also a key factor. The larger the hailstones and stronger the wind the greater the damage.

During the Great Depression, whether or not to carry crop hail insurance was another expense and decision farmers had to fret over. One year in late May, a hail insurance salesman drove in our yard and started giving Dad his sales pitch. Detecting Dad's hesitancy he chimed in, "Sold some to Larson and Johnson." (Nearby neighbors). Dad didn't take kindly to him blurting out our neighbors' business. We kids were amused the way the salesman had a "roll your own" cigarette dangling from his bottom lip. He didn't make a sale.

One morning in late July 1937, news traveled fast over the telephone party line that a severe hailstorm hit six miles south of our place toward the town of Alta. At Dad's suggestion, Mom and some of us kids piled into the car to go see the damage. We couldn't believe our eyes! Six-foot corn stalks were chopped down to six-inch stumps. Oats in shocks and soybeans fields were obliterated. A few dead farm animals lay in pastures and around the farmstead. Farm building roofs were damaged and windows shattered. Two- and three-inch-diameter hailstones were reported.

That day we really learned what "hailed out" meant! Though we lived with and understood the vagaries of weather, we couldn't help but wonder: Why not our farm? At the same time we were thankful to be spared. A glum sorrow hung over us as we drove back home.

Farmers are generally optimistic, but must be able to accept what nature serves up. Like most storm or flood victims, they roll up their sleeves and go to work, getting on with living and building. These farmers, with volunteer help from their neighbors, did just that.

I've never forgotten that sudden, devastating event—tragedy striking down from heaven!

The Infamous 1940 Armistice Day Blizzard

Though we listened to the weather forecasts faithfully, predicting it before radar and other technology involved a lot of guesswork. Consequently, the infamous November 11, Armistice Day blizzard came without warning and with a fury. This early in the fall farmers had not completed winter preparations and livestock were out in open fields grazing on cornfield residue.

It snowed steadily for a day and a half, accumulating from sixteen to eighteen inches. Gale-force winds piled snow into three- to five-foot drifts, blocking all roads and stopping our futile efforts to shelter and feed livestock. Temperatures dropped close to zero. Many farmers lost cattle that were driven by the severe blizzard into farm fence lines. They became stranded and froze to death or suffocated when ice covered their face and nostrils. A few people in the upper Midwest became stranded while traveling and died of exposure.

That fall, I was feeding thirty-two lambs for a 4-H Club, western "feeder lamb" project. During the blizzard, I frantically battled drifting snow while stacking hay bales to keep the lambs' shed from becoming inundated by snow. By keeping the lambs dry, from crowding and piling on one another, I was very lucky not to lose a single animal.

The Armistice Day storm proved to be the worst early storm on record. You can be sure, after that, we were not as complacent about preparing for winter.

On The Other Hand

In contrast to the turbulent stormy weather, were perfectly clear black nights. With no electric lights to blur our view, the night sky was awash with sparkling clear stars. Lying on our backs on the lawn, we imagined ourselves navigating the celestial heavens as we identified the Big and Little Dippers, a few lone stars, the Milky Way and other galaxies. The fall's spectacular northern lights seemed to make the sky shudder!

At these times, we could clearly hear coyotes in the timber a mile and a half to the north. Their shrill, primeval howling sent chills down our backs.

The familiar old saying: "Everybody talks about the weather but no one does anything about it" is of little solace. Farmers had to cope with it, and did. We survived.

Figure 6.2: Red-tailed hawk.

Figure 6.1: Hen pheasant.

CHAPTER 6
WILDLIFE

Hawk and Pheasant: Real Life Drama

It was a hot July day when Dad asked me to take a team and mower to cut a small, wild hay patch surrounding a two-acre "prairie pothole," typical of glacial drift soils. These depressional areas often had standing water or remained muddy all summer. Consequently, they were good wildlife and nesting habitat. At times they were infested with mosquitoes. On that day, even with temperatures at ninety degrees, I had to wear a light jacket to keep from being "eaten up" by the hoard of mosquitoes. The horses were restless, constantly tossing their heads. On checking their face and necks, I was shocked to see them matted solid with mosquitoes. My glove became red when I attempted to wipe away the blood-engorged mosquitoes. I hurried to finish the mowing and find relief at the barn for both the horses and myself.

While mowing the field, I observed a large red-tailed hawk circling in an ever-tighter circle. It finally plummeted from 200 feet and landed on a hidden hen pheasant brooding her nest of eggs. The hawk arose, wings flapping wildly, with the hen pheasant clutched in its grasp. The hen was frantically trying to escape, cackling loudly with wings flapping. They climbed to about one hundred feet when the hen freed herself from the hawk's deadly claws and a cluster of hen feathers erupted. The hen, floundering from shock, circled back to her nest. This time, the hunted won.

Regretted now by many that have a new appreciation of wildlife and habitat, this pothole and thousands of others were drained of water, falling victim to tile drainage. The constant urge of farmers to cultivate every square foot of land may now appear misguided. A classic conflict of Western man's religious ideology: "taking dominion of the earth" versus empathizing with a balance of nature.

Wildlife Can Be a Pleasant Part of Our Lives

Though we now hear much about protecting wildlife habitats and sanctuaries, the farmstead, with its large grove, orchard, and spacious buildings, was a haven for wildlife. My folks taught us to cause no harm or disruption to songbirds or other harmless wildlife. We enjoyed the sight of them and their songs. Starting in early spring, each species of songbird—with no advance warning—appeared over the course of several days. Their individual chirping and calls were a welcome sound confirming the calendar: spring was here! Robins, the "early birds," were always among the first. They made themselves at home in the house yard getting the "first worm." One year, a white Robin among the gathering caused so much curiosity that I took a picture of it on my ninety-eight-cent Brownie camera!

Robins were soon followed by red-headed woodpeckers, who announced their arrival with a "rat-a-tat, tat" on the trees and wooden buildings and—somewhat disquieting—on the roof's metal ridge cap. Rancorous blue jays, quiet brown threshers, downy woodpeckers, and flickers all busied themselves building tree nests, hurrying to answer nature's call to reproduce another family.

Figure 6.3: White robin.

We took special note when barn swallows suddenly returned to build new mud nests in the cow barn and livestock sheds, where they were assured an abundance of flies and other insects. The blue dart-winged swallows would swoop in and perch—unconcerned—a couple of feet above our heads as we both went about our work.

Getting special attention from our family was a swinging, sack-like nest that held a pair of bright-orange-blazed Baltimore Orioles. Yearly they built a nest in a tall box elder tree near our house.

Goldfinches, wrens, and hummingbirds were elusive. The trumpet vine by our open front porch attracted hummingbirds that gathered to feed on the succulent nectar. When they came to feed, someone would excitedly call for us to come quickly and watch. The diminutive birds would dart about, then stop in mid-air and insert their long beaks in the trumpet-like flowers, feeding on the nectar.

Meanwhile, the songs and calls of killdeers, bobwhite (quail), and meadowlarks announced their return to the cow pasture. Blackbirds and kingfishers gathered by creeks and swampy areas, as did the large—gangly but graceful—blue herons.

English sparrows, pigeons, crows, owls, and red-tailed hawks, having stayed over the winter, did not add as much to the spring drama. However, their activity increased as they each set about raising new broods. Most exciting was a huge bald eagle in flight or perched high in a giant cottonwood tree. Seen only two or three times in my youth, the sight of our national emblem flying freely gave me a feeling of pride!

Our entire family would hurry out to the farmyard when the first large "V" formations of Canada geese flew over on their migratory flyway. The formations flew with a steady urgency, landing only to feed and rest in isolated farm fields. They flew north to Canada each spring to raise a new clutch of goslings and then south in the fall to overwinter in southern Gulf States. We clearly heard the haunting sound of their honking communication, as they navigated through the night at 1,000 feet or more of altitude.

I remember one mild winter day, when I was about four years old, Dad excitedly called us to come and look out of the window. There, perched on top of a haystack about 150 feet away, was a rarely seen prairie chicken. Abundant in pioneer days and delicious on the dinner table, they were hunted relentlessly—almost to extinction. Their short flying range made them easy targets. The demise of the prairie chicken is another example of humans not giving much thought about sharing the earth with even the harmless and beautiful of God's creation.

The Peculiar Balance of Nature

There are exceptions to this nostalgic presence and pageantry of wildlife. Many humans have a long and unseemly hatred of snakes. It probably goes back to biblical prophecy that snakes

Figure 6.4: A bull snake.

were condemned to crawl on their belly and also to our fear of the few poisonous snakes out of hundreds of harmless and beneficial species. As a part of God's creation, I have always felt that snakes got a bad rap.

One day, we were standing in the farmyard observing a group of young half-grown chickens that had gathered around. To our surprise a large, four-foot-long bull snake came slithering through the flock. It was obvious that the snake wasn't doing any harm. The chickens showed no concern. But we humans impulsively panicked— "That viper was about to do in our chicken flock!"

Ken ran to the house, got the 12-gauge double-barreled shotgun and—with the apparent approval of all—shot the head clean off that bull snake! I felt a peculiar remorse. There was no justification for killing that innocent snake other than our own—in part, superstitious—fears.

We have since learned the benefit of snakes for controlling overpopulation of rodents and, fortunately, now we are not quite so quick to destroy another of Mother Nature's contributions to wildlife.

The family farm was profuse with wildlife. We lived in harmony, except for the few times when they posed a threat to our livelihood. Thirteen-striped gophers were harmless inhabitants of our pastures. When above ground, they quickly darted about searching for an insect lunch. A sentry would stand erect on rear haunches, on watch for predators such as a circling hawk or a red fox. A short, sharp whistle would signal their family and neighbors to swiftly pop into the nearby gopher hole. Red timber squirrels gave their noisy "Pish! Pish! Pish!" as they scrambled and jumped between tree limbs in the large farm grove. We often paused to enjoy the familiar sight and sound of an attractive ring-necked cock pheasant and were always startled at the restrained, then explosive, flush of the partridge covey. Nervous cottontail rabbits' quick eyes and radar hearing alerted them to any danger and their speed easily outran predators. Though they occasionally took advantage of Mom's garden, the baby "Easter bunnies" livened up Easter celebrations! When disturbed, larger jackrabbits accelerated with ten-foot leaps, bolting across open farm fields.

Looking back fifty-plus years, it seems amusing now how we "lived" what, today, is taken in by "armchair adventurers" watching television!

Figure 7.1: Dad and three youngest boys play in the yard. It was special to us kids when Dad took a few minutes to play with Howard, Art, and me. Our always present dog, Scot, nearly missed the photo. (circa 1927)

CHAPTER 7
INVENTING FUN AND ENTERTAINMENT IN THE 1930s

Television and structured community programs, even Little League baseball, rob today's children of their creativity.

With a little radio programming, we created our own entertainment. Other than Buck Rogers who, with a jet-powered backpack, flew through space, the paper's comics were of homespun characters in droll situations we readily related to—and often incorporated into family teasing. When my older brother Howard, about age 14, took a shine to a neighbor girl, we mimicked the homespun and hokey comic strip "Out of Our Way," teasing "Big boy loveth Ikell Perkins somethin' terrible." Howard betrayed his fluster by pounding Art and me, which, much to his chagrin, only amplified the laughter!

Comic's character "Nebs" invented an atom pill, a drop into the car's gas tank, that provided unlimited mileage—harnessing atomic power years ahead of the scientists!

Mom got caught up in the original "soaps," so nicknamed because of their persistent advertising for Rinso and Oxydol for laundry and dishes. "Use Life Boy, get rid of B.O." We kids laughed when Mom's Swedish accent pronounced it, "bay-ooo!" Advertising took about half of the fifteen-minute radio segment. Between the sales pitches, stories told of the daily dilemmas in the lives of *Ma Perkins*, *Mary Noble—Back Stage Wife*, and others. Every broadcast ended with enough suspense or intrigue to draw Mom back to the next day's broadcast.

We boys looked forward to the late afternoon 15-minute radio serials. Favorites were *Jack Armstrong—The All-American Boy* and *Renfrew of the Mounties*, a story about the Royal Canadian Mounted Police who "always got their man." In *I Love a Mystery*, three young, adventurous men engineered frantic escapes—even from giant vampires in a haunted castle! All of this was dramatically told by sound alone (the radio) plus our imaginations.

In listening to these programs, we had several strikes against us: weak broadcast signals, unreliable radio receivers, weak batteries, and farm chores to do! The first three strikes resulted in static or fade-out—always at the crucial moment! Again, about half the broadcast time was advertising for Wheaties, Postum, and other "store bought" goodies. And there was always a pitch for some "gimmick," requiring that we send in cereal box tops for a cheap pin or ring. The final strike: youth adventure programs were broadcast around 5:00 P.M.—chore time. You can be sure chores got priority!

Neighborhood Social Life

Taking cream and eggs to town for "trading," to get groceries and supplies, resulted in regular trips to town. Trips were made on Wednesday and Saturday nights in summer but only on Saturday night in winter, during school months. Many towns, including Rembrandt where we traded, held concerts in summertime in the

town park. Farm families and others would gather around the perimeter of the park, sitting in their cars, to visit and enjoy the music. The band was made up of local high school and adult musicians. The end of each musical number was greeted with a loud honking of car horns. With such a variety of cars, the *"oogaa, oogaa"* of the Model Ts, and the "beep, beep" and "honk, honk" of others made a symphony of their own!

Some towns offered free outdoor movies to attract customers. In Rembrandt we could go to a movie theater for ten cents, sometimes a nickel. The movies were mostly cowboy shows and a *Little Rascals* comedy.

We farm kids were not as streetwise as the town kids, and there were a few attempts to bully us by a couple of town roughnecks. Ironically, the town cop's two boys were the most threatening. Only once did it come to fisticuffs, but when an adult stepped in, it was called a draw. We stood our ground well enough, but weren't completely comfortable on their turf.

My Dad, along with some of his friends, would stop in at the local tavern for a beer. I remember listening in on their lively discussions about farm matters, politics, and solving world problems. If we were lucky, Dad would give us a nickel to buy an ice cream cone at Albertson's drug store. Albertson's was pretty plain, compared to Norman Rockwell's *Saturday Evening Post* magazine versions. There were a half dozen porcelain-topped barstools along the soda fountain. Four heavy, wire-framed chairs accompanied each of the three small, round serving tables. Mr. Albertson's sparse store and cautious outlook were common among small-town storekeepers trying to scratch out a living during the Great Depression.

In the summertime, social life often meant picnics with friends. In addition to heaps of potato salad and fried chicken, summer picnics included ball games, pitching horseshoe, time for visiting (talking), and other activities.

Before machines took over much of the hard work and drudgery, farming was done with muscle power. Brute strength was valued in the farm culture. Young men competed to see who could lift the most. A neighbor, supposedly, could lift the rear wheel of a Fordson tractor. Two men would stand opposite one another trying to twist a pitchfork handle to determine which had the strongest grip. Tug-of-war contests were popular. Physical strength was admired and envied. This changed dramatically after WWII as hydraulic cylinders replaced biceps!

The County Fair Expands a Farm Kid's World

Going to the county fair—with its variety of displays, entertainment, and chances to visit with friends—was an annual event. Our showing 4-H calves or market hogs aroused our parents' interest in attending. Many families would meet and share a picnic lunch with fried chicken. Later, church-run food stands were popular.

When taking our 4-H calves to the huge Clay County Fair, it was a big deal to bunk through the week in the second story dormitory of the 4-H barn. During the week we had spare time to wander around the fairground displays even if we didn't have money to spend on Midway rides or on the "freak" or "girlie" shows. But we got some insight into some of the scams and ever-present pitchmen also known as "barkers."

One vendor was selling a small "spark booster" that plugged into the top of the distributor used on all, 1930s vintage car engines. The gadget supposedly increased engine power and gave better gas mileage. We were intrigued at how the motor speeded up when the spark booster was plugged in. After watching the vendor for some time, we detected a fine wire attached to the throttle linkage that he pulled simultaneously with inserting the spark booster. Any doubt about the ongoing scam was dispelled when we noticed—on several occasions—that as the vendor was completing his pitch about all the benefits, a man dressed in bib-overalls waving a dollar bill would call from the back of the crowd, "Give me one for my Chevy pickup." Then, later in the day, a man—yup, this same man—called out, "Give me one for my Oliver tractor"! When this act was repeated through the week, a few farm boys went home a little wiser. And the word "shill" (a phony accomplice) was added to our vocabulary.

Home Entertainment: 1930s Style

In the winter, card parties were the most popular home entertainment. Often two or four couples would come together and play "500." Because they couldn't afford it, little or no alcohol was served; however, coffee and food were always served. We kids "stayed out of the way." We played our own games and usually lay down on the beds or davenport (couch) and went to sleep long before the adults were ready to quit playing. Games often lasted to midnight or later. Of course, getting the cars started on a cold night was always of concern.

By the time I was of junior high age, the occasional neighborhood dance was awkward to avoid, even though most of us kids lacked confidence to participate. That was no excuse when the flirtatious and fun-loving, neighboring Stanley girls took control. With the old phonograph playing a scratchy record, they yanked us out on the "dance floor" and soon began jumping around with the musical beat. We were dancing! Of course games, charades, and spontaneous humor got nearly every one involved. Not all of us could overcome our country shyness at the first attempt. Even after a glass of cherry Kool-Aid!

Mixed in with these activities were a variety of church and public school programs to expand our "social experience."

Winter

Entertainment was governed largely by outdoor weather. In winter, because of school, our only free time was evenings and weekends.

The school bus was an old fashioned, cumbersome, wooden bus-body mounted on a farm truck chassis. When arriving home at our farm in late afternoon we kids got off and made a "beeline" for the kitchen. Mom, anticipating our appetites, often had a fresh loaf of homemade bread and occasionally some leftover dessert waiting. After a quick change from school to work clothes (newer blue denim overalls to patched ones), we boys were headed outside, each assigned chores according to age and capability. The girls stepped right in beside Mom and helped with kitchen and household chores.

During the week, time for entertainment was limited to the evenings, after school homework was done! Miss Jeppeson's long division assignments often left little time for games.

Playing games was confined mostly indoors during those long winter nights. My brother Art and I, avid basketball players, had to "make-do." A ball was made of tightly rolled up wool socks and a heavy wire towel holder mounted near the top of the kitchen door served as a hoop. We shot many games of "twenty-one."

Of course, the pool hall in town was fascinating to us young boys, but we weren't allowed to go in. That didn't stop us from improvising! With the tablecloth removed from the large dining room table, we lined it with books, placing bindings toward the inside for cushions. Corner and side pockets were formed by gaps between the books. From our marbles collection we selected about fifteen larger "shooters" for cue balls and selected a couple of straight maple sticks for cues. We shot many competitive pool games!

We could always fall back on "Hide the Thimble" and dominoes but they often weren't exciting enough. By making a checkerboard out of a flattened corn flakes box and borrowing white and colored buttons from Mom's sewing basket, we played checkers. That checkerboard was used for years before a fancy red and black one showed up under the Christmas tree. By using lamplight we made hand shadows on the wall: a dog's head, horse's head or a scampering rabbit. Accomplishing these challenged us to make more imaginative images, such as a flying bird. Everyone got involved.

We waited for an empty, wooden, sewing thread spool from Mom. A rubber band was threaded through the spool and anchored with a thumbtack at one end. The other end was inserted through a pearl button (a bearing!) and looped around a matchstick, making a "tractor." When wound up, it would propel itself across the linoleum floor, which of course led to races and distance contests.

When a blizzard or severe cold kept us in the house, we sat around the dining room table where Dad taught us to play six-point pitch; high, low, game, jick, jack, and joker were all "counters." Even with no financial stakes, it got competitive! Keeping track of plays and points improved our memory skills. Dad also taught us a card game he played in Sweden called "casino." Swedish terms identified cards and

Figure 7.3: Coasting sleds provided much of our winter entertainment.

trick points were: "lil-on" a duece, "stur-on" an ace, and "sisston" a ten. Another simple card-matching game was called "schmelta schmeen."

With Dad in his mid-forties, tired from a day's farm work and me the youngest kid, it was a special treat when he took time to play with me. At three or four years of age, I felt excited and cared for when Dad held me on his knee and we clasped hands for a horseback ride. Going through the different gaits (Swedish named): "sen-it-so snit" was a gentle walk of the preachers horse, "scrit-ity scrit" was a more bumpy trot of the banker and then came the farmer at a wild gallop, "gallop-ity, gallop-ity." I went flying up in the air and was gently let down to the floor—exhilarated.

Prairie potholes, not yet eliminated by tile drainage, provided great skating ice. Dad brought a pair of "clamp on" steel skates from Sweden (of course Swedish steel was the best) and we paid ninety-eight cents for another pair at the local hardware store. These skates were clamped on our work shoes by a screwing device. Even though emulating 1936 Norwegian Olympic star Sonja Heine was futile, we had hours of fun despite an occasional body-bruising fall.

Our coasting sled with steel runners was always kept handy for a few runs down a snow-covered hill in the pasture. Even more exiting, was a school "coasting party" on a choice hill in the community. A favorite neighborhood hill was a winding public roadway providing nearly a half-mile run. A bonfire at the hilltop was welcomed for hand warming and for toasting marshmallows. We built homemade sleds with wooden runners, which were used to haul pails of feed and firewood at chore time.

With our occasional "daredevil" stunts, I'm surprised we all grew up without serious injury—or worse. One time, brother Art decided the snow-covered corncrib roof would provide an exciting ride. Our steepest coasting hills along Brooke Creek had only about a 20 percent slope and we flew down those at breakneck speed! The crib roof was more than twice that steep—but it looked so inviting! Dressed in his blue

Figure 7.4: Donna and Mickey got skis for Christmas. (circa 1941)

mackinaw jacket and Lindy cap, I couldn't believe it when Art managed to climb, carrying the sled, to the top of the crib roof—much less get on the sled pointing in the right direction. I'm not exaggerating when I say he made a "blue streak" down the crib roof, over the lean-to shed roof, clearing a farm fence, barely missing a tree limb—and landing in a huge snowdrift! Physically unhurt, mentally in shock, we agreed not to tell anyone. But after several days, and with no apparent damage, we did tell. There were some chuckles, but mostly rolling eyes that said, "How stupid!"

In the summer of 1937, because of job scarcity in the farming community, my oldest brother Nels went to St. Paul, Minnesota, and worked for Dad's fellow immigrant, Dan Zackau in his hardware and furniture store. Nels brought us four pairs of wooden skis for Christmas. Short, four-footers for Donna and Mickey and six-footers for Art and me. We had never seen skis before, and you could be sure ours were the only ones in the neighborhood. We immediately had to try them on nearby coasting hills. As bindings were only a strap over the arch of the foot, it was quite a balancing act! We may have made it to the bottom of the hill—still standing—one time out of ten. There were plenty of laughs at the falls and a few "hurrahs" when someone made it down without falling. Fortunately, falling in the snow didn't bother much until our clothing became soaked through. We soon learned that with a rider on the galloping pony and a forty-foot rope, we got some good ski rides in the level pasture. Of course, the temptation of being pulled behind the car was too much, as was the challenge of more speed. More than once I let go of the towrope to escape a headlong plunge into a steep road ditch! Daredevils, or a mite foolish? Probably both.

Trapping Mice

Our farm house was a typical two-story structure sitting on a stone foundation, which enclosed an earthen cellar. Because the cellar didn't freeze during winter, it provided good storage for garden produce and canned foods.

Though the stone foundation joints were tucked with mortar, it was still a poor barrier to rodents. Occasionally, a family found a polecat (civet cat) had taken refuge in their cellar. I remember more than one summer when a snake found a cool, comfortable haven in a rock wall crevice. The snake didn't seem to cause much alarm.

For us kids the real excitement began every fall when field mice, after living in farm buildings in summer, sought refuge in the warm cellar during winter. Mice soon learned there were even better "accommodations" upstairs in the living rooms.

Consequently we set up a "mouse trapline." Six or more traps were baited with cheese and placed in the soon detected mouse "runs." We set traps after supper. In the evening, as people quieted down, the mice became bolder. It not only interrupted our school homework, but also caused a howl of excitement some evenings as the traps went off two or three in succession, like popguns!

During the depth of the Depression, we trapped for survival—us against them! They ate or contaminated our food. By the mid 1930's, when times got a little better, Mom came up with a bounty system. Paying us a penny a mouse! With the buying power of a penny (a wood pencil, an "all day" sucker, or a small toy), we were in big money.

Mice kept migrating to the warm house as it got colder, so our trapping season would last for several weeks. The dead mice were always a welcome meal for our mother cat.

By the end of "trapping season" we had accumulated twenty-five cents or more. Spent carefully, it lasted for several trips to town.

Trapping: Big Game! Big Money?

Looking back as adults, we laughed about the enthusiasm we had displayed and at the great preparations we made for the fall trapping season. We poured over trapping supply catalogs. We sterilized our traps in an old cream can filled with water and some stove ashes mixed in, supposedly to neutralize any scent. This solution was brought to a boil over a bonfire. When the season opened we set traps in burrows, animal trails, and culverts scouted out a few weeks beforehand. The next morning we were up early, full of optimism, to check the trapline. We were prepared to skin our catch and optimistic that the catalog fur prices would fulfill our dream of getting a $3.79, .22 caliber, single-shot rifle! After a few days with empty traps, it became laughable how fast our enthusiasm faded. One time my brother Art and I caught a skunk. We managed to kill it with a hammer and proudly came home, alternately carrying the skunk, slung over our backs. Unfortunately, the smell preceded our arrival and Mom wouldn't let us near the house! We had to take our overalls and jackets off in the wash house and hang them on the clothesline to air out! We got an unscheduled soap and water scrubbing in the tin bathtub in the cold washhouse.

Despite the fun we had during the winter, there is little wonder that we welcomed the first warm and sunny days of approaching spring!

Spring and Summer

Come spring, we couldn't wait to get outside where plenty of work awaited—but also some time for games. A game with marbles placed in a circle drawn in the fresh spring dirt was a favorite. We played catch with a softball, batted out fly balls, and—often on weekends—had enough neighborhood players for a game of "work-up." We played softball on and off from early spring until late fall.

After somehow acquiring an old, battered, leather basketball, we made a hoop out of an old, metal bucket, cutting out the bottom and nailing it to a tree. Even in the "open-air arena" we had some heated one-on-one competition and neighborhood pickup games!

We later laughed at ourselves for having "fits," that is, abruptly changing from one game or fad to the next. Nearly all our toys and gadgets were homemade. For a week or two, we wouldn't be without a slingshot protruding out of our back overalls pocket. Slingshots were made from a crotch carefully selected from a tree in the grove and rubber bands cut from a ruined tire inner tube. Then we made rubber band guns. Next came the bow and arrow phase: we made bows from plum brush saplings and arrows from wooden lath. Our enthusiasm for homemade archery may well have sprung from seeing a Saturday afternoon *Robin Hood* movie. Though seldom attended, movies inspired many adventures on the farm. *Mutiny on the Bounty* led to taking "stations" in our favorite climbing tree and sailing the seven seas! My older brother Howard would mimic Captain Bligh: "Avast, you blasted swabs!" "Enemy off starboard!" and "Fire!"

We played a homemade version of "cowboys and Indians" or "Tarzan" in the barn. A rope swing tied at the peak of the haymow led to some daredevil attacks!

The large house yard with its lawn, bushes, and trees, provided a great place for foot races, ball games, or an evening session of "hide and seek." Reversing roles we played "gray wolf out," where the person being "it" (the wolf) would hide and the others would hunt it.

Every summer we built wooden stilts. Strange how standing eighteen inches taller gave our surroundings a different perspective. We copied county fair acrobats and developed proficiency for some competitive races.

We were lucky to have had our pony, Dixie, said to be an Indian pinto. Dixie was used about every day, except in winter, for bringing in milk cows, carrying water to workers in the fields, going on errands to the neighbors, and just for fun. Our greatest pride was in neighborhood pony races: Dixie had a terrific competitive instinct and was never beaten in the many sixty or eighty rod (quarter-mile) races. Bicycles became popular in the later 1930s, but because ponies were more useful on the farm, there were few bicycles. We never had a bicycle until Nels brought two nice ones home for Donna and Mickey in about 1941.

When not needed to drive the elevator, the iron (one-inch-diameter by twelve-feet-long) tumbling rod was placed across the corncrib alleyway. It made a great chinning bar, for playing "skin the cat" and emulating the accomplished acrobats!

Mimicking county road building, we kids built a great network of "roads" for our toy wagons and trucks in mellow soil in the grove. Similarly, our sisters were always setting up their playhouses in the grove or in a temporarily vacant building. For some strange reason, we boys had an irresistible urge to "raid" the girls' playhouse! The horseshoe diamond was set up all summer for an after-dinner game before going to the fields or for entertaining Sunday visitors.

With a large grove of trees at our disposal, we couldn't resist climbing them. Of course, this led to challenges over who could climb the highest. Dad or Mom's stern warnings usually kept us from getting too far out on a limb—a lesson that likely

bolstered our common sense. That may have restrained us from accepting foolish challenges later in life.

Spring was met with a siege of kite flying, and I don't recall a summer when we didn't have one or more tree swings. The swings remind me of a funny story: After listening to incessant quibbling over whose turn it was to use the tire swing near the house, Mom stepped out on the porch, and for a reason I never understood, said "It is Dorothy's turn." Lois, Howard, Art, and I went off some distance to play ball. After a while, Dorothy apparently decided having the swing all to herself wasn't so great. She came sauntering over to where we were, mustering newly-learned sixth grade vocabulary, haughtily announced, "Important: I am done. Imagine: who wants the swing?" We rolled on the ground laughing and Dorothy was teased about her pompous comment for years.

Buena Vista County straddles the east-west Mississippi-Missouri watershed divide. The eastern two-thirds of the county drains to the Mississippi River and western part to the Missouri. Brooke Creek originating only a couple of miles northwest of Storm Lake, runs north to the Little Sioux River and eventually to the Missouri. Brooke Creek was one mile east of our farm and provided adventure for neighboring farm kids. We often waded and swam in the creek—surrounded by a large cattle pasture, occasionally a "cow pie" floated by!

In Brooke Creek we caught "craw-daddies" (crayfish), sometimes at the expense of having a bloodsucker (leech) attach itself to our leg. We fished and seined, proudly carrying home a half-dozen six-inch bullheads, which Mom dutifully fried—and we feasted! A catch of only one or two fish would be "saved" and became residents of the livestock watering tank. There we kept close track of their growth and aquatic life style.

It seems like a youngster's imagination is quite spontaneous and unpredictable. Acquiring a metal hoop or a small wheel, leftover from machinery repair, soon resulted in making a "T" (a stick with a cross-piece nailed at the bottom end. We often had races in pushing the rolling wheels. Even the simplest of "machines" were devised when we were given the opportunity.

After local gravel pits were mined, they usually refilled with ground water, making a tempting, if dangerous, swimming hole. Dangerous because the steep outer banks with no beach area could make it difficult to get out of the water. There were enough drownings to make this a valid concern, and we boys got solemn warnings

Figure 7.6: Two boys playing marbles.

from our parents and older sisters. Using caution, I learned to "dog paddle" in the neighboring Honsbruch gravel pit. Though my swimming skills improved, I've carried that gravel pit fear and respect for water ever since.

Sounds and Noises: The Farm Had a Variety

I suppose mimicking or copying animal sounds has been a part of human culture since prehistoric times. It was likely used to lure game during the hunt for food. It certainly could have evolved by children playing and pretending to be animals! Things haven't changed much, as grown men use duck calls when hunting and people hold hog-calling contests at the county fair!

We kids were drawn to this challenge. Mimicking the whinny of a horse was quite difficult, while copying the sound of a crowing rooster came easy. For me making animal sounds was easy as a juvenile, but I lost some of that ability when my voice began to change at age sixteen. One spring evening, my sister Dorothy and I were home with Dad while the rest of the family went to a school function. For some unknown reason, Dorothy and I started imitating a crowing rooster. Dad, usually preoccupied with other concerns, wasn't quick to join in our kid games. But on this particular evening, he broke into laughter at our flawless rooster crowing. When our car turned into the farm lane, Dad said we should hide in the next room. When the rest of the family gathered in the large dining room, Dorothy and I began doing our rooster crowing. Mom, my sister Lois, and brothers, Art, Howard, and Ken looked startled and then broke into uproarious laughter as Dorothy and I perfectly mimicked crowing roosters. We were all surprised and pleased to have Dad join in our fun, doing "what came naturally" out on the farm.

With no television to spoon-feed us trivia, we relied on our imaginations. I am convinced it made us more innovative in our adult lives. It gave us memories that brought hilarious laughter years later at family gatherings. Now, thirty to forty years later, I can recall few memorable television programs.

The following parody about homespun entertainment is from my "Philosophies" column:

Losing our Marbles, in a Modern Way

At consolidated country schools in the 1930s, we improvised our own recreation. There was no organized sports program to spoon-feed us. Lacking enough players for two softball teams, we played "workup." A game ran continuously—morning recess, noon hour, and afternoon recess—throughout the week. Monday we started over. There was no umpire. By settling close calls and other disputes, we learned about human character and about governing.

We played other games according to the season—"keep away" ball, an unrefined brand of soccer; basketball, if gym room permitted; and, come spring, a peculiar frenzy of marbles! Quite often the more athletic girls played ball and occasionally we had to recruit girls to have enough players. However, girls seldom played marbles.

Marbles were sometimes played on a smooth floor but, most often, on bare ground. In either case, the set-up was similar: two to four players and a two- to four-foot circle or ring, in which each player placed one or more marbles. Each player had his favorite "shooter." The shooter was larger than the smaller marbles, sometimes called "mibs." To start, players "lagged," tossing their shooters toward a line scratched in the dirt. The player whose shooter stopped closest to the line got the first shot.

A player's shooter was held curled in the index finger and flicked out by the thumb. Players won marbles by knocking them out of the ring.

As the shooter didn't roll very well in the dirt, a few (very few) players developed the "snap shot." Though I never mastered it, my brother Art was an expert at the snap shot, as was the janitor's kid, John Wayne Ring. Only two out of some twenty to thirty kids, all hoping to win a bag full of marbles! To execute the snap shot, the shooter is held at the tips of the index and big finger and snapped out by exerting thumb pressure. The resulting flat, arcing projectile "zapped" a marble out of the ring with amazing accuracy.

Art and John Wayne took marbles unmercifully. With his marble bag overflowing, Art gave me some of his winnings so I could keep playing.

For those of us lacking snap shot skills, "equalizers" were invented. "sweeps" or "clears" meant you could remove twigs or stones from your shooter's intended line of travel. Another was "rounds," meaning the shooter could be moved in an arc equal distance from the target marble for a more advantageous position. There was also "knucks-down," in which the shooter's knuckles had to touch the ground.

The imagination having no limit, it soon developed that the shooter had to call out his options, such as "rounds" or "clears"! And, contrarily, the opponent could block this move by calling out "no rounds" or "no clears." Whoever called out first prevailed. The game turned into a verbal shoot-out. A kid named Eugene was fastest on the "vocal draw." Physical skill or adroitness was replaced by an unrelated aptitude.

In that schoolyard, a microcosm of civilization, man's value system became somewhat corrupted. The value of one skill eroded. It was replaced by an unrelated skill.

Similarly now, exacerbated by the electronic age of radio and television, a brain exercise known as thinking has been replaced by diatribe. Normally polite and considerate people become rude and argumentative, drawn into boisterous shouting matches. Witness *Crossfire*, *The McLaughlin Report*, *Limbaugh*, and most other talk (shout) shows. Politicians are not immune either.

A clue to our discontent lies in our love for sports. We silently and subconsciously admire the players who, with no waffling, have to produce results. Arguing with the umpire doesn't put points on the scoreboard.

So how do we restore some intelligence and respectful discourse to the public dialogue? To start, participants must be more considerate. People in charge must demand a higher standard. Finally, we the audience who are "turned off" need to act—by turning it off!

Come to think of it, the shouting added to the original marble game might have something to do with "losing your marbles!"

CHAPTER 8
RURAL SCHOOLS: NO FRILLS EDUCATION

Rural Schools: No Frills Education

Fortunately for America, our founding fathers and the immigrants who followed believed strongly in educating their children. This was accomplished first at home by parents and private tutors, then in school classes formed by churches. By the mid-1800s, public tax-supported schools were becoming prevalent. This, in part, was motivated by immigrants' resentment of restrictive educational opportunities in their native lands. Many immigrants felt handicapped by a poor education and wanted a better lot for their children.

This was demonstrated early in rural America through establishment and support of country schools. In the Midwest, the one-room country schools and the consolidated rural schools that followed played a crucial role in the educational, social, and economic advancement of rural people between 1860 to 1970. During this time, farm kids—caught up in the inevitable and continuing migration to industrial cities—found that their rural education put them in equal stead with their city cousins.

The Country School

One-room country schools were rapidly established in western Iowa during the early 1870s. They were the principal, if not exclusive, education providers until around 1915, when many country school districts began to combine into consolidated districts.

The typical one-room country school district was comprised of four square miles (four sections of farmland). One acre near the center was dedicated for building the new schoolhouse. The kids walked to school, but districts were generally organized so no youngster had to walk more than two miles. The teacher, usually a single female, roomed and boarded with a farm family near the school. School started in September and continued through harsh winter weather to end in late May—in time for students to help with summer farm work. In addition to teaching the "three R's" ("readin', ritin', and `rithmetic"), the curriculum included geography and other subjects. The teacher was janitor (keeping the schoolroom in order), fireman (attending the wood-burning stove), and disciplinarian. During winter, field mice sought shelter in the warmer schoolhouse. It wasn't unusual for classes to turn into pandemonium when a mouse, more startled than the kids, started scurrying about the classroom. There were chortling reports of a panic-stricken teacher standing on a chair and screaming for relief! In disciplining eighth grade boys (who were often taller than she was) the teacher's salvation was strong parental support. Corporal punishment in the way of a spanking with a wooden paddle was quite common.

The schoolyard usually had a shallow well, or a nearby farm well was used for the daily water supply. Students carried water to the schoolhouse in a pail. Toilet facilities consisted of a small wood-frame "two-holer" outhouse, usually located as far from the schoolhouse as the one-acre site would allow. The temptation to sneak over and

Figure 8.1: Highview Consolidated School opened in 1915, with the first graduation (twelfth grade) in the mid-1920s; it closed in 1961. The third floor was a residence for the superintendent and his family, and for five or six women teachers. Men teachers roomed with nearby farm families. This school, like others, was a symbol of pride and progress for the community.

knock on the side of an "occupied" outhouse was too much for some boys. Recreation at recess and noon was mostly outdoor games, everyone being involved, with little regard to the often inclement weather.

One teacher taught all eight grades; enrollment usually ranged from eight to fifteen students. Teacher qualifications were not demanding: the county superintendent certified a young man or woman who had some schooling beyond eighth grade, such as two years of high school or summer school classes in teacher training. In reality, a lot of education was disseminated between grades by listening and observation in the open schoolroom and by older students helping younger ones. A creative teacher used resources at hand. From all evidence, most students finished eighth grade with a fairly good knowledge of the subjects taught. Rather than the broad brush of a seamless landscape that later came to be called "social studies," students were taught clearly definitive subjects such as reading, arithmetic, history, geography, writing, and classic literature.

Years later, while President of the Buena Vista County Historical Society in Storm Lake, I was involved in preserving one of the last remaining country school buildings in the county. At the dedication ceremony in the summer of 1996, I was amazed at how many former country school students lauded the quality of education they had received in country schools sixty to eighty years earlier.

Consolidated Schools

Starting around 1915 and continuing into the 1920s, many one-room country schools combined to form larger consolidated districts. From sixteen to twenty-five

Figure 8.2: Highview students from grades one through eight pose beside the school. The close-knit nature of the rural community is reflected by family enrollment: four Freeman kids, four Christiansens, three Bengstons, three Schomakers, three Andersons, three Mickelsons, three Sturgeons, and three Waldsteins—me: second row, second from right, Art: fifth row, third from right, and Dorothy: fifth row, fifth from left.

country schools formed larger districts that served twelve grades and offered more extra-curricular activities such as sports, band, vocal music, and drama. Indicative of changes in priorities was that when people compared schools, the size of the gymnasium was duly noted.

When we attended Highview Consolidated School, our day followed a pattern. We were up at 6:00 A.M. in the fall and spring, but closer to 7:00 A.M. during the winter. We boys had morning chores, mostly feeding livestock and milking the cows by hand. We hurried in for a breakfast of cooked oatmeal and dressed-up by changing patched-up for newer and cleaner blue denim bib-overalls. We then hurried out by the road to meet the school bus.

We each carried our noon lunch to school in a lunch box, an empty gallon syrup can or a paper sack. Everything in my lunch pail was homegrown or homemade! My lunch always included some fruit, usually an apple (or occasionally a store-bought orange), sandwiches, and a cookie. A few students occasionally had fancy store-bought cookies. One girl, a friend, must have read my envy and offered me a bite of her sugar cookie with a large crown of marshmallow covered with a sweet pink frosting. I gagged! No more envy!

In consolidated schools, students were grouped by grade in separate classrooms. Grades one and two, grades three and four, grades five and six, and grades seven and eight. One teacher in each room taught both grades. The four high school grades, nine through twelve were grouped together in a large "assembly hall," but most individual classes were held in separate rooms. As in country schools, we always recited the "Pledge of Allegiance" to the flag at the start of each day. On certain occasions a prayer was said. No one disputed, and all seemingly welcomed, this custom. Far different now fifty years later, when disputes over separation of church and state caused courts to stop prayer in school.

School started in early September, right after Labor Day. After only five or six weeks of classes students were dismissed for a two weeks "corn-picking vacation"! The school students were needed at home to help with the arduous job of harvest—handpicking the corn crop. Going back to school was a welcome relief!

My parents made it clear they expected us kids to study hard and behave. We knew if we got in trouble in school, we would likely be in bigger trouble when we got home. Time was set aside in the evenings to do homework.

There were a variety of extra-curricular programs. I remember one (as it was quite an excursion) when the sixth, seventh and eighth graders were loaded into school buses and taken to the insane asylum located in the town of Cherokee, about fifteen miles west of Highview School. It was commonly referred to as the "crazy house." Both of those names became socially incorrect later on when "mental health institute" became the more accepted term. We kids, having heard horror stories about the crazy house, were a little fearful of what lay ahead. No one was joking about it. We all took note of the security as we were escorted through the hallways. Guards communicated with employees by rattling their key chains; the frightening look on some of the "inmates" faces and an occasional scream kept us pretty subdued. The memory of that experience remains vivid.

Education Is Harvested from Experiences

A humorous incident happened on that trip to Cherokee. I happened to be sitting toward the front of the bus near our teacher, Miss King, a very nice and seemingly shy young lady. Riding along I saw a highway advertising sign for Nehi (pronounced *nee high*) soda pop. Unthinking and innocently, I asked Miss King how that was pronounced. First, her discerning smile and then a full blush told me she thought my question was mischievously motivated. I laughed it off trying to confirm my innocence. Her reaction alerted me that what children say and what adults hear can be quite different. And why adults often find so much humor in a young child's communication.

Another, more disturbing, experience occurred when I was in third grade. Although it was unusual to have married women teach, a Mrs. Ruth Johnson taught third and fourth grades. Our school day seemed to be going quite normally when I saw Mrs. Johnson put her head on her desk and start crying. I approached her desk, as did another boy, Vinton Freeman. We awkwardly tried to figure out what to do and quickly agreed to inform Superintendent Runnings. I hurried out and up a short flight of stairs to his office and explained the best I could. Mr. Runnings promptly came, calmed the worried students and, at the same time, gave assurance and comfort to our teacher. He handled the situation well. Mrs. Johnson left the classroom and the teacher in the adjoining classroom monitored both rooms as we continued with our study assignments. My parents told me Mrs. Johnson had a nervous breakdown. I didn't grasp its full meaning, but the grim symptoms left an indelible mark.

The superintendent, principal, and two other teachers taught various high school subjects. In 1935, the average elementary teacher's salary in rural Iowa was $646 for the school year. High school women teachers got $800 and men $841. In the depth of the Great Depression, some schools ran out of money and had to pay their teachers in script, a voucher they could use for their absolute necessities at local stores. Little wonder my folks remained silent when my older sister told of a teacher who wore the same dress every day of the entire school year.

In the tenth grade, boys took Manual Training (later called Shop) where we learned woodworking, use of a wood lathe, wood finishing, and built a farm wagon box as a class project. Girls took Home Economics to learn cooking, canning, and sewing—practical skills for many future farm wives.

At monthly Community Meetings, a forerunner of the Parent-Teacher Association (PTA), students were given a chance to show off to their parents and peers by participating in the evening's program. There was always singing, but musical instruments were limited to piano, accordions, and marimbas. I took part in several one-act plays. One time, after playing the role of a German doctor, I was surprised but privately pleased when adult acquaintances complemented my accent. It was a great time for parents to be involved in school matters and visit with neighbors. Having the run of the schoolhouse and grounds, a few boys and girls managed some flirtation not possible during the school day.

A Midwestern rural consolidated school was located at the fringes of the nationwide automotive and petroleum marketing network. This led to a need and economic opportunity for rural gasoline stations. In the spring of 1937, Russell Jensen built a small (twelve-by-eighteen-foot) wood building and opened a DX gas station across the road intersection from Highview Consolidated School. In addition to gasoline and oil, Jensen sold bread and a few other provisions. He also sold Mars, Oh Henry! and Baby Ruth candy bars for a nickel. A few candy companies had small penny bars. There were a few students whose families could afford such an indulgence, but I never got one. Jensen's station was often a gathering place for a few farmer neighbors who needed a loaf of bread or a can of tobacco—or more likely, to rehash local news. While many rural schools prompted the opening of neighboring gas stations across America, school closings later in the century, likewise, led to their demise. The Jensen station closed in 1990 after fifty-three years in business.

Consolidated schools initiated another phenomenon—high school basketball. Acute inter-school rivalries developed. Basketball teams, cheerleaders, and band uniforms raised the spirit and excitement within the school. Basketball games provided entertainment for the parents and adults of the community, as well as social contact between districts. My brother, Art, was a "star" on the Highview team. Basketball team rivalries inevitably led to competitiveness, which led to tournaments and newspaper publicity for unheard of farm kids. The county tournament was the pinnacle for most schools and players. The tournament broadened our horizons as we played alongside "big town" Class A teams.

While the small consolidated schools did not have enough boys for a football team, during the school year we played baseball both in the fall and spring. We became quite proficient at the game. County tournament playoffs were held each spring. Because my brother, Art, was a good basketball player, he was "recruited" to attend Rembrandt while I finished high school at Lincoln Lee Consolidated. It got considerable notice in the sports page when, by coincidence, Art and I pitched against each other during a highly contested tournament game. Though Rembrandt won, I never conceded it was due to the pitching!

School sports can be character-building. For me, it stimulated my empathy for the underdog. Across America, unfortunately, we shifted emphasis to extra-curricular activities (band and basketball) rather than academics. Fifty years later, the 1983 "Nation at Risk" education report alerted America that we had let public school education drift off course.

Graduation, High School Diplomas, and Class Rings: A New Fad

In contrast to country school days when eighth grade was the end of the line, graduation and earning a high school diploma took on added significance. It was necessary for college entry and very helpful in opening doors to employment. A high school diploma conveyed some status, which was embellished by getting a "graduation ring." The cost of a ring was a considerable hurdle in the midst of the Great Depression. However, the ring salesmen had a way of portraying the class ring as an essential show of accomplishment, and he hinted that not getting one noted your family's economic status. Were you the hardest of the "hard up"? This quickly translated into social pressure.

When my brother Howard was about to graduate in 1936, my folks really didn't have the $6.75 to squander on a class ring. However, they felt the pressure. It didn't help Howard's cause that my sister, Lois, who graduated in 1934, lost her $3.50 class ring while helping to gather mulberries! Being on the school board, Dad may have felt some pressure to support the school fad. Even at age eleven, I felt the tenseness of economic reality versus social display. Howard got his ring. But in the weeks and months that followed, I remember he became quite indifferent about the ring. It lay on the dresser unused. That had a lasting affect on me. I didn't graduate until 1943 when times were better, but after a short discussion, I told my parents that I didn't want a class ring.

Perhaps that was an early sign of my inclination to make my own decisions rationally and avoid trying to keep up with social pressure—or "the Joneses"! Never for a moment have I regretted my decision.

Cornfield Job Interviews

From about 1935 to 1939, my dad was on the school board and served as president during the last two years. There were always one or more teachers to hire for the upcoming school year. Teacher resignations were usually presented in the spring, toward the end of the school year, so interviews of applicants started immediately. It seems the President of the Board did the initial board interview. I remember, when Dad was planting corn, a teacher hungry for a job drove right out in the field. Dad stopped planting and held a "formal" interview while nudging a clod of dirt with his toe or minding the horses while analyzing the young applicant, usually fresh out of college and anxious to get their first teaching job. I suspect Mr. Runnings' familiarity around the horses helped him get the superintendent job!

Getting Expelled was Not Uncommon

I entered first grade at Highview Consolidated School in 1930, at the age of five. With two older brothers and two sisters in school, I had plenty of sibling support, as was common among the large farm families. More than once in a school dispute, family presence made sure it was settled fairly. We upheld a "family code"—you had to do your own fighting. A few families didn't follow it, and a school fight could turn into a family feud!

Raised in a large family and having to stand up for my rights, I fought if necessary. I never looked for fights at school, but Dad never discouraged us boys from having wrestling matches at home.

For some reason, I felt sympathy for a mouthy, fat, fifth-grade classmate everyone seemed to pick on. He was a "smart aleck." Being an adopted, and an only child, he had better clothes and school supplies than most of us, including a pair of leather "high-cut" boots we boys all wanted but couldn't afford. While we were riding home on the bus one afternoon, putting up with the usual teasing and pestering, one boy— a regular antagonist—knocked his books on the floor. Sitting across the aisle, I instinctively stooped over to pick up his books. Overreacting, he kicked me in the face with his envied high-cut boot. I lost my temper and came up slugging, hard and fast. About that time, the bus stopped to let us off at our farm. I didn't think much more about the scuffle.

The next morning, the boy wasn't on the school bus. But an hour later, his dad and mother brought him to school. Within fifteen minutes, I was called before the Superintendent and Principal. To my surprise there with his parents was the boy with two obvious black eyes! The conversation implied I should be expelled from school. I was in big trouble, but was given a chance to tell what happened. The superintendent gave me the obligatory lecture about fighting, but I detected a glint in his eye, indicating he had a pretty good reading of the situation. After some stern looks and harsh words, I was sent back to class. Interestingly, several students, some older, casually let me know they were on my side. I was not proud or boastful of what happened and was fearful of what my parents would say. Thankfully, and suspecting Dad and Mom knew more about the incident than they let on, I never got the expected reprimand. But neither did I get their approval—only a cautionary comment about behavior.

The School Bus

In the mid-1920s, my older brother, Nels, drove one of the horse-drawn school buses, a wood box-like structure mounted on a wagon chassis (running gear). It had side widows, a roof, rear steps to an entry door, and bench seating along each side. During the day, horses were tied up and fed in the horse barn, located on the school grounds. At 4:00 P.M. they were hitched up to take the kids home.

By the 1930s, a number of farmers had purchased trucks to haul grain, livestock, or farm supplies. The truck box and cab would be removed from the Chevrolet, Model A Ford or International truck and a school bus body similar to, but larger than, the horse bus was mounted on the truck chassis. Farmers owning trucks would contract with the school board to handle a bus route. My older brother, Kenneth, using Dad's Model A Ford, had a route for a couple of years. These outfits were used until the later 1930s, when they were replaced by yellow steel-bodied manufactured buses, a smaller version of the school buses used after WWII and since.

After getting off the bus and getting a whiff of Mom's newly baked bread, we went straight for the kitchen. After a snack of bread, butter, and homemade plum jam, we quickly changed clothes and set about doing our assigned evening chores, boys outside and girls inside helping Mom.

End of School Celebration

At the end of the school year there was always a school district potluck picnic. The day held some apprehension for us students, as we got our final report cards telling whether or not we passed into the next grade.

The picnic provided an opportunity for neighbors and friends to visit and catch up on news. The younger kids played some organized games and used playground equipment: swings, toboggan slide, and the merry-go-round with abandon. There was always a baseball game; often, the high school team played a men's "pickup" team.

To shelter the three bus bodies, owned by the Highview District, they were removed from the trucks and stored in the school horse barn for the summer. With no cab, the truck chassis resembled the speedy dirt-track racers that excited county fair crowds.

Farm boys and young men were not immune to daredevil antics. Revving up their "racers" with the mufflers removed, issued a not too subtle challenge. This led two of the more assertive drivers to assemble about a half mile down the adjacent gravel road and then come roaring back, racing side-by-side past the school ground packed with excited onlookers! With my brother being one of the contestants, the race was surprisingly emotional for me. But when he won by a half-truck length, my worry turned to elation. No doubt a few older folks considered it mere foolishness, but I surmised many secretly enjoyed the excitement!

Completion of rural consolidated high school with average or better grades qualified students for admittance to most private liberal arts and state colleges. For the most part, the education students received at the rural consolidated schools served them well in their lives and careers.

CHAPTER 9
THE COUNTRY CHURCH: BAPTISM TO BURIAL

Farmers Had to Have Faith in Nature, Most Believed in God

Although I firmly believe that a person's religion is, at best, a private matter, residing in a human soul, I sense a spiritual thread running through the generations. This thread certainly helped hold rural farm communities together, and in a larger sense it can bind civil society as well.

Rural churches filled an important niche in the social life of farm families from the late 1800s into the early 1950s. Then, large labor-saving machines (like combines) replaced neighborhood group undertakings (like threshing runs). Big machinery led to bigger farms and less neighboring. There became less need for community. We begin to see the close-knit fabric of the rural Midwest, of which church congregations were a vital thread, come apart.

When I was young, no dramatic experience or incident made me expressly aware of my religion. It blended into my life as did other family events.

I grew up a member of a typical country church. Little Sioux Valley Lutheran was three miles northwest of Rembrandt, Iowa. Early Norwegian settlers founded the congregation in the fall of 1868; most were farmers. The attractive wooden structure was built in 1887. It is a testimony to their religious roots and pioneer community achievements. I remember it as impressively large, but it became mysteriously smaller when I returned to visit years later! Four arched, frosted-glass windows on each side directed our attention to the worship service rather than allowing us to gaze out at attractive grave headstones, or white clouds drifting in a blue sky. A tall, impressive steeple held the church bell. I was thrilled when allowed to pull the steeple rope and hear the loud *clang, clang* of the bell. Four or five wide concrete steps at the base of the steeple led to large double-entry doors into the sanctuary. Families, following a peculiar herding instinct, usually sat in the same places in plain wooden pews on either side of the center aisle. My attention was always drawn to an impressive altar at the front of the sanctuary. Time and again, I pondered the large painting of the crucified Jesus Christ on the back wall over the altar. Nailed to the wooden cross, his blood trickled from the spike wounds. It was captivating to a young child. The communion rail, covered with splendid red-velvet cloth, surrounded the altar and painting. A baptismal font was on the left. On the right, four stair-steps led to the ornate, elevated pulpit from which, preacher Reverend Theodore Lerud, dressed in an impressive black robe, gave stern sermons straight from biblical scripture. I don't ever recall an attempt to incorporate any humor.

The church's partial cellar contained a large wood-burning stove positioned under a four-foot-square floor grate near the center of the sanctuary. Though it took some of the chill out of the large open room, most people wore their overcoats during winter church services.

This farm kid was impressed by an ornamental wire fence which surrounded the church and adjacent cemetery. Brick pillar gateposts, each topped with a basketball-size masonry ball, added stature.

Figure 9.1: The Little Sioux Valley Lutheran church.

The two-acre cemetery lay just to the east of the church. Some old, gray, small, limestone markers dated back to the early 1880s. The cemetery contained many grave markers that varied in shape and color—large, four-foot-tall granite stones, small stones, and a few modest military markers. The quiet country setting gave the church and cemetery a pleasant distinction. The markers had familiar names of congregation members, neighbors, and friends. That gave pause to a young lad trying to understand the cycle of life and death. A few years later, the scene became more personal for me when a headstone for my parents' graves took its place among the others.

Behind the church was a deteriorated wooden shed, leftover from earlier days when it accommodated teams of horses that members drove to church services. On occasion teams were driven some distance when family and friends attended a wedding or funeral.

The People Worship

In our rural area, most people had some religious ties and church affiliation. Some good people didn't. They may have felt they couldn't afford either giving money to

Figure 9.2: The cemetery was usually adjacent to the rural church.

the church or buying dress-up clothes. There was a scattering called "holy rollers" who didn't seem to be bothered by these limitations. They sometimes held "tent revival" meetings. A friend invited me to attend his church, which turned out to be a holy roller meeting. The animated "Amen" and "Yeah, brother" responses, different from our Lutheran Church's more reserved services, took me aback. Though I didn't feel threatened, I was in fear of being noticed for not "getting into it." I was relieved when the meeting was over. The few Catholics in our neighborhood were generally thought to be a little "stand-offish," keeping any "church talk" to themselves. Even at a young age, scattered seeds of religious prejudice were unwittingly planted in my mind.

At our Lutheran church, families gathered just before Sunday morning worship started. Men wore their "Sunday suits," and women's apparel included a hat, always worn in church. We boys dressed in trousers—we didn't think wearing bib-overalls to church was proper. After church, especially in nice weather, the men stood outside and visited about farm matters and current local news.

Communion, with bread and wine, was a rather sacred ritual served, customarily, only a couple of times a year. The participants, often husband and wife, met briefly beforehand in the preacher's small, barren sacristy to reaffirm their beliefs. The preacher asking: "Do you renounce the devil and all his works and all his ways?" I presumed all answers were affirmative!

When I was about four years old, I remember leaning against my mother and looking over the back of the pew, where I saw a mother uncover her breast and start nursing her baby. It was taken as a natural thing to do. Farm kids continually saw nursing by farm animals and I had no trouble relating this to the highest of mammals. In later years and as an adult, it always perplexed me that some people were made to feel uncomfortable in doing the most natural thing necessary for human survival.

Figure 9.3: My parents' headstone.

Condensed milk, developed in the late 1920s, made bottle-feeding babies the stylish thing to do by the 1930s. Women's magazines frowned on fashionable ladies breast-feeding. I remember my parents, along with a neighbor, chuckling about a new young mother trying to tell crusty old Dr. Herron that she didn't want to breast-feed her newborn baby. Dr. Herron scolded her: "Do you think God gave you those breasts for ornaments!" This incident foretold of the oncoming sales campaign by the bottle and formula industry, a conspiracy to outdo Mother Nature.

Reverend Lerud, a dedicated minister, served two bodies or congregations: the Little Sioux Valley rural church, and Our Saviors—the "town church"—in Rembrandt. The Preacher lived, with his wife and family of one son and three or four daughters, in the parsonage located at Little Sioux Valley. Though we heard stories about "preachers' kids" either being too straight-laced or, oppositely, too wild, the Lerud kids seemed quite normal.

Kids Take A Part

At grade school age, with some indifference, I attended Sunday school classes. There were four to six kids per grade, usually taught by a high school-age or older girl. Looking back, I gained some education and religion from the effort. That Sunday school added to my moral underpinning is evidenced by a Sunday school lesson and Bible verse that I've never forgotten: John, Chapter 3:15: Anyone who hates his brother is a murderer.... In a large family with closely-aged siblings, disagreement and anger may spill over into momentary feelings of hatred—a word not tolerated in our home. That Sunday's lesson came on the heels of a typical sibling dispute with my brother, Art. This Bible verse struck home and I felt deep remorse for my brief hateful feeling toward Art. As a result, I have refrained from using the word "hate" toward another person all my life.

A high point in the year was the Christmas program. Each kid had to memorize a "recitation." Some of them I can still recite, sixty-five years later:

"I gave a gift to Jesus,
The best gift that I had,
I gave my heart to Jesus
I know it made him glad."

Some years we took part in a pantomime or joined a trio in song. Not wanting to embarrass our parents, we memorized our lines. Some kids, not so concerned, were noticeably coached from the wings. We were excited about being treated with a popcorn ball, an apple, or a bag of hard Christmas candy after the program. Riding home to the farm in a cold car, we were pleased when our parents said we had done well.

Our family took the team and bobsled to church a few times when the roads were drifted with snow and my older sister's part in the church service required attendance. We lay down on fresh straw bedding and covered up with heavy robes as the bobsled glided along smoothly and quietly. Occasionally when the sled runners screeched across a gravel patch it sent chills down my spine. Following the Swedish tradition at our house, it wasn't mandatory that we attend church every Sunday. I assumed this to be a general Protestant view—that attendance should emote from desire rather than edict. Except for harsh weather or occasional urgent farm work we attended quite regularly.

In summer there was no Sunday school, but in August the congregation held a well attended "Ice Cream Social" at the parsonage. The parsonage, adjoining the church lot, included a nice, substantial house and yard with Norwegian spruce trees and shrubs. Plenty of rich, homemade ice cream and freshly baked cakes were relished. We kids were organized for games or invented some mischief on our own.

Confirmation

In 1938 at age thirteen, I was confirmed after two years of confirmation class. The purpose was to reconfirm baptismal vows, learn the Lutheran Doctrines, and confirm adult church membership. It was commonly called "preacher school." Our class of twelve met at the town church on Saturday morning under the tutelage of Reverend Theodore Lerud who was respectfully called "Preacher." The preacher, a big and authoritative man, clearly had us all intimidated. We memorized our lessons out of fear. Instruction was very parochial, leaving little opportunity for questions or discussion. Having some understanding of gravity, I had doubts and questions about Jesus' bodily ascension into heaven—taught as fact then. Worse yet, I had the audacity to ask Preacher about it. Exhibiting noticeable fidgeting with his reading glasses, when pressed with "worldly" questions, the preacher didn't tolerate much inquiry. He gave

Figure 9.4: 1938 Confirmation class. Twelve obedient confirmands, under the watchful eye of Reverend Theodore Lerud. Front row: me, Cornelia Hickman, Preacher, Hazel Herrig, Joe Lorenzen, Eugene Grodahl. Second row: Orin Peterson, Pauline Olson, David Enderson, Dorothy Olson, Art Waldstein, Marvel Herrig, Paul Haraldson.

me a mild censure about believing the word of God and then quickly moved on. I reasoned that being created with an inquisitive mind, it was natural to ask about rigid parochial teachings or anything else you don't comprehend. But I learned that my view was not universally held!

During this time, I observed a contradiction in human nature. A confirmation classmate stole a candy bar from Rystad's general merchandise store and wantonly chewed it down while walking from the store to the church for confirmation class! While my classmate's stomach apparently welcomed the candy bar, I had an empty, hollow feeling in mine. Learning the "Ten Commandments," including "Thou shall not steal," was a requirement of confirmation class. I said nothing at the time, but days later told my older brother who expressed disdain for the thief.

After confirmation we were allowed to take part in communion along with older adults. I could not reconcile doctrine with reality when the preacher insisted that, without question, the wine was Christ's blood! In later years, I accepted it as symbolism.

In confirmation class the preacher made a point of men being "called" to the ministry, as if they would and should receive some mystical message. I never understood it, nor did I receive one. I knew two or three young men around my age that went into the ministry and apparently served the Church well. Years later, I got a little different take on the process from a young man who was in the same age group as—and high-schooled with—our own kids. John (not his real name) had some college and some entry-level job experience. Like many, he seemed to bounce around some. I was pleased to see John one day at a café and inquired about his status. John said, rather straightforwardly, that he had decided to go into the ministry. I was a little surprised but hinted I'd like to know what motivated his decision—truly anticipating hearing of a profound, higher call. I was taken aback when John somewhat matter-of-factly said, "It seems like a good deal"! Hard-working and dedicated preachers I've known surely have been spiritually motivated.

Religion and Life Come Full Circle

In this Little Sioux Valley Lutheran church, I experienced some agonies of life. One was my mother's funeral when I was only twenty-five years old. Then I learned a truism: no matter how much you anticipate a loved one's death, it is traumatic when it happens. Though I believed myself to be a realist about death, I was overcome for a brief time with grief and tears at my own mother's death.

Without realizing it at the time, I made lifelong friends in the church congregation. A sprinkling of weddings and anniversaries marked other "growing up" experiences. I became aware that moral temptations were an element of life and that church teachings could help me take measure of my own behavior.

With the decline in rural population and consequent consolidation of church congregations (similar to that of rural schools), we have lost most of our rural churches. Little Sioux Valley closed and combined with Our Saviors town church at Rembrandt in 1954. Today, there is a stone monument set amidst the cemetery markers, commemorating the location of the old church.

I wasn't brought up to "wear my religion on my sleeve." At the same time our parents cautioned that we should never be irreverent. I've pondered religion all my life and have struggled to settle on a body of beliefs that may constitute a viable faith.

While being taught in the Lutheran Church's rather parochial doctrines, I was increasingly exposed to secular, scientific views. Though there is an ongoing melding, these two sources of instruction come into conflict when the Bible is mistakenly taken too literally or as a book of science. For example, regarding the age of the earth or the time and method of creation.

I remember struggling with the philosopher's dictum: "Know thyself." How was I to know myself? In later years, I concluded that a simple but succinct interpretation is: "What do I stand for?" Our beliefs and actions tell us and our community what we stand for—who we are. We can, "Know thyself." And that knowledge can be a beacon.

Christmas Memories: From "Philosophies"

"Merry Christmas!" Hearing those words is magic in uplifting the spirit. Seeing Santa Claus still makes me feel good.

As a small child, I believed in Santa Claus. Though I subconsciously perceived an underlying mythology, it was wonderful to believe in the myth. Though aware of the inevitable as I advanced in grade school, I clearly remember wanting to hold onto that belief.

My parents, with the help of older brothers and sisters, went to some length to keep Santa Claus alive. There were real sleigh tracks in the yard on Christmas morning and, one year, strange marks in the snow on the roof of our farm home. Material gifts were sparse in those Depression years, but faith was plentiful.

Without deliberate planning, Marianne and I perpetuated the belief in Santa Claus in our own children. We fell into various schemes. For many years, a tradition was going to Grandpa and Grandma Aust's home for Christmas Eve dinner. German "weinerschnitzel" was the main dish. But rather than veal, it was delicious breaded pork chops.

When loading the car to leave for our grandparents, Marianne (Mom) always "forgot" something. So it was back into the house and a frantic scurry of getting toys from all the hiding places to under the tree. I'm still amazed she didn't break a leg rushing up and down the stairs.

At Grandma's, the Christmas tree had real candles. Beautiful! When the room lights were turned off, we sang Christmas carols. The universality of the spirit was felt when joining German grandparents in "Stille Nacht, Heilige Nacht."

Dinner prayers were never from memory. It was time for the heart to speak. The meal was savored with wholesome food and joyous anticipation. When the latter could no longer be contained, we concluded it was time to go home and see if Santa had indeed gotten there.

Each mile of the seven-mile trip home brought a higher level of excitement. One beautiful starlit night, we stopped perchance of seeing "Old Saint Nick" and his sleigh. Yes, miracles do occur. There, clear as the celestial Yuletide traveler, was a space satellite in orbit.

Another time we came upon three beautiful deer standing still on the road. Santa's deer, resting? It took no prompting to excite the imaginations of four bubbly little children. Even Dad and Mom got a little choked up at their innocent enthusiasm.

Yet another trip greeted us with a magnificent, dense snowfall of cotton-ball snowflakes, floating slowly down in the still night. In the quiet, remote countryside, we stopped the car and stepped out into nature's grand cathedral. We could hear and feel Christmas—Christ's mass.

Arriving at home, fumbling around until grandparents drove in, and then trying to orchestrate some semblance of a simultaneous entry into the house—turned into a stampede. Yes, Santa Claus had been there. Gifts were piled under the tree.

My grandchildren sometimes ask, "Grandpa, do you believe in Santa Claus?" Reassured by the late scholar and philosopher, Joseph Campbell's, proposition that in the civilizing process, "Myths become truths," I unhesitatingly say "yes!"

Believing now that a spiritual component is a fundamental part of human character and of our religious embodiment, I further explain that Santa Claus, the jolly elf, epitomizes the spirit of Christmas. This is reflected in good cheer, generosity, friendliness, charity, and the good side of human beings. This is Christmas.

Merry Christmas.

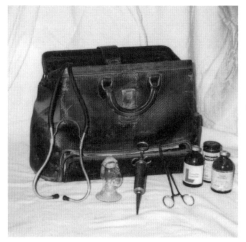

Figure 10.1. The doctor's "black bag" was symbolic: a trademark of the confidence we held that the doctor would help us.

CHAPTER 10
RURAL MEDICINE: COUNTRY DOCTOR

By post WWII standards, rural medical care during the Depression years of the 1930s was primitive. The most dramatic changes came after the development of antibiotics and miracle drugs during and after the war.

"Country doctors" were held in high esteem and relied upon whenever sickness struck a family. While those doctors had good medical schooling for the times, much medical science was still on the brink of revolutionary discovery. The doctor's supply of remedies was quite limited. His most often-used medicines could be carried in his ever-present "black bag," along with essential diagnostic tools: stethoscope, thermometer, blood pressure cuff, otoscope (for ear and nose exam), tongue depressors, and cotton swabs.

Remedies stored in our home medicine cabinet included a small bottle of iodine for cuts and scratches, a thermometer, aspirin for fevers, adhesive tape, gauze, Vick's Vapo-Rub for colds, clear alcohol for a disinfectant, a "patent medicine" healing salve, a bottle of cough syrup, a bottle of liniment, castor oil laxative, and Denver mud for a poultice to draw puss out of a boil or an infection. We also had a "Doctors Book," two inches thick and well used.

The sharp sting (and impulsive "ouch") from the iodine made us forget the hurt of the injury! The distinct smell of evergreen-based liniment assured us healing was underway.

Back then "house calls" also meant farm calls, which could mean a challenging trip over muddy or snow-drifted dirt and gravel roads. For a family with a sick child with a 103-degree fever, the doctor getting out of his Model A Ford, black satchel in hand, was a mighty welcome sight.

The most common sicknesses in the 1930s were measles, chicken pox, small pox, mumps, whooping cough, scarlet fever, common colds, influenza, typhoid, rheumatism, diphtheria, and ear and other infections. Seems like our family had most of them! The list reminds me of how many sicknesses vaccination and modern drugs have practically eliminated. Emergencies such as appendicitis and farm accidents proved the importance of having a doctor in the community. It wasn't unusual to see a boy with his arm in a sling, broken while handling animals, or falling off the pony or out of a tree.

We never thought of farming as particularly hazardous, let alone dangerous. It wasn't until agricultural colleges, such as Iowa State, started compiling farm injury data in the 1930s, that farming was indeed found to be accident-prone. Statistics proved there were many more animal-related injuries than farm people realized. Frequent injuries resulted from getting kicked while milking a cow. Most animals are somewhat "territorial," exhibited by a mother cow charging a man in defense of her newborn calf, or by a sow protecting her new litter. More serious, an ill-tempered and angered bull has injured and killed a number of farmers while they were attending to the cattle herd. Most were sure their bull could be trusted! Because of their size and strength, horses unintentionally, caused injuries (such as stepping on a man's foot) and needed to be handled with care.

In developing early farm machines, it seemed that safety was secondary to accomplishing a given purpose. However, as tractors and mechanical-powered machines became more prevalent, so did serious injury. Metal shields were added to isolate turning gears and chains. An exposed power take-off shaft injured many and killed a few men before these shafts were adequately shielded.

One of the most hazardous machines was the mechanical corn picker. Most accidents happened when the operator attempted to clear cornstalks or leaf trash from either the snapping or husking rollers. Because of the speed of turning machine parts a gloved hand can be instantly drawn into them. In every community it was not uncommon to see a man with an empty shirtsleeve or a metal hook and clasp protruding from it. The most unthinkable was a neighboring farmer who lost a hand in his corn piker and then two years later lost the other one! I was startled when first seeing Carl with two artificial lower arms!

Sickness Strikes At Home

In January 1936, at the age of eleven, I came down with a fever and rheumatic symptoms. For a month or more I had signs of listlessness and fatigue while doing my assigned farm chores. By custom, I hesitated to complain. Along with the nagging fever, I began to have some obvious swelling and some pain in my joints. My family developed immediate concern, and I remember my folks poring over the Doctors Book, looking for symptoms like mine.

To complicate matters, the winter of 1936 was one of the worst on record, with heavy snowfall and continuous winds; rural roads were drifted shut for weeks.

Our family became increasingly alarmed that we couldn't get to Alta, eleven miles south of our farm, to see Doctor Herron, our family doctor. A day's break in the weather in mid-January allowed my oldest brother Nels, my Dad, and I, to travel to the doctor's office in Nels' Model A Ford. The car was equipped with tire chains, and we carried shovels to scoop snow if needed. I clearly remember the strenuous climb up a long flight of wood stairs to the stark doctor's office. The doctor's frown told me that he didn't like what he saw: fever of 102.5, joints badly swollen with white cartilage lumps, and raised reddish patches of skin rash over my body. Dr. Herron sat on a stool and took medical books from a cabinet. Sitting there, I suddenly felt lonely and, for the first time, a little scared.

After about fifteen minutes, which seemed like an eternity, the doctor spoke in his oddly high-pitched voice; "I think the boy has arthritis." Not knowing anything about it, I was bewildered. On hearing a diagnosis my Dad was relieved. Dr. Herron was direct in prescribing my treatment: a pint-sized jar of aspirin discs that effervesced in water to be taken twice a day (tasted awful!), a quart-sized jar of large reddish-brown cod liver oil capsules to be taken twice a day, some wintergreen liniment, and absolute bed rest for three months!

Dr. Herron took these medicines from a small storage closet and handed them to us as we prepared to leave. Neither his diagnoses nor treatment was questioned. We did it.

During that visit to the doctor's office, another event left an indelible mark. A siege of boils running through family members was quite common. Both Dad and Nels had some nasty inflamed boils on the inside of their forearms. Dr. Herron told Nels to lay his arm on a table. Using a scalpel, the doctor quickly split the boil open. Bloody pus squirted out. Nels grimaced at the pain. The doctor bathed the wound, applied iodine, and wrapped Nels' arm with gauze. Then it was Dad's turn. They healed well and got rid of the boils.

An army cot was set up for me by the south double windows in the living room. Heat from the low winter sun sure felt good. I was carried from the downstairs bedroom to the cot every morning. From the cot, I watched for my siblings to come home in the school bus. I listened when Mom talked to neighbors and occasionally butted-in on the telephone party line to visit. I remember my excitement on April 15, 1936, when the implement dealer delivered a John Deere GP tractor to our farm. This was a few years after the worst of the Great Depression when our Fordson tractor had been repossessed to settle a bank debt. Now, worn-out draft horses would have some much-needed help.

In the winter and early spring, after school homework, our family would play games at night, such as "hide the thimble," or word games or riddles. One spring night when I joined in with the laughter and excitement, I clearly remember my Dad saying, "It's great to hear our boy laugh. He's getting better." That was true. But, a typical after-effect of childhood rheumatic condition can be heart valve damage, a heart "murmur." So I was restricted from some activities and exertions for several years after my illness.

An Uplifting Visit

In mid-May, our sixth grade teacher, Miss Barkley and her whole class walked three miles to visit me, their sick classmate. Miss Barkley was a wonderful teacher and a very fine person. I've never forgotten that day. Because of my sickness, I had to repeat the sixth grade, but took it in stride.

For years afterward, I read everything I could about arthritis and heart murmurs: causes, treatments, and cures. Deductively, I made a "diagnoses" of my own sickness. In the summer of 1935, I'd had a rotten baby molar and remember spitting out decay waste. Back then Dad pulled our teeth with an ordinary pair of pliers, carried in the bib-overalls side-plier-pocket for instant machinery or fence repair. We exaggerated the pain and fear of getting a tooth pulled, so I didn't tell anyone of my bad tooth. Years later, I surmised from my reading, that decay organisms had entered my bloodstream and caused the rheumatic disease. Incidentally, I didn't go to a dentist until I was a junior in high school.

In November 1943, I went to Omaha to enlist in the Army Air Corps. World War II was in full force and, because of my earlier heart murmur, I was worried about passing the rigid flight training physical exam. Though I didn't show or express it, I was exhilarated when I passed with "flying" colors!

Sadly, a few schoolmates and acquaintances were burdened their entire life with crippling rheumatism and arthritis.

Country Doctor: An Unsung Hero

The wisdom of a country doctor using rudimentary medicines and a caring family following the doctors orders may have pulled off a miracle. Miracle or not, I've never stopped giving thanks for my cure, a blessing I received.

CHAPTER 11
DRIVING: FROM HORSES TO CARS

Driving: From Horses To Cars

The transition from horses to automobiles and tractors resulted in many humorous situations for farmers as well as other Americans. We often heard about a farmer who got into an emergency situation while driving the tractor and—reverting to driving horses—hollering at the top of his voice, "Whoa! Whoa! Whoa!" Use of the tractor's clutch or brake had completely deserted his mind.

I remember our family having the following cars during my growing-up years: A Model T Ford. A 1926 Dodge four cylinder, four-door sedan (dubbed the "sun parlor" by my sisters because of its square box-like body and large windows), a 1933 four-door Chevrolet with wire spoke wheels, a 1935 two-door Pontiac with front opening "suicide" doors, a 1937 Buick, and a 1939 Buick four-door, "straight 8" cylinder engine. In the early years of the Depression we had a Model T truck, which sat idle (not driven) in the garage for several years because there was no money to buy license plates. In 1937 we traded this truck for a 1931 Model A Ford farm truck, needed to handle the school bus route. During the Great Depression town people could forego owning a car, however, it was practically a necessity for farmers to have one. It is noteworthy that all of these cars named above were "used" when purchased, except the first Model T. My parents were not able to buy another new car until after WWII!

There Were Always Some Qualms About Whether the Car Would Start

Starting the Model T was no simple matter. It worked best with two people. With no electric self-starter, one person had to turn the hand-crank located at the front of the car. Seated inside, the "driver" would push up the spark-retarding lever, to avoid "kicking" the cranker, (which could result in a sprained wrist or even a broken arm), press the clutch pedal down, slightly advance the gas lever, and pull the choke—all at the same time! He then had to be ready to make rapid readjustment of these same controls the moment the engine started! A welcome addition to later Model Ts was battery driven self-starters.

Once the motor was running, getting the Model T to move was not simple either. Model Ts had three pedals: a clutch, brake, and shifting pedal. Letting the shifting pedal halfway out was "low," and clear out was "high" gear. All Model T drivers developed the habit of "riding " the shifting pedal halfway out to get the car moving and then all the way out after gaining some speed. This proved to be a bad habit when Model T drivers started to drive the clutch-controlled three-speed transmissions. Riding the clutch while revving up the noisy engine, Model T wise, attracted plenty of attention and some ribbing from younger, more savvy drivers.

"Hey, your engine's missing," wasn't an unusual warning because the early ignition systems (spark plugs and distributors) were not too reliable, causing one cylinder to miss fire. It was readily apparent on the four-cylinder Model T and Model A Fords and even on the six cylinder engines. It was strange how car incidents often

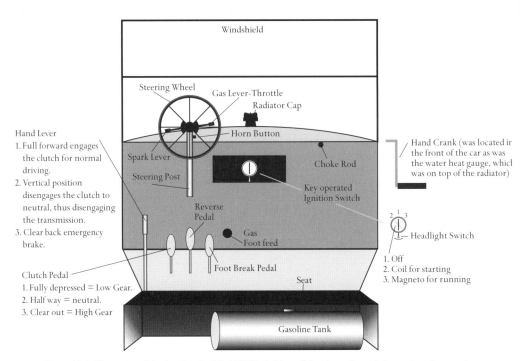

Figure 11.1: Illustration of the interior of a Model T Ford. Most of these controls needed attention when starting a Model T Ford—no wonder the older horse-drivers were intimidated and sometimes confused!

turned into local humor. One Saturday evening, a local character eased his car into a diagonal parking spot in front of some pool hall bench sitters. One kibitzer called out, "Hey, Charlie, your engine's missing." Charlie said, "Dats funny; it vas dare ven I left home"! Jesting put-downs were ample in the country vernacular.

Model T Fords were built so gas would flow from the gas tank by gravity to the engine. This worked fine when designed on the level factory floor but someone forgot to tell the engineers about hilly country roads. To climb certain steep hills, the accepted procedure was to turn the car around and back up the hill, allowing gasoline to flow to the engine.

Driving It Was Another Matter

Dad was never a good driver. Many men his age never made a complete conversion from horses to cars! Most farm wives, including Mom, did not learn to drive a car—even though most could handle a team of horses. When a few, often younger, women learned to drive, they were considered a little risqué! Dad was content to leave the driving up to us boys, and we were more than happy to comply!

We boys learned to drive even before reaching teenage years. It was partly out of necessity, partly because we had easy access to field lanes and open fields to practice on, but mostly because of our eagerness to drive. Necessity included hauling hand tools or fence building materials where needed, or the water jug to thirsty workers. In addition to field lanes, the stubble field from a newly cut oats crop allowed plenty of room to maneuver and learn about turning corners. I'm still amazed at Dad's willingness to ride along as he let us drive the car around the farm. What a thrill when we were only ten years old!

In the 1930s, before pickup trucks were common, many farmers pulled a two-wheel trailer behind the car for light hauling. My Dad and many farmers his age never learned to back a two-wheel trailer without jackknifing it. Many times, Dad drove the car and trailer loaded with five hogs to the Rath Packing Plant's hog buying station in Rembrandt. He drove into the parking area, got out, and my brother Art, age fourteen and with no driver's license, slid behind the steering wheel and effortlessly backed the trailer up to the unloading chute!

One Saturday, Art and I had to go to "preacher school"—confirmation class. Art, age fifteen was driving. Dad sat beside him in the front seat and I sat in the rear with a full, wooden egg case to deliver to the store. A short distance from the farm, they discovered a mouse scurrying around on the front floorboards of the car. Near panic set in as they tried to stomp on the elusive mouse. Not paying attention to the road, Art drove right into the ditch. I was busy trying to keep the eggs from flying out of the egg case! They finally stopped the car, opened the door allowing the mouse to escape, and then drove back up on the roadway and to town. We were none the worse for the excitement, but our family had many laughs over what would have qualified us for a scene in a *Keystone Cops* comedy movie. Especially when I exaggerated about catching eggs in mid-air and stuffing them back into the individual egg pockets!

Love of Cars was a Learning Process.

Looking back sixty-plus years, I realize how primitive those 1920s and early 1930s cars were, especially when compared with improved models that followed. For example, we always carried a spare tire mounted on a wheel rim. We fully expected to have a flat tire from time to time, and used the spare fairly often, especially on longer trips—meaning thirty miles or more from home. A small packet of inner tube patches, cement (glue), and a hand (air) pump were always kept handy to repair a flat tire at the side of the road. Headlights for night driving were very poor, limiting safe night driving to speeds of thirty miles per hour. Until the late 1920s, only the rear wheels were equipped with small mechanical brakes, which provided only limited stopping ability. Then "four-wheel brakes" were advertised as a major advancement. It wasn't until the later 1930s that much better hydraulic brakes came into general use.

Engines were hard to crank when heavyweight engine oil became stiff in cold weather. When combined with six-volt batteries weakened by cold temperatures, winter starting was always uncertain. If need be, we pulled the car with a team of horses to get it started. When the engine finally started, with a couple of *huffs* and a *bang!* we kids running alongside gave a cheer! Before permanent antifreeze, we had to rely on methyl alcohol added to the radiator water. Since alcohol has a low boiling point, it would often boil and evaporate, allowing water to freeze in the radiator. The result: no circulation for cooling and an overheated engine, in the coldest of winter. Passenger compartment heaters were skimpy tin ducts, which attempted to capture heat from the engine manifold; these heaters delivered little warmth, so passenger comfort required the use of the same "buffalo robes" of horse and buggy days!

For years I've laughed at how we school boys argued about cars, sometimes the discussion turned into shouting matches! Whatever kind of car the family had was the best. With our limited knowledge, the truth was, we didn't know what the heck we were talking about! But some adult conversations were not much different when cars were the subject. Once when talking cars, our German neighbor, Rudy Beckman, chimed in, "I've had a *Boo-eeck* [Buick] for seven years and never had a wrench on it." My older brothers laughed when surmising that Rudy probably didn't drive his Buick over 500 miles a year.

We boys not only knew every make of car, but what model everyone in the neighborhood drove. Some days not a single car went by, but when one did we always commented "There goes Rueben," or whoever. A strange car was promptly noticed, leaving little chance for a salesman to surprise an unwary farmer!

Improved roads and better cars played a key role in overcoming the Great Depression. They helped farmers save time, get more work done, and made life more enjoyable.

It is interesting how men are taken up with cars and 'car talk'. My brother Art, haveing good mechanical skills, kept his cars in good running order. One day, years later, we were engaged in the usual car talk and listening to a minor noise in my car's engine. I expected Art to confirm it was a loose tappet or something. I was taken aback but then laughed at his droll comment, "The best thing to do with some of these engine noises is to turn up the radio!"

Airplanes Yet!

Exciting developments in travel were not all confined to the ground. In the late 1920s and early 1930s, airplanes and "barnstorming" pilots became a more frequent sight. Their planes were several steps better than the old "Jennies" flown in WWI. At small-town celebrations, rides in the planes were offered for one dollar. Air passenger service was in its infancy. The newness of airplanes and flying was evidenced by us kids dashing out to the farmyard whenever the drone of an airplane's engine was heard. They were either single-engine biplanes (two wings) or monoplanes. We always watched from the yard until the plane was out of sight. It must have been amusing to the pilot to see kids run out to watch at every farm home he flew over. Of course, this interest and insatiable curiosity soon led to us kids to make some hard landings while equipped with homemade wings and jumping off the cattle shed roof! We finally settled for building model airplanes.

CHAPTER 12
THE FARM: A PLACE OF EVOLVEMENT

From "Philosophies": "One thing I've never understood: why each new generation that comes along, having discovered sex, act like they invented it."

Inevitably every child asks, "Momma, where did I come from?" The familiar "brought by a stork" yarn was readily taken to be mythical humor. In our family the question resulted in a variety of responses, a different story for each sibling. Being born in January, I was "found in a snowdrift." Even at three or four years of age, because of a wink or smile, I perceived it to be in jest—but did not fully disbelieve it. I envisioned being wrapped in a baby blanket for warmth. Even though told by family members I trusted, subconsciously I knew it was not entirely true. I was mildly perplexed for a year or so. Then, with more open laughter and reaction by my older siblings, I accepted—without much concern—that I had been spoofed. When I become an adolescent, sex was not talked about openly in our family.

On the farm, mating, breeding, and birthing of animals was an economic necessity in order to grow produce for the market—for income. As a young boy growing up on the farm and observing these reproduction cycles, I saw sexual reproduction as a natural and essential part of the farm operation. This was unconsciously translated to mammal reproduction—to human life.

During the 1930s and before, in every farming community there was a man with a stud horse. Before tractors took over, farmers had to raise a colt now and then in order to have ample workhorses. Roy Rosdail with "Mon," a handsome and assertive bay stallion hitched to a two-wheeled Sulky cart, drove around the farm community. His goal was to find—simultaneously—a farmer needing a foal who had a mare in heat. Though not a sole means of his livelihood, stud-fees at ten dollars for a foal helped support his family.

It struck me strange how our other horses became excited when the stallion came on the farmyard. They milled around the barn lot, whinnying loudly, as if acknowledging that a different kind of intruder had moved in on their territory. This didn't happen when a neighbor drove an ordinary team of geldings or mares into the farmyard. More than once Roy arrived at our farm in late afternoon, surmising there could be another place set at the supper table and a spare bed. We kids were both curious and fearful of the large, aggressive stallion kept in our barn overnight. At times it took a firm hand and a short whip to keep the rambunctious stallion under control as Roy led him to the water tank or was hitching him to the Sulky cart. The stallion sired two colts by our mares over a period of five years to raise horses needed for farm work.

There was a peculiar double standard, an obvious contradiction in the sexual attitudes toward sons and daughters. There was a subtle acceptance of sons being aggressive in their sexual prowess. Bragging rights paralleled a peculiar rite of passage. Jokes about boys "sowing their wild oats" were permissible. However, a girl involved in such behavior was "loose" or "fast." Daughters were expected to be virgins. Not a very realistic probability when those restraints didn't apply to boys. My Dad was very

Figure12.1: Roy Rosdail with his large, assertive stallion, Mon. (circa 1934)

strict when it came to my older sisters dating. He knew whom they went with and when they were expected to be home. My Dad, like many other fathers, scared suitors away. No doubt parents were sincere and did shield daughters from unwelcome situations.

But not all young women or men escaped. "Shotgun" weddings were not uncommon. In this exaggerated scenario, the pregnant bride's father stood at the back of the church with a shotgun to "encourage" the groom and soon-to-be father to dutifully assume his responsibility. A mocking joke was often heard in these instances: the first child was born "prematurely"; however, subsequent babies took nine months.

Years later, when there was much fuss and confusion about teaching sex education in schools, I realized how much education we farm kids got by observing Mother Nature first-hand. And I observed that town kids could be quite ignorant about it. Efforts to "modernize" sex education in public schools swung toward the application of psychology and biology in the absence of any moral teaching. With the high rate of promiscuity and babies born out of wedlock, we must not have it right—yet! The situation changed with the advent of birth control pills in the 1960s.

Over the years I've wondered about the effect of culture, customs, religious hang-ups or deep seated instincts on the inability and discomfort in explaining sexual reproduction to youngsters—even to our own children. One commentary may relate; in the early 1960s television talk show host, Jack Parr, was interviewing the witty and mirthful British intellectual Malcolm Muggridge. Their conversation drifted to sex and Parr's question of why we humans, particularly Westerners, are embarrassed to talk about it. Muggridge's response was in a humorous vain, "Well if you think about it, the act itself is funny! The peculiar contortions we go through to propagate the human race!" In some way, Muggridge put it in a down to earth perspective. Something a farm boy, often observing animal reproduction, could relate to.

Figure 12.2: Otto Aust and his prize angus bull. (circa 1942)

The Civilizing Process

The mores and customs of farm life fit, in a small way, into the centuries old trek (starting about 3,000 B.C.) of striving for a higher level of civilization. That level has been predominately measured by man's advances in culture, science, industry, and government.

For many centuries, philosophers and scholars have been redefining the meaning of civilization. Advances are often related to group living (cities-governance), growing of crops (food), domesticating animals (food and draft power), and learning crafts (tools). One of the most essential driving forces supporting all of these efforts is developing an alphabet and writing. If we substitute farm neighborhoods for historical population centers, all of the above-mentioned advances mesh with and compliment the family farm.

In the early 1900s, Sigmund Freud wrote that man's sexuality had much greater impact on the civilizing process than previously considered. While gaining considerable acceptance, Freud's work has also been under continual examination and some dispute.

With continuing advancements in warfare—means of killing people—any thoughtful person can't help but wonder if we really understand civilization very well. When we daily read and hear the litany of man's brutality, irrational behavior, and a variety of sex-related crimes, I wonder about our self-acclaimed, elevated status. How elevated are we?

From the 1930s and beyond we have accelerated our claim to a higher civilization based on mechanical accomplishments such as automobiles, tractors, radios, clothes dryers, television, nuclear bombs, and many other "gadgets." While most of these things intend to make life more convenient, actual civilization must be measured in humanitarian accomplishments. In short, this means a maximum of individual freedoms and the minimum of individual suffering while living under government by the people.

The singular most important and most-heard voice, over the last two millenniums, to speak out for ingredients of civility among people is that of Jesus Christ. That gives some confirmation to teachings and disciplines instilled, in my youth, at the Little Sioux Valley Lutheran country church. That, in large measure, is why I attempt to live by and practice Christ's teachings.

Part One

Part
Two

Plants
The Wealth of Man Starts with Food Produced from the Soil

Morning on the Farm

Arne Waldstein

Vintaged in chilled morning air,
Leaves come unstilled
Whispering about the new day.
Sun sparkling,
Refreshed from the night away
Warming air and me.

Farm boy leather high shoes
Tread lightly over the dirt yard,
Audible in the morning.
This dirt I walk on, whose is it?
A part of earth? I'm pondering.
An enigma shared by God and me.

Lifted barn latch
Brings muffled crescendo
From friends inside.
Old Bill rasps at a stroke on the nose
And Jim snorts, impatient to abide.
Acknowledging oats and me.

Flared nostril breath,
Horse odor and sweated leather.
"Aroma Nostalgia"
Five dollars a moment.

On the other side Roany, moos just audible
In chorus are
Essex, Pontiac, Wippet, and Red.
Cows named after cars
Epitomize epochs ahead.
Foolish dreams of machines, space men, and me.

Cow's tail flits as a baton,
Milk squirts zing the bottom of the pail.
Mother cat purrs hopefully
By old tin pan.
A cowbarn symphony
By beasts and me.

Hogs argue over new thrown ears
Rudely tearing away dawn's mantle.
Day won't wait

Kennut, "Bring the hammer."
Art, "Open the gate!"
The farm becomes now and me.

Breakfast homemade,
Potatoes from the cellar
Sizzled in smoked bacon grease.
Eggs gathered last night,
Hot coffee gulps allow a pause.
In the morn I reflect on the farm and me.

Part two is about the reality of farming, making a living through the production of plants and animals.
Responding to those endeavors demanded work—often, hard work.

CHAPTER 13
POTATOES: "A FEAST FOR THE MASSES"

A small potato patch was often planted in the house yard in early spring to provide tender and succulent, though small, "spuds" for the dinner table by late June. In addition, most farmers grew a larger patch in a nearby farm field. A goal religiously followed by many families was to have potatoes planted by Good Friday. Seed potatoes were taken from leftovers of last year's crop. This runs counter to the common practice of selecting seed from the most productive plants. However, the genetic benefit from a tuber (potato) seed is not readily predictable.

The first step in preparation for planting fell to us kids. We sat on a stool by the potato bin in the cellar, selected a potato, and cut it in three or four slices or sections—made sure that each slice had an "eye" or bud—then placed it in the seed pail.

A joke was told about neighbor Victor wanting to ease up on his hard-working hired man, Steve, by letting him cut the potato pieces. Vic advised Steve to be sure that every piece had an eye or seed bud and went about other chores. Stopping by after awhile Vic was surprised to see Steve in quite a fluster. Vic inquired, "What's the matter? I thought you would enjoy such an easy job." Steve responded, "It ain't the work; it's having to make these darned 'one-eyed' decisions!"

In the selected field, a horse-drawn cultivator was used to dig four-inch furrows about forty inches apart. With bucket in hand, we walked in the furrow, dropping a seed eye about every ten inches and pressing it into the soil by stepping on it. A team pulling an eight-foot drag harrow covered the seeds with dirt.

With good moisture and (hopefully) a timely rain, the potato sprouts pushed through the ground in a week. Using a regular corn cultivator and hand hoeing controlled weeds. A real threat to the crop was potato bugs (Colorado beetles), which seemed to come out of nowhere by the hundreds. The potato bug would devour the plant foliage, leaving the stems and branches barren of leaves. In desperation, we kids walked the rows carrying a gallon can with an inch of kerosene in the bottom. We picked the tan, black-striped beetles off the plants and dropped them into the can. As this proved to be a futile control measure, Dad and other farmers started spraying plants with a poisonous arsenic-of-lead solution that gave quick and complete control.

In mid-August using a five-tined pitchfork we dug potatoes from the field for daily eating. The new tender spuds were flavorful! In September we harvested the main crop. A team pulled the potato plow to bring the tubers to the surface. Running the shovel-shaped plow blade shallow, it lifted the potatoes out of the ground and onto an attached grate-like shaker, separating dirt from the potatoes. Walking with a pail in hand, we picked potatoes up from the ground, and dumped them into a wagon, hauled and unloaded them into the house cellar. Safely stored, they were a nurturing staple for our long winter diet.

Though we carefully preserved them, our parents allowed us to use a few potatoes to carve funny human faces, busts, or small animal likenesses. When dried, our amusing carvings were displayed for several weeks on a windowsill, the clock

Figure 13.1: Potato plow or "digger" was used at harvest.

shelf, or on the bookcase. We occasionally took our "pieces of art" to school where the teacher put them on display along with those of our classmates.

Another cycle of annually producing a crop, in this instance potatoes, was completed. This practice, although of different crops and by different people, has been duplicated by farmers around the world for thousands of years.

Figure 13.2: Picking potatoes (or spuds) was a tiresome job. We kids created some comic relief. In this photo, Art is more interested in our dog, Scot; Mom seems to tolerate our antics; Dorothy proudly points to a fruit of her labor; and nieces Donna and Mickey "ham it up," while I'm pretending a potato can be interesting! (circa 1937)

Figure 14.1: A buzz saw, when belted up to the tractor pulley, will cut logs into stove-sized firewood.

CHAPTER 14
BRINGING IN THE WOOD SUPPLY

Being the youngest of eight kids, I usually ended up with the most menial farm chores. Often, my brother Art and I worked together bringing in "burning" (fuel) to last the winter night and next day. This meant filling the cob box, splitting wood into small pieces for the kitchen range, and splitting larger stumps for the "parlor furnace"—heating stove.

Though wood was our main fuel source corncobs (a by-product of the corn crop) played an important part. When ear corn was shelled from the crib, we were left with a sizeable cob pile. We took cobs directly from the pile to the house for burning or stored them in an empty building, often the smokehouse. Cobs were used daily to start the fire in the stoves and for added fuel. At times we ran short on cobs from the sheller and resorted to the hog lot for cobs left after the hogs had eaten off all the kernels. To the uninformed, this may seem unsanitary, but hogs are instinctively clean animals in many ways. Given a choice, they never defecate (manure) near where they eat, so the hog lot cobs were clean and, unlike sheller cobs, were full-length—handy for stoking up the fire.

Getting It Together

Gathering the winter's wood supply started in late fall after corn harvest. Dad, my oldest brothers, and sometimes a hired man, would gather up timber from groves and windbreaks that early settlers had the foresight to plant. They would always fell the dead or dying trees first, but occasionally cut poorer live trees to get enough wood for the winter. Hardwoods such as ash, walnut, elm, maple, or box elder were preferred. Cottonwood and willow made poor firewood and were harvested only when dead or damaged by lightning.

Using an axe, Dad selected and notched trees to fall in the desired direction. Starting opposite the notch, aggressive strokes with a two-man crosscut saw brought the reluctant giant crashing to the ground. Sometimes I felt a sense of guilt in slaying a majestic friend.

The men immediately set to work cutting the limbs and logs into ten- to fifteen-foot lengths, then loading and hauling them to the farmyard with a team and wagon or bobsled when there was snow. The usual grain box was removed and logs were stacked on the bolsters of the wagon or bobsled running gear and were tied down with log chains or rope. Getting to ride on top of the teetering load, when my older brother drove the team, was a big thrill. I observed that the wagon chassis and wheels squeaked and groaned under the heavy load while the bobsled skimmed along smoothly and silently.

When ample logs were piled, two or three neighbors joined in to buzz-saw the logs into about fifteen-inch lengths to fit the stove. My dad owned the buzz saw, which was staked down near the log pile and near where they wanted the stump pile to be, usually in close proximity to the house. The buzz saw was belted up to a farm tractor. In the 1920s that usually was the Fordson, but ours and many other tractors were casualties of the Great Depression of the early 1930s. A few farmers could afford to keep a 10-20 McCormick-Deering or a John Deere D plow tractor, which was used to power the neighborhood buzz saws and other belt-driven machines such as the grain thresher, corn sheller, silage chopper, or feed grinder.

Buzz-sawing was quite dangerous. With the open, unguarded, spinning thirty-inch steel saw blade, only grown men worked at it. Occupation and Safety Hazard Administration (OSHA) laws were not yet conceived, but today's OSHA inspectors would have gone wild at the lack of safeguards! The job required five or six men: two carried logs to the saw, two handled the logs on the saw table and one threw the sawed stumps onto a pile. Another man usually tended the tractor and was ready to help carry an extra-heavy log. The shrill *whine* and *zing* of the steel buzz saw blade and cackle of the straining tractor engine could be heard around the neighborhood. The freshly cut sawdust had its own pleasing aroma. The newly-cut stump pile grew like a pyramid, reaching about eight to ten feet high.

Finally A Warm Reward

From fall sawing until spring, we boys selected, split, and hauled-in the day's burning. We soon learned which stumps split easiest. Come spring, only knotty, tough pieces remained, requiring the use of a mall and steel wedges.

Wood was hauled to the house in the coaster wagon or sled and stacked neatly in the back porch. Mom's quick glance let us know if we had enough wood to keep the house warm in spite of prevailing winter temperatures—often below zero.

As corncobs and wood were the main farm fuels, it was a real luxury to occasionally have a few pieces of coal that were used sparingly to "bank" the fire during the coldest winter nights.

A quip heard in the neighborhood was about getting several "heats" out of the wood: first, from cutting the trees; then, from hauling the logs; then, from buzz-sawing the logs; then, from splitting the logs; then, from hauling the resulting firewood to the house; and—finally—from when the firewood was burned! Even after that, we had to carry out the ashes! Years later in college economics classes, I easily related some farm work to the term "labor intensive."

From the foresight of pioneers to plant trees, to the labors of settlers who followed, harvesting firewood was an important part of survival and economic gain in the farming community until after WWII. Then, farm families switched to furnace oil or propane—both fossil fuels. In the process, farm families lost some of their interdependence, becoming less self-sufficient and more beholden to the corporate energy giants and world oil cartels. For convenience, we gave up another bit of freedom!

CHAPTER 15
HAY: MAKING HAY WHILE THE SUN SHINES

Hay acreage in the Midwest peaked in the early 1900s. Thereafter it gradually decreased. By 1930 approximately 20 percent of Corn Belt cropland was used for growing hay needed on family farms to feed livestock. In those early "hay days," from 1907 to 1937, hay acreage dropped 40 percent in Iowa. Two events quickened this change: in the early 1930s tractors were rapidly replacing hay-eating horses, and more profitable soybeans crowded out hay land acreage.

Small native grass (wild hay) areas were left in drainage ways (draws) to prevent soil erosion and gullies. Fields of wild hay were also left in wet, poorly-drained sloughs and on some lighter upland soils. Fields seeded to alfalfa, clover, and timothy were known as "tame" hay and came to make up most hay land acreage.

After corn and small grain crops, haymaking was the major job in terms of time, labor, and equipment. The first of three cuttings of alfalfa was done by mid-June, the last in August. Other hay crop varieties, such as red clover, were harvested at various times during the summer.

Days before cutting hay, we repaired mower sickles with new sections and fitted the mower's cutter-bar with new ledger plates. Sitting on the metal seat and pedaling to turn the whetstone grinding wheel, Dad looked as though he was riding a tricycle. The high-pitched complaint of the hardened steel sickle acknowledged that it had surrendered to sharpening.

"Putting up" alfalfa hay started by mowing the field—with a typical five-foot sickle-bar riding mower, pulled by a lively team of horses. By maintaining good momentum, the mower cut better. Mowing always started at the outside (perimeter) of the field and worked in toward the center. Dad taught me how to keep the corners square by cutting clear through the standing swath before making a sharp ninety-degree turn and proceeding alongside the remaining standing crop.

One of the sweetest aromas of the countryside was a newly mown alfalfa field. Often, local town folks would take an evening drive in the country just to enjoy the fresh smell of newly-mown hay.

Farming has long been known as a rather dangerous occupation in terms of accidents and injuries. The sickle bar of a mower or grain binder claimed a finger or two from rushed or careless farmers. It was a sickening feeling to see a brooding hen pheasant flee her nest and barely escape the sickle bar, knowing full well that her clutch of eggs or newly-hatched chicks were devastated.

As haymaking progressed, farmers kept a wary eye out for any thunderheads, hoping to avoid rain and thereby harvest the most luxurious green hay crop.

After cutting, hay was left to dry for twelve to twenty-four hours, before windrowing with a side delivery rake. Often, if raked in the morning, the first hay loads were hauled in that afternoon. Although anxious to get the crop in, there was a constant concern about getting it dried down enough to avoid "heating," that could result in a spontaneous combustion fire, which destroyed barns from time to time.

Figure 15.1: Mower.

Reports of barn fires in the area kept farmers' nerves on edge as they tried to outguess Mother Nature.

A hay loader was drawn behind the hayrack (hay wagon), pulled by a team of horses. The hayrack was a wooden structure sixteen-feet-long by seven-feet-wide with thirty-inch high side rails. It had considerable capacity for loose hay. The hay loader

Figure 15.2: Side Delivery Rake.

Figure 15.3: Hay loader and hayrack.

gathered the windrow from the ground and delivered it by means of a slat and rope conveyor to the hayrack. As a boy, my job was to drive the team on the hayrack while Dad and an older brother stacked the oncoming hay to get the biggest load possible. This usually and mischievously resulted in the driver, even while standing high on the front-end driver's ladder, getting covered with hay!

When loaded, the hayrack was pulled to the barn for unloading. In older and smaller barns the hay was pitched off by hand. But most barns were equipped with a track and carrier whereby hay was unloaded with a mechanical hayfork or rope slings. One of the hottest and hardest jobs was "mowing" (mouwing) which meant spreading the hay out in the barn haymow so it wouldn't become overly packed and difficult to remove when feeding livestock the following winter.

Figure 15.4: All hands welcome, as Dad and boys load the manure spreader. Circa 1930.

In addition to barn storage, large haystacks were located along fence line mangers for convenient winter feeding. The stacks were usually "capped" with wild, tall grass hay to protect legumes from rain and snow. When feeding the hay to the livestock, a "hay knife" with a three-foot serrated blade, was used to help remove the tightly-packed haystack.

As with most farm enterprises, growing hay continued beyond harvest, resulting in a year-round cycle. By spring, wasted hay dribbled by livestock feeding along the hay mangers was mixed in with animal excrement and trampled into a two-foot-thick manure pack. Manure accumulated in straw-bedded cattle sheds, leftover haystack, and straw pile "bottom" waste. All of this left a challenging job to contend with each spring. Using four-tined forks, we "bent over and strained" for a few long days loading the manure spreader. A three-horse hitch was needed to pull the whirring spreader to fertilize nearby hay fields, where a new hay crop was already starting to grow! The next crop cycle, another season, was already underway.

We kids, though growing bigger and stronger, were hoping the next harvest would prove just a little easier.

That hope was spurred when, in 1939, we got our first glimpse of what lay ahead—*hay balers*. The job of handling bulky, loose hay was hard work, time consuming, and required costly storage (often in huge gambrel-roofed barns).

New Holland Machinery Company of New Holland, Pennsylvania, was a leader in designing efficient portable hay balers. The baler was pulled behind a farm tractor and either powered by the power take-off shaft or an auxilary gasoline engine. Rather than the cumbersome horse-drawn hayrack, a flat rack was hooked up and towed behind the baler.

As the machine moved across the hay field it picked up hay from the windrow, compressed it into sixteen by sixteen by forty-two inch bales, and bound it tightly with two strands of fine wire (later twine was used). The machine then conveyed the bales back to the flat rack. Usually two men rode on the flat rack, stacking sixty or more bales to a load. The bales were about one-sixteenth the volume or bulk of loose hay, which greatly reduced handling and storage needs. In winter, feeding livestock by bales proved more efficient than loose hay.

Shortly after WWII, hay baler machines took over hay harvesting and storage. Another new and innovative farm machine took yet more drudgery out of farming.

A colloquialism conceived by a farmer while making hay was: "Never pitch hay against the wind." The reproach, "He pitches hay against the wind," simply meant that that the man didn't use common sense. It was a short, poignant bit of jargon that was readily understood by country people.

CHAPTER 16
GROWING OATS: SEEDING TO THRESHING

Oats raised by individual farmers, started in early spring, became a cooperative neighborhood endeavor at threshing time in late July.

While oats was the dominant small grain crop, some barley and rye were grown for livestock feed. Because the spiked beards on barley heads irritated the skin when shocking and threshing, farmers were reluctant to grow it. Rye, seeded in the fall, offered some early spring growth and light grazing. Flax was grown during WWII for needed linseed oil and linen straw to fabricate heavy battle-gear cloth. A flax field, in full bloom of blue flowers, was truly a waving sea.

Oats seeding was done in late March or early April. Equipment included a team, pulling a "triple-box" wagon with an endgate seeder mounted on the rear end of the wagon box. A chain driven by a rear wagon wheel powered the seeder. It was one of the first important fieldwork jobs we kids could help with because two people worked best: a driver for the team and a scooper to keep the seeder filled with oats. Oats were seeded on prior year's corn stalks still standing in rows. The endgate seeder would scatter oats over nine row widths, about thirty feet. I remember the seeder's wearisome whirring, synchronized with the horse's pulsing, rhythmic stride: *imm-ya, imm-ya, imm-ya.*

An eight-foot, single disk pulled by four horses was used to cover seed and hasten germination. Because of my youth, I drove a four-horse span less than a dozen times before tractors took over. While riding on the disc's concave-shaped steel seat I was only six feet behind the four horses. Their harness creaked as tugs strained at every step while the dust cloud from tilled dirt was at times stifling. After disking, the seedbed was leveled with a sixteen-foot-wide spike-tooth harrow (drag) pulled by a span of four horses. We often walked behind the drag, but on larger fields a riding cart was attached—some luxury.

Mother Nature Does Her Miracle

Only 110 days after seeding, plants matured around July 10, and the fields turned into amber waves of grain! We sowed oats of different maturation rates to spread out harvest time: Iowa, 105 days to maturity; and Green Russian, 112 days to maturity.

It was exciting to get the grain binder out of the shed and take care of necessary repairs in preparation for harvest. Invariably, canvas had to be patched, sickles sharpened, and binder twine bought. Twine came in sacks of six rolls each and had that distinct aromatic smell of hemp. The twine rope binding the sack was useful around the farm.

The binder, pulled by three or four horses, cut an eight-foot swath, starting at the perimeter (outer edge) of the field and working in to the center. In the mid-1930s farmers were losing good horses to "sleeping sickness," leaving older and poorer teams. Because the binder had to maintain a steady momentum to cut well, I rode— at the age of nine or ten—on the back of one of the draft horses using a short whip to

Figure 16.1: The binder is stopped and a burlap-wrapped water jug is passed around for a cool drink. (circa 1934)

keep the team at a steady pace. I could feel the horse's strain, hear the tugging leather harness squeak, smell whiffs of sweat and an occasional smell of rank gas from the horse's habit of farting! Though Mom sympathized, little concern was given to blisters I got on my rear from riding the horse all day. What a relief and improvement it was when Dad bought the John Deere GP tractor in 1936. As older brothers were faster at setting up shocks, at age twelve I got to drive the tractor, pulling the binder operated by Dad. Maybe it was a reward for riding a horse pulling the binder!

The binder's sickle mechanism cut the oats, laid it back on the platform canvas, elevated it to be gravity-fed to the packer arms, mechanically tied it into bundles with a "ker-chunk" sound and then kicked the bundles into a cradle-like carrier. Dad would systematically trip the carrier dropping four or five bundles in windrows. Older brothers and often sisters helped set six or eight bundles into shocks. It was slow tedious work on the hottest July days. Often in life, pure enjoyment, expediency, and the realities of nature come into ironic conflict. We kids went barefoot most of the summer, partly out of the sheer, unfettered, *Huckleberry Finn* liberation. But mostly because there were too many other needs for "shoe" money. Iowa's state flower is the wild rose, a small, thorny, spiked bush that flourished in oats fields. Treading barefoot through the oats stubble, while avoiding the needle-sharp thorns of the rosebush, was a challenge to be reckoned with. Occasionally, someone would have to sit down on an oats bundle to extract a thorn or sliver from his or her foot. Whenever anyone took too many "sliver breaks," a call went out across the field: "Sleeever"!—goading the guilty party to get up and help with shocking.

With the WWII labor shortage everyone had to pitch in and help.

Figure 16.2: Niece Donna drove the tractor under the watchful eye of Art on the binder. (circa 1944)

Neighbors Pull Together

Oats shocks were left standing for a week or longer to "sweat," or cure, before threshing. Threshing provided camaraderie among neighbors in the "threshing run," or "threshing ring." Usually, one or a small group of farmers owned the threshing machine. A farmer having a tractor best adapted to the job provided power. Usually a "three plow" tractor was needed. The tractor was "belted up" to the thresher with a forty-foot-long fabric belt. Fed by bundle-haulers with a steady flow of bundles, the big machine with its rhythmic vibration quietly hummed along hour after hour as it separated oats grain from the straw. In the thirties, a few steam engines were still being used to power threshing machines.

The threshing machine was moved from neighbor to neighbor until all eight to twelve farms in the threshing run were finished. The script was about the same at each farm. The "host" farmer's wife would always make sure her meal, or rather banquet, was better than the neighbors'! My older sisters would often help neighboring farm wives when they had to prepare the meal. With the threshing machine shut down for noon dinner, men would wash up in several wash basins set up temporarily on sawhorses and planks under a shade tree near the house. Young, hungry men devoured the wholesome spread of food. Dinner table conversation was rather mundane, but it fascinated a young boy clinging to every word and nuance.

The threshing crew was a rather complex social and economic arrangement. One man tended the threshing machine; another was responsible for the "engine" (tractor). The host farmer was responsible for hauling his grain away from the "separator" (as threshing machines were sometimes called) to a granary located on the farmstead. There was nearly always a "hired man" who followed the threshing machine to "stack" or shape the large straw pile to best preserve it for feed and bedding

Figure 16.3: Mickey, age twelve, works alongside grandpa when shocking newly cut oats bundles. (circa 1944)

during the long winter to come. There were usually eight or more bundle-haulers, each having a team and hayrack. Lively competition existed between the young men hauling bundles to see who could go to the field, get loaded, and get back the quickest. For the fastest, it meant some relaxing or "horsing around" time—as after the first load of the day bundle-haulers never got out of their "rotation." Skill was required in shaping a full-square load in contrast to the smaller "peaked" loads referred to as "raindrop splitters"! Haulers with smaller loads of bundles were taunted with friendly jests.

Farm work crews often provided an interesting study of human nature. A few "dressed up" landlords, apparently worried about getting their share of the crop, would hang around on threshing day. Stories were told about a landlord grasping the topside of the wagon box, pulling himself up as if to inspect the grain and thereby bulging out the sides—getting more bushels in his load! Naturally, farmers and workers of the "threshing crew" were resentful. Some would smear black, sticky axle grease along the top of the wagon box. An overly assertive, grease-smeared landlord got the message.

At our place, Dad, with the help of two of us kids, hauled oats to the granary. That job was quite involved. With two teams and wagons, one wagon was always at the thresher being loaded while the other was hauling a full load to the granary. The loaded wagon would be parked at the elevator hopper and in the "jack" (or hoist) to speed unloading. A team on the horsepower, walking in a thirty-foot-diameter circle, powered the gears that drove the elevator and hoist.

During the ten-year period from 1931 through 1940, oat yields in Iowa averaged 31.6 bushel per acre. Threshing time presented the farmer with the first opportunity of the season to sell a cash crop. The ten-year August price average of 24.6¢ per bushel ($7.75 per acre) reveals how difficult it was to develop significant farm income during the Great Depression.

Figure 16.4: Threshing machine.

It usually took two weeks or more to complete the threshing run, depending on rain delays. In the later 1930s when farmers began to get out from under the worst of the Depression, they would celebrate completion of the last job with a case or a keg of beer. That's when I had an early introduction to beer, probably at age eleven or twelve! Being there as a worker with the men, it was a "rite of passage" to be offered a beer. Somehow I managed to conceal that the beer made me queasy, but you can be sure I never admitted it until years later.

Time to Settle Up

A week or so after threshing was finished, farmers gathered at the threshing machine tender's (often owner's) house for a potluck supper, which always included fresh watermelon. The real purpose of the meeting was to settle up accounts for threshing which cost two to three cents per bushel.

At a yield of thirty-two bushels per acre, and at .02 per bushel, that's 64¢ per acre. Take that and multiply it by eighty acres, and it comes to a $51.20 cash outlay for the entire threshing job. Of course, the labor was paid by exchange of work within members of the "threshing run." This exemplifies how the scarcity of cash and "trading labor" sharply curtailed monetary outlays during the Great Depression.

Another interesting chapter in farming, growing the oats crop, came to a close until the next spring. Then, again signaled by the "whirring" seeders, planting a new crop will have started.

Figure 17.1: Primary tillage: six horses pull a gang plow.

CHAPTER 17
GROWING CORN: KING OF THE CORN BELT

During the Great Depression, corn (in varying amounts) was grown in every state in the Union. It was by far the most important crop in the Midwest. Soybean acreage increased rapidly in the late 1930s, and it replaced small grain and hay; however, corn remained number one.

Preparation

Producing a corn crop covered a long time span, starting when oats stubble or hay land was plowed the previous fall. It was concluded fifteen months later when corn harvesting was finally completed. Fall plowing was usually accomplished by using a gangplow having two fourteen-inch moldboards or bottoms and pulled by either five or six horses. Smaller farmers often used a one-bottom Sulky plow with three horses. Both were built so the driver could ride on a round, concave metal seat—pretty luxurious. Most farmers kept a one-bottom walking plow for small jobs such as the garden. Real luxury, enjoyed by a few farmers was a "plow tractor," often a standard tread, steel-wheeled 10-20 or 15-30 McCormick-Deering, a John Deere D, a Fordson, or one of several other makes. Tractors could be heard chugging a mile away late into the evening, long after horses had to be fed and rested. Tractors were the envy of farmers still using horses.

A well-plowed field was black and clean. The newly turned soil had an organic smell from prior crop residue. The plowed soil had a mellow, damp feel. Usually, large flocks of seagulls would hover closely over the moving plow, eagerly feeding on exposed earthworms. Friendly banter advised the plowman to wear a wide-brimmed hat to avoid seagull droppings. These black fields were quite different from forty years later when plant residue was purposely left on the surface to help control erosion—a lesson learned from the dust bowl of the 1930s. A lesson missed when Indians earlier cautioned, "White man turn earth upside down!"

Although spring plowing worked quite well in the loess soils of western Iowa, fall plowing was preferred in the black glacial drift and other heavy soils prevalent in most of the Corn Belt. Here spring-plowed soils turned over in slabs, often resulted in a cloddy, poor seedbed. Because plowing corn stalks under in the spring did not allow enough time for decomposition, corn stalks were often raked into windrows and burned. During a calm spring evening it appeared as if the whole countryside was on fire. Though expedient and a striking scene, it was a terrible waste of valuable organic matter.

After the freezing, thawing, and decaying of crop refuse during winter, the fall-plowed field would be nice and mellow come spring. Loose dirt would fluff up, dusting our shoes when walking in the fields that were ready for the new corn crop. Seedbed preparation started in mid-April after oats were seeded. First tillage was with an eight-foot disk pulled by four horses, straining and leaning into their harnesses. Early weed seed germination often made a second disking beneficial. Disking was followed within a week and just before corn planting with a sixteen-foot-wide spike toothed harrow or "drag" pulled by four horses.

Figure 17.2: Planting corn. Note check wire.

After the drought and dust storms of 1936, simultaneous with the rapidly increasing number of tractors, farmers and scientists started looking for improved tillage tools. In addition to a mellow seedbed, reducing soil erosion became a priority. This resulted in the design and development of the "spring tooth harrow." It met the tillage needs but required the now available farm tractor to pull it. Within just two or three years about every corn farmer had a spring tooth harrow. It became the choice for final seedbed preparation. After harrowing, corn was planted as soon as possible before weeds started to germinate again.

Planting Corn: A Meticulous Job

Planting corn was one of the most exacting jobs for the Midwest farmer. Two forty-inch-wide rows were planted with each trip across the field. The farmer always used his best, most spirited team and kept them walking fast and straight. People noted how straight neighborhood cornrows were planted; the straightest were recognized during small talk among neighbors. Planting about fifteen acres in a day was typical; but with long hours and an exceptional team, eighteen acres could be planted. Occasionally, an eager farmer would change to a fresh team at noon.

Wire-checking meant stringing a planter wire through the field, from end to end. The wire had a curled wire button every forty inches. The wire threaded through the planter's yoke mechanism as it traveled through the field made a familiar and shrill *cli-ick, clack—cli-ick, clack*" that could be heard several hundred feet away—all day long. Each wire button tripped the planter valve, dropping seeds at forty-inch intervals. On entering the end rows, the check wire would be released from the planter yoke, and the team and planter were turned around and headed back in the opposite direction. The operator jumped off the planter, pulled up the check wire stake, held the wire tight, moved over, and reset it in line with the planter. This procedure was repeated at each end turnaround.

No wonder my Dad came in from the field bent over. I recall Dad trying to stand up straight, straining while lifting a pail of feed or getting comfortable in a chair. He never said ouch but let out a loud "I—*iii!*" (probably from his Swedish vocabulary) when getting a piercing pain in the back. Nearly every corn planting season, he suffered attacks of lumbago (back trouble) necessitating a trip to Linn Grove to see Doctor Hughes, the chiropractor where he obviously got gratifying relief.

Nearly all corn was wire checked with three seed kernels per "hill," every forty inches. The corn was "checked" so the crop could be cultivated crossways (crossed), for maximum weed eradication. However a few small fields would be drilled without using check wire, dropping a single kernel every foot. These fields could not be cultivated crossways and often led to exhausting hand hoeing.

Corn planters could be set up for forty-two- to thirty-six-inch-wide rows. Check wire was also available in these widths. But forty inches was the most common. When asked why corn was planted in these wide rows, the farmer's uncomplicated answer was, "That's what a draft horse needs to avoid stepping on the corn plants."

Three or four days after planting, farmers would start scratching around in their fields to see if kernels were starting to germinate (sprout). It usually took from a week to ten days for corn plants to emerge. We anxiously looked for the first field in which corn could be "rowed"!

Pests: Worms to Weeds

Cutworms were the first of several hazards to threaten the crop as the season progressed. Cutworms chewed the new seedling off at ground level killing it. Often patches of two or three acres of low ground had to be replanted, or a whole field if following hay sod. Incidentally, this was a minor threat compared to the European corn borer plague that invaded Iowa cornfields in 1949.

Another common pest was the gray ground squirrel, which was about two-thirds the size of a common timber squirrel. Going down the row with uncanny accuracy, ground squirrels dug up planted seed for a lunch at every hill. Fortunately, as they lived in sodded areas they only damaged the field border rows.

Two other animals, the thirteen-striped gopher and the common crow, were maligned for destroying seedlings, but I never saw it actually happen.

Hopefully the crop would be three or four inches tall before cultivation started in late May or, more likely, early June. Occasionally, because of early weed germination a farmer had to "blind plow," that is, cultivate, before the corn emerged. I remember riding in the concave seat of the steel single-row cultivator. This meant driving the team while straddling the cornrow. Then, with feet in metal stirrups and grasping wooden handles, the operator controlled the two (left and right) three-shoveled gangs. The gangs, positioned on each side of the cornrow, had metal "shields" to keep dirt from covering the young corn plants. When such happened, we carried a five-foot-long wooden stick to rescue (uncover) the fragile plant. We also had, as did quite a few farmers, a two-row cultivator pulled by a span of three or four horses.

Enter Farm Tractors

During the 1930s, the major machinery companies were improving and selling "row crop" tractors, which could readily be fitted with a two-row, mounted cultivator. Some popular models were the Farmall F-20, John Deere Model A, Allis-Chalmers WC, Oliver 70, and others. The need for tractors was intensified in 1935 and 1936 because of the loss of draft horses from "sleeping sickness."

My older brothers wanted to use a tractor as soon as practical, because of the reduction in good horses. The John Deere GP Dad bought in 1936 had high-clearance front and rear axles for straddling a cornrow. Thus, it could be equipped with a three-row mounted planter and a cultivator. It was a good idea, but it didn't blend well in making the transition from the standard two-row planters, which more easily configured and fit with two- and (later) four-row tractor cultivators. This limitation didn't stop my brothers. They rigged up an offset hitch so our two-row horse cultivator could be hooked up and pulled behind the tractor.

It worked quite well, but few farmers tried the idea. Of course, it took two men (or rather a man and a boy) to operate it. At age twelve I was quite a "big shot" driving the "Poppin' Johnny" tractor while my brother Howard rode the cultivator, steering it to stay on the rows the best he could! Occasionally, when I drifted off row-center, he would shout above the tractor—and loud enough for neighbors to hear—"Get over!" or "Wake up!"

In mid-June we got a break from the cornfield to put up the first cutting of alfalfa hay, but that's another story.

Although hailstorms could occur throughout the growing season, mid-June was the peak period for them. I remember us kids joining our folks, anxiously watching as mountainous thunderheads and dark clouds boiled in threatening skies. Nearly every year some farmers in the area got hail. Occasionally, it destroyed an entire crop.

Starting in June, the summer-long job of hand weeding began. Morning glories, an early pest, had to be hoed or pulled by hand. Their vines would climb and strangle growing corn plants. Other emerging broadleaf weeds would be cut at the same time.

Late in June we would start "crossing" the corn. Then, we learned how straight the wire-checking job was! If crooked, some kidding often resulted: "Watch out! You'll spring the cultivator frame dodging through those crooked cornrows!" As corn was now seven or eight inches tall, shields were removed from the cultivator.

A Little Time To Socialize

By the Fourth of July, we were ready for a break from the daily toil. The national holiday often resulted in a potluck picnic with neighborhood friends. We looked forward to a feast on new "spring fryers,"—chickens we started in early spring from incubated eggs. Softball games, tug-of-war, pitching horseshoe, and other activities provided entertainment. Lemonade was the popular drink and, though considered an extra treat, the older men occasionally had a bottle of beer.

By then, farmers hoped their corn reached the goal of "knee-high by the Fourth of July" and was about ready to be laid-by—the third and final cultivation—before it

Figure 17.3: A team, wagon equipped with "bang boards" and one or two hard-working huskers get one load before dinner and another before supper! (circa 1933)

got hip-high. A wire nose basket was fixed to the horses' bridle to keep them from eating green corn plants as they walked through the field. Though weeds often were no longer a threat, laying-by was a custom to be followed and it leveled the cross-cultivated rows for easier harvest come fall. As learned in later years, this late cultivation probably did more harm than good due to mechanical root pruning.

The corn crop wasn't home-free yet and neither were we. Hand weeding continued for many days in August as we walked the fields to eradicate cockleburs, velvet weed, sunflowers, and other weeds that escaped the cultivator. Dad usually walked with us, I suppose to maintain some discipline. But he dared not get too far ahead, evidenced by a wild hemp or sorghum stalk turned into a javelin or spear, resulting in "sneak attacks" among us kids! The tall corn provided great camouflage!

Another interlude occurred in mid-August when field corn in early milk stage was ripe for roasting ears. We checked individual ears to get a succulent batch. As the roasting ear season was short, we devoured it daily for a week. Although it wasn't as tasty as today's hybrid sweet corn, we relished it.

In early September when the cornfields were beginning to turn brown, we kids were getting scrubbed up and a new pair of overalls in preparation for school. Seems like we just got a good start at school when it was time for "corn picking vacation." In early to mid-October, we were let out of school for one or two weeks to stay home and help with corn harvest.

In the meantime, many farmers had cut, bundled and shocked a few acres of corn fodder to be left in the field until winter when it would be hauled in for cattle feed.

Harvest: Corn Picking Time

Husking corn by hand, most often called "corn pickin'" was a main event, and the longest stretch of hard work during the season. All the family and "hands" were

Figure 17.4: Unloading corn with an elevator. One man drove the team, one tended the machines, and another fed corn into the elevator. (circa 1934)

involved. We got up at 5:00 A.M., fed and cared for livestock, harnessed the horses, ate breakfast, and headed for the field by 7:00 A.M. In the fall weather, we started the day wearing heavy jackets, but they were shed as the day—and the worker—warmed up. Cloth husking gloves used to protect the hands were double-thumbed and reversible, thus extending their use. Mom sewed hand-to-elbow length "sleeves" to pull over and protect our blue chambray shirts. A metal husking hook riveted to a leather pad was strapped over the husking glove. It was used to strip husk from the corn ear. Good corn pickers made the husking motion a rhythmic art: left hand grabbed an ear, the right hand striped loose the husk, grabbed the bare ear, snapped it off, and flung it into the wagon. All this was done in three or four seconds.

It was a matter of pride to have a clean, bright-yellow, husk-free load. A team and wagon was needed for each one or two huskers. The standard triple-box wagon was equipped with high "bang boards" on the side opposite the huskers. Hearing the tossed ears hit the bang boards in rapid succession, we did not need to look up from the steady pace of grabbing and husking the next ears. In early morning we could hear the *bang! bang!* from neighboring fields as every farmer was out getting the crop gathered before snow and cold weather struck. The team of horses, driven by verbal commands, pulled the wagon alongside the huskers. A welcome break and nourishment came from a small box attached to the wagon. It held the water jug, apples, and a few pieces of cheese or sausage. When picking alongside my Dad, he took two outside rows and I took the inside row next to the wagon. I soon learned to lag back a little to avoid getting "beaned" when Dad tossed an ear. When he didn't exude much sympathy, I soon concluded it was my responsibility to stay out of the way! Small, half-barren ears ("nubbins") were left for livestock to glean. We would expect to fill the wagon by noon and then again in the afternoon, totaling around eighty bushels for the day's work.

Corn picking contests were common, and young men were always trying to set a new record. Picking one hundred bushels per day was a threshold occasionally reached. When better yielding hybrid corn was planted in the later 1930s, 130 bushels and more were reported.

Wagonloads of corn were unloaded in the corncrib. I sympathized with a neighbor and friend, who though having fewer acres, had to scoop his loads off. Most farmers had a mechanical elevator, which delivered ears to the crib cupola and spouted it to different bins. A team walking in a circle turned a "horse power" with gears driving a tumbling rod, which turned the elevator flight chain. Another tumbling rod extended to the hoist or jack, raising the front wheels of the wagon causing corn to flow out the rear into the elevator hopper. It took about fifteen minutes to unload a wagon.

From 1930 through 1936, Iowa corn yields averaged 33.7 bushels per acre. The first major improvement in corn yields came in the later 1930s as farmers adopted the new "hybrid" seed corn. After the drought in 1936 proved the advantage of hybrid corn, farmers shifted dramatically to planting hybrid in 1937. Corn yields from 1937 through 1939 jumped to 47.7 bushels, a dramatic 40 percent yield increase. Before hybrid seed was developed, Dad would stand at the elevator and select out the best-looking ears to be hung and dried for seed next year. Later, when scientists learned more about genetics and corn breeding, this ear selection was proved to be of little or no value.

Handpicking would last from two weeks to a month. When done, we could finally breathe a sigh of relief knowing this crop season was over. Dad saw that we prepared for the oncoming winter by putting away all hand tools and storing supplies where they were safe from being covered by snow. With corncribs full, oats in the granary, a huge straw stack near the cattle lot, the barn haymow full plus two or three haystacks outside, we were ready for the oncoming long and harsh winter. It also meant it was time for butchering a hog or two.

Corn Picking Contest: An Athletic Event

Physical strength and endurance were a necessary qualification for much of industry and especially farming before the strong swing to mechanization by the mid-1930s, the decade of the 1940s, and thereafter. This was reflected in feats of strength carrying over into entertainment and games. Hand corn husking was a good example when later, in the decade of the 1930s, it swelled into local, state, and even national corn husking contests.

In 1938, a major corn husking contest was held at Hartley, Iowa, some forty miles north of our farm. Friend and neighbor Engebret Grodahl called Dad wondering if he would care to go and suggested they each take one of their boys along. His son Eugene and I got to go. Just to be included with our dads was an infrequent treat and adventure. It was exciting to witness the carnival atmosphere: banners, food stands, a public address system, and the corn picking contestants treated as celebrities. The contestants lined up on cornrows at the starting line. The corn huskers worked in narrow "lands" only a dozen rows apart. The anxious contestants launched into the challenge at the sound of the starting gun!

Figure 17.5: Nels drove a Fordson tractor pulling a one-row corn picker. Nellie and Bill pull the wagon alongside as it filled with ear corn "on the go." (circa 1928)

I remember Dad and Engebret talking about this man's strong shoulders, another's intense concentration. They compared the husker's smooth and rapid motion in grabbing the ears, ripping loose the husk, snapping off the shanks. We were fascinated by the rapid *bang! bang! bang!* as ears were flipped into the wagon box without the contestant ever taking their eyes or mind off seizing the next ear! Approximately thirty contestants picked corn for an intense eighty minutes, until the ending gunshot. Drivers took turns weighing in each load. The heaviest load, the most bushels picked, won! It was very straightforward.

While riding home in the backseat of the two-door Ford, Gene (fourteen) and I (thirteen) thought we were pretty important among all those men and a scattering of farm wives watching such a pageantry.

Young Men Captivated by Machines

In the prosperous 1920s, Dad bought a one-row McCormack-Deering corn picker and pulled it with the Fordson tractor. Though few did, it could be pulled with four horses. A team and wagon driven alongside the picker was filled with corn ears delivered by the picker elevator. It sure beat handpicking! On a good day, 300 or more bushels could be harvested with the mechanical picker. When the Great Depression shut down farm tractors, it also shut down mechanical corn pickers. Our corn picker was parked in the cattle shed for several years. We kids played on it during the summer. In 1937, the same brothers who hooked a two-row cultivator behind the tractor, and even though Dad was skeptical, figured the old corn picker could be resurrected. After a grease job and minor tune-up, they hooked it behind the John Deere GP. We were forever rescued from the drudgery of handpicking—forever, because the machinery companies were rapidly developing two-row pickers to be mounted on row crop tractors.

Figure 17.6: A 1939 John Deere two-row mounted corn picker. Tractor-mounted corn pickers, built in the later 1930s, were the first major advancement in corn harvesting.

The following incident exemplifies the anxiety and stress during corn harvest. I pressed the team into a trot, hurrying to get an empty wagon to the field and take the loaded wagon home to the corncrib for unloading. Just as I pulled up, Howard, driving the tractor pulling the corn picker, hollered with alarm when, as he pulled the tractor clutch lever it broke off! He held the two-foot-long lever up like a useless wand. He couldn't stop and was headed for one of a string of forty-foot-tall willow trees along the field boundary fence. Reacting with some panic he simultaneously pulled back the throttle lever, stepped on the brakes, and hit the willow tree! The tree shook violently until the tractor engine died. The drama lasted no more than ten seconds but we were terrified that the tree would snap off onto the tractor—and driver! With a quick trip to Alta, the blacksmith welded the broken lever and we were back picking corn within a couple of hours.

Corn Meant Feed for Livestock

To fatten up butcher hogs and feeder cattle, corn was usually fed "on the cob," which meant whole ears of corn (with the kernels still on). Hogs picked kernels clean off the cobs when ears were scattered on the ground. There was little or no waste. Corn ears were broken by hand over the edge of the feed bunk into smaller pieces while cattle lined up on each side to feed. Cattle, having a ruminant digestive system, ate it all—the cob along with the kernels of corn. Milk cows were fed a daily ration to improve milk production. Whole ears of corn were fed into the hand sheller by one of us kids while the other turned the crank to shell the corn kernels off the cob. When the shelled corn was mixed with oats it made a good ration for the egg laying flock of hens. Except for the team we used for winter chores, the other horses "roughed it," gleaning the fields.

We had a "burr mill" feed grinder that was turned by a team walking in a thirty-foot-diameter circle. Bushel baskets of whole ear corn were dumped into the round metal hopper on top of the grinder and the resulting ground ear corn "meal" dropped in a basket under the grinder. The grinder was also used to crack shelled corn and to pulverize whole oats for a more palatable feed.

With more tractors, belt-driven stationary burr mills replaced the horse-powered models. By the late 1930s belt driven hammer mills came into general use.

In the depths of the Great Depression, with no money for wheat flour, some farmers used these same machines to grind corn meal, to make cornbread for the dinner table. It was rich in carbohydrates and with maple syrup made a tasty, healthful meal.

The annual cycle of growing corn always overlapped from one season to the next. While the current year's crop was maturing and filling out ears during August, fall plowing of oats stubble in preparation for next year's crop was getting underway.

Yes, in the Corn Belt, "corn is king." It was not only the main source of income it demanded the greatest amount of time and work by the farm family. Corn was a big part of our life!

CHAPTER 18
GROWING SOYBEANS: A NEW CROP

In the 1930s a new crop, soybeans, came to the Corn Belt. Soybeans had been grown as a forage crop on limited acreage in northeastern states for decades and for centuries in China. Soybeans were new to the western Cornbelt. The first seed varieties my Dad bought had strange-sounding Asian names like Mukden and Manchu.

Soybeans had been grown in China and the Orient for the protein-rich food known as tofu and for cooking oil. In addition, the green leafy legume made an ideal forage crop for farm animals. Meanwhile, Corn Belt farmers relied predominantly on feed grain crops: corn and small grains such as oats, barley, rye, and some wheat. Income from soybeans, a cash crop, would be welcome. Cash crop meant it would be marketed as produced, rather than fed to livestock.

Agricultural college research stations expanded study of soybeans because they offered diversification in crop production and good potential for expanding the market for American farm products.

Iowa soybean yields from 1930 through 1939 averaged 16.8 bushels per acre. Confirming its newness to Iowa, the first price-reporting data started in 1933. Prices from 1933 thru 1940 averaged 91.4 cents per bushel. The acceptance of soybeans as a crop and food source is reflected by a yield increase of about 30 percent from 1935 to 1955 and the price per bushel more than tripling.

Corn Farmers and Soybeans Come Together

Corn being the most profitable and widely grown crop resulted in corn following corn in the absence of a good alternative rotation crop. Because a corn crop depleted soil moisture and nitrogen, second-year corn yields usually declined. Even the corn-oats-hay crop rotation was lopsided; too much hay and not enough corn. Soybeans, a nitrogen-producing legume, offered a good addition to the crop rotation. They could be planted and cultivated with corn-growing machinery the farmer already owned. Meanwhile, development of effective harvesting machinery was delayed until it was determined how the new crop could be best utilized—as hay forage or a seed crop. Strangely, a more rapid expansion of soybean production was hindered for two reasons: 1) the uncertainty of how to best utilize the crop, and 2) lack of effective harvesting equipment.

Contributing to soybean's value as a cash crop was the growing demand for protein and cooking oil in the U.S. In addition to adding soil nitrogen to benefit the corn crop that followed, farmers liked spreading out the workload; this allowed them more time to plant and harvest the different crops, and soybeans left the soil and seedbed mellow for the following corn crop.

With The Help of the AAA—"Triple A"

Soybean production also fit in with the Great Depression-era of government economic recovery programs such as the Agriculture Adjustment Act (AAA). The

Figure 18.1: Grain combine (circa 1938 model). We bought this McCormick-Deering (six-foot, cutter-bar) combine in 1943, primarily to harvest soybeans. However, these combines also hurried the end of oats shocking and threshing runs.

AAA reduced corn acreage (supply) and thereby lifted the corn price above the extreme lows of ten to twenty-five cents a bushel. Soybeans were first planted in significant acreage in 1933. They were most often planted on "government" acres that were restricted from corn planting. It was a new crop and farmers were not sure how to handle it. Our first crop was stacked like hay and fed to livestock as roughage. I remember my Dad and neighbors being surprised and pleased at how the cows really liked that "soybean hay." Even after a cash market for the soybean seed crop was developing, farmers were somewhat reluctant to grow them because of uncertainties about harvesting and storing. Soybeans didn't lend well to cutting with a binder, shocking, and threshing as was customary with oats and other small grain.

Large wheat (grain) combines had been in use in the western Great Plains since the early 1920s, but not in the Corn Belt. Through experimentation it was learned those large combines worked satisfactorily for harvesting milo, alfalfa seed, peas, and other seed crops. Why not soybeans? In the 1930s those large twelve-foot (cutter-bar) machines were not well adapted to the Corn Belt's small fields. However, in the mid-1930s the major machinery companies began to design and build smaller six, even four-foot, cutter-bar, combines. By the later 1930s, farmers began to buy the new small combines and—simultaneously—soybeans as a seed crop expanded rapidly. Farmers who bought a combine (usually with a six-foot cutting sickle) could get all the custom combining they wanted as soybean acreage exceeded harvesting capacity.

Because no soybeans had been grown on Iowa prairie land previously, an inoculate, growth-stimulating microorganism was needed for the survival of young seed sprouts. A special black, dust-like inoculate was mixed in, giving an even, black coating on the seed. While helping Dad, our hands and arms got black; however, the inoculate washed off easily.

Soybean planting started in late May, a week or more after corn was planted. The same planter was used. Seeds were drilled (planted without check wire) in forty-inch rows and were cultivated twice rather than three times like corn. In late July and early August when soybeans were eighteen- to thirty-inches tall, we kids spent days walking the fields to cut out broadleaf weeds such as cocklebur, velvet weed, and sunflowers.

In early September, the soybeans matured rather quickly. If there happened to be an early frost, they turned from a dark green to golden brown in one or two days! Harvest was just around the corner and got underway in late September.

Harvested soybeans were usually stored on the farm or occasionally delivered from the field to the elevator in town. Farmers preferred to store soybeans, as prices usually improved within a few months after harvest. Or, they might be sold at harvest if income was needed.

Mother Nature Keeps Us Humble

Typically farmers get a little nervous as harvest approaches. After investing in seed, labor, machinery, and living with seasonal weather threats, they are concerned that something could happen before the crop is safe in the bin. That's why farming is a gamble! Many years later, I had an interesting experience: It had rained and drizzled for a couple of days on a farm I was managing, soaking the standing soybean seedpods. Tension mounted as harvest was delayed. When it cleared off, I was anxious to get out and see if the crop was ready and if indeed the farmer was ready to harvest. About 10:30 A.M. when I was walking the field, the sun came out bright and unusually warm. Suddenly I heard a snap and rustle, not unlike popping popcorn. As the hot sun quickly dried the wet seedpods, they shrunk, exploded, curled inside out, and threw the three or more enclosed seeds into the air. I could hardly believe what I was seeing as 5 to 10 percent of the pods popped open. In fifteen minutes, it stopped as quickly as it started. I estimated four to five bushels per acre were lost.

The new soybean crop gave additional diversity to the now expounded, "diversified" family farm.

Part Two

Three

Animals

Animals Empower Man: Draft for Heavy Loads—Food for Energy

Animals Empower Man: Draft for Heavy Loads— Food for Energy

It is not known when humans first domesticated animals. It was probably more than 15,000 years ago. Dogs may have been the first because of their docile nature, hunting ability, and protection as "watchdogs." Bovine species such as goats, sheep, and cattle, raised for their meat and milk, followed. Domestication means taming (to control), assumed for people's benefit. Species and numbers of domesticated animals grew steadily as agriculture developed; for example, oxen and then horses were the primary draft animals for centuries, through the first third of the twentieth century when tractors took over.

As providers of food, meat and milk, and draft (pulling power), animals played a key role on the family farm up through the Great Depression. This has changed drastically in the last half of the twentieth century when tractors completely took over draft needs and factory farms took over meat, egg, and milk production. It is evident that man still has an affinity for—and a special relationship with—animals.

The following chapters tell about our indispensable need for farm animals during the Great Depression.

CHAPTER 19
FARMERS AND HORSES: A STRANGE CAMARADERIE

Even though we developed an attachment to all farm animals, there was a special feeling toward horses. Maybe it was our ability to domesticate, tame, and control an animal so much larger and stronger than we humans. A horse is capable of severely injuring any one of us with either a brutal kick from a hoof-appended, muscular rear leg, a strike from a front hoof, or a chisel-toothed bite. A runaway team could wreck whatever was in tow and seriously injure the driver or passengers. Our bond with horses is reinforced because a good horse will never do any of these things.

We were more in communication with our horses than any of the other animals except for our farm dog. We had to be in communication to handle the brutes, such as always letting them know when approaching. We avoided surprising them by speaking as we entered the horse barn and by giving them a gentle pat on the rear before entering the stall to harness them or for any other reason. Sociably, most horses responded with a gentle rasping, deep-throated reply.

All the horses had names they recognized and responded to: Bill, the stocky Belgium; Jim, the big bay "coach horse"; Nellie, an indifferent gray mare; Jennie, a black Percheron mare often teamed with Jim; Cap, a smaller nervous gray; Pat, an unfriendly strawberry roan; Ben, called Ben-jam-in; and Dick, an impressive bay with a "club foot." Dick's club hoof and irregular stride resulted from a bad barbed wire entanglement that happened when he was a colt being boarded at a neighbor's pasture. The timber pasture was isolated and had escaped daily checking. It was another incident giving credence to the remark "farming is a gamble." Then there was Dixie, our Indian pinto, the fastest pony in the neighborhood!

The different temperament of horses was vividly demonstrated whenever we rode Dixie in a neighborhood race. As two or three ponies trotted to the "quarter-mile" starting line, Dixie became increasingly nervous and agitated. By the time we lined up at the start, she was prancing, vibrating with excitement. At the starting signal Dixie was always out a quarter-length ahead of the other ponies, neck outstretched and nostrils flared! Always riding bareback I leaned forward, legs clutching her sides and hands grasping her mane to stay on. Though we raced dozens of times, Dixie was never defeated. Years later, I fully understood the announcer as he described the Thoroughbreds being jockeyed into the starting gate at the Kentucky Derby. Though a little mysterious, we humans can relate to a horse's competitive instincts.

Each horse had a different personality and temperament. The friendly horses would nuzzle us with their noses to get attention and, of course, were always rewarded with a few rubs on the nose, pat on the neck, or nibble of feed. The horses' appreciation of the mild scratching of a brush or currycomb was obvious by their relaxed manner. Their soft *hrr, hrr, hrr*, was heard when grain was placed in their feedboxes.

Of course, communication was essential when a team was hooked up for work. Although the reins signaled direct commands, these were nearly always accompanied

Figure 19.1: It's "lunch time" as Dad holds Lady with foal. (circa 1940)

with voice commands. Some teams were driven almost exclusively by voice. Voice sounds were "get-up" or "giddap" to move ahead; "whoa" meant stop; "gee" left turn; "haw" right turn, and "baaack-up," in conjunction with a tug on the reins, to back up.

We fed our horses according to how hard they worked. When not working, pasture grazing was ample. When working, they were kept in the barn stalls and their ration included hay, fed in the stall manger. Grasses such as timothy were favored over legumes. A sturdy wood feedbox held small grain—oats, barley or, more often, corn—usually fed by the ear. I was always amazed at how their powerful jaws and sharp front teeth would bite the corn kernels clean from the cob. Oddly, most horses ate cleanly and kept their feedboxes dry, while a few slobbered all over it.

Coming in from the field at noon or supper time after a half-day's work in the hot summer, the horses were thirsty. When unhitched from the cultivator, teams were promptly led to a large wooden water tank near the windmill. Immersing their mouth and even their nostrils six inches into the cool water, they quaffed down huge gulps to quench their thirst. It was curious how large a plug of water, at two-second intervals, pulsed up their jugular-like esophagus. I remember placing my hand under a horse's neck, gently cupping the esophagus and was startled at the largeness and force of each swallow. Six or seven large draft horses would lower the water level three or four inches (sixty gallons) in just a few minutes.

Farmer Healer

Horses required regular care to remain in good health and working condition. Farm horses always walking on soft dirt were not shod with iron shoes. We trimmed and cleaned their hooves every couple of months, disinfected scratches, and salved horse collar abrasions promptly. Our mare, Pat, developed a fistula—a gigantic, saucer-sized boil—on the side of her neck. Reddish inflammation confirmed how sore it was, and she would bolt at the slightest touch or attempt to doctor it. In an effort to relieve the inflammation we brought the haltered mare alongside a farm wagon. As I held her head tightly against the wagon box, Dad used a razor-sharp knife to lance a five-inch gash in the fistula. Pat jumped and tugged back, but I held fast as nasty white puss squirted the wagon box. Once the extreme pain was relieved, she was less touchy and we began several days of treatment with a lime-based solution, using a large syringe. In a month Pat was healed, harnessed again, and working faithfully. In those days a farmer had to be a horse doctor, too.

Getting Too Attached

Our sentimental attachment spilled over to sadness at times. Dad had our nicest young black mare, Babe, bred to produce a foal. When the very cute, white-maned, bay colt arrived, we kids fell in love with the curious little rascal. Foaling always has some risk, but after the second day when we thought any crises had passed, we found Babe dead in her pen. She had bled to death during the night from internal injury. We were all shocked, saddened, and Dad was distraught—losing our finest young mare.

We kids were immediately determined to save the colt by bottle-feeding. Mom called the veterinarian to check the formula for diluting cow's milk. We were confident that we would save the colt and have a lot of fun doing it. When after about one week the colt died, we kids were devastated. At our insistence, Dad let us have a "funeral" and bury the colt near the barn. We dug the grave and cried as the little colt was laid to rest. We set a cross marker over the grave. For several years, I never walked by or over the grave without thinking of the poor little colt.

The following story is from my "Philosophies" column:

The Death of Old Jim

Horses provided the power on nearly all Midwest farms, including ours, for most of the 1930s. This was somewhat of a comeback for horses after being partially replaced by a surge of newly developed farm tractors in the prosperous 1920s. My Dad had a Fordson tractor during that time. However, during the worst of the Great Depression (from 1931 to 1935) farmers did not have money for new tractors or even fuel for the ones they had. More than a few were left parked in the shed, or sometimes repossessed to satisfy a bank loan.

While farming 240 to 320 acres, we had eight to ten horses (four or more teams) and Dixie, our pony. The horses all had names and were thought of as individuals—each having a different appearance, character, and even personality. Some were quiet, others skittish; some were gentle, others assertive; some were trustworthy, others would bolt at a slight commotion. Some, easy to drive, would lean into a heavy load or could back a wagon up steadily. Most fell short on one or more of these traits.

Old Jim had the best of all these traits. He seemed to crouch down for easier harnessing. No worry about Jim ever kicking or stepping on your foot. He always acknowledged his eight ears of corn with a low, deep rasp, as if to say, "Thanks, Boy." Jim was no purebred. He was a big, dark bay with a blazed face. My Dad said he must have some German coach horse breeding because he was flat over the rump. Dad, having served in the Swedish Calvary, surely knew about coach horses! Old Jim had a peculiar gate, a long stride—always just a little ahead of his teammate. Peculiarly, his rear hooves tracked ahead of his front ones. We all loved old Jim.

Dad had Jim a long time and he was getting on; as a horse's life span goes, Old Jim was maybe seventeen years old. One morning we found Jim standing by himself, a little way out in the pasture. We approached him and readily saw that his left front leg had been broken just below the shoulder. Horses have their pecking order like most other farm animals, and Jim was always the barnyard leader. I've witnessed some pretty severe kicking duels between horses trying to establish their territorial dominance. But as the younger horses got bolder and more vigorous, one apparently challenged old Jim with a devastating kick, breaking his leg.

It was one of the very few times I ever saw my Dad show any emotion. He turned and looked away. Dad knew Jim had to be destroyed, but could not bring himself to do it.

All of us kids stood dumfounded, discomforted by the lump in our throats. One of my older brothers got our neighbor Bill Green to come over. I remember peeking around the corner of the barn. I couldn't stand to watch, but neither could I look away. Bill Green stood ten feet in front of old Jim, leveled a 410-gauge shotgun, aimed at the center of an imaginary "X" drawn between the ears and eyes. The shot was deafening and fatal. But even with tears in my eyes, I'll never forget how old Jim's legs seemed to draw up quickly to his body, causing his massive weight to hit the ground with a deadening thud. As if an image of finality, a visible cloud of dust ascended.

Somehow on that day a young boy became much older, witnessing a moment in the drama of life and death.

CHAPTER 20
FARM BUTCHERING

Of Late: A Fading Art

For thousands of years prior to the late 1930s families butchered, processed, stored, and ate both domesticated and wild animal meat. This story tells of the last decades of that practice: butchering in the late 1920s and 1930s on the farm. While we occasionally butchered a steer, often sharing half with a neighbor, we always butchered two or more hogs a year. The number varied with family size, but with our eight kids, providing meat for the table was no small matter.

Come late fall, when cool temperatures would preserve fresh meat, spring farrowed pigs had grown into nice fat 220-pound butcher hogs, ready for market. Dad walked among the one hundred or so hogs calmly sizing up ones that would make the best pork chops!

Butchering was an exciting time, and like many farm customs, it was part ritual. Favorite places to hang the hog for butchering were outside, using the wagon hoist (jack) or tying a block and tackle from a tree limb or in the corncrib alleyway on an overhead joist. It was strange how on butchering day the needed paraphernalia quickly came together: scalding barrel, planks for a table, buckets of water, scrapers, a singletree, block and tackle, knives, wash basin, towels, and pails.

As the hog had to be "scalded" for easy removal of bristly hair, a scalding barrel was located near the butchering area. Some folks had a large, cast-iron kettle, but we used an ordinary fifty-gallon steel drum (barrel) that had one end cut out. Water in the barrel was heated over a cob fire. A makeshift table was set up nearby using a couple of sawhorses and three or four short planks.

Getting Down To Business

As soon as the water was steaming hot, the "victim" was herded near the scalding barrel and killed with a well-placed .22 caliber rifle shot. I felt queasy if the pig gave out a weak squeal while dying. Immediately, Dad would slit its throat to assure ample bleeding. Very quickly, two husky men or boys put the carcass in the barrel of hot water. It had to be turned end for end to be completely scalded. Scraping to remove the hair started as soon as the carcass was pulled from the barrel, using a cup-shaped metal scraper with a wooden handle and broad blade knives. The men worked rapidly. The hog was soon hoisted onto the table where final scraping and hair removal was completed. Care was taken so the carcass never touched the ground. In the cool air, the steaming carcass gave off a pungent, but pleasant, odor.

The hog was hung "spread eagle" (shackled), by inserting singletree hooks in the strong tendons in the rear ankles. With block and tackle attached to the singletree, the carcass was hoisted up, head down, for butchering.

With sharpened knives, starting at the tail, Dad quickly slit open the belly exposing the viscera (guts) and internal organs. Care was taken not to sever the stomach or intestines. Nothing edible was wasted. The heart, liver, and kidneys were

Figure 20.1: Scalding a hog. Careful and quick work prepared the hog carcass for butchering. (circa 1933)

all saved in clean milk pails. The head was left attached. The small intestine was saved for pork sausage casings.

The dressed carcass was hoisted up, out of reach of the family dog and cat! It was left to chill overnight in preparation for carving up the next day.

"Processing"

The next morning Dad used a special meat saw to split the spine lengthwise from tail to snout, forming two halves, so it was ready for "processing," or carving up. At our house this was a family affair. The dining room table was covered with several layers of newspaper and then a bed sheet.

A carcass half was placed on the table and we all gathered around while Dad and Mom quickly assigned us tasks to help cut it up. After thick layers of lard were peeled off, we kids cut them into small squares, placed them in a boiler over a hot fire to separate the clear fat from crisp crackle tissue, a process called rendering. The main use for lard was in cooking, but Mom also used lard in making large pans of light brown soap that—when hardened—was cut into two-by-three-inch bars. Slow to lather, it didn't work well as a hand or face soap. However, when soap shavings were added to the hot soft water in the washing machine, the laundry became quite sudsy. But it didn't compare to the new detergent soaps, such as Oxydal, Rinso, Lux and others as advertised on the radio soap operas.

It was a fun time, spiced with laughter and conversation. Invariably the pig's tail was slyly pinned on the back of someone's overalls, followed by an outburst of friendly teasing!

The different carved-up cuts of pork were processed, canned in two-quart jars, or salted down in wooden barrels for curing and preserving. Roasts were wrapped for storage in the cool cellar; sausage meat was ground and stuffed into casings made from cleaned and boiled small intestines. The variety of edible body organs (heart, liver, brains, and tongue) was preserved to be turned into delicacies. Hams and bacon sides were hung for curing in the smokehouse.

It seems archaic now, with modern supermarket meat counters, that Mom would send me, maybe seven years old, out to the smokehouse. There I used a small ladder to retrieve a cured ham that was held by a piece of twine, looped over a spike nailed in a two-by-six ceiling joist. With the hide left on, the flavor and juice was held in, giving bacon and ham the "country smoked" taste. Slices of the ham hide and bacon rind offered tasty chewing long after the meat was eaten. Store-bought pickled pig's feet of today don't come close to those we made on the farm!

"Cracklings" leftover from the lard rendering were doled out as a delicacy. When we over indulged, it resulted in a bellyache! Even allowing a little nostalgic exaggeration, all of the hog was turned into healthful and tasty food. The commercial meat packers used to say, "We use everything but the squeal!" At home there was one exception: the head, which was used to make headcheese. Lardy headcheese sandwiches in the Depression day's school lunch box almost made me gag. Learning later that headcheese was a high-energy nutritious food didn't stop my revulsion of even thinking about it.

That's how it was done in the era of home butchering on the family farm.

An Afterthought

From the late 1930s until about 1965, many farm families rented a large freezer compartment from the town "butcher-locker plant" operator. Locker plants sprang up for several reasons: farmers had less time or desire to butcher, sons didn't learn the skill, and with home refrigerators, housewives were glad to quit home processing, canning, smoking, and curing meat.

Locker plant operators took over butchering and provided freezer storage boxes for individual families to store meat from their butchered hog or beef. We kids remember the shock of going from a hot summer day into the locker plant freezer for several minutes to get packages of meat. We came out shivering! And we understood why the plant operator always kept a jacket by the freezer door.

Three key factors forced the locker plant out of business: In the early 1950s farm families rapidly bought deep freezers and put them in the basement or back porch, filling them with frozen pork, beef, chicken, and garden vegetables. Farm families, like their city cousins, also enjoyed the selection and convenience of the supermarket. In addition, the intrusion of government into private business included a myriad of locker plant regulations and inspections. Faced with the hassle and extra expense, many struggling butcher-locker plant operators became discouraged and closed. Many communities lost another service and small towns lost another business.

Figure 21.1: Mom looks over the chicken flock after gathering eggs in the hen house. Four farmyard ducks pause to get in the picture! Mid-1920s.

CHAPTER 21
CHICKENS AND THE EGG LAYING FLOCK

On a family farm in the 1930s, a flock of chickens provided food for the dinner table and hard-to-come-by cash income for family needs. The chicken flock was an important element in adding diversification to our farm as were milk cows, hogs, horses, sheep, ducks, geese, and any other venture that held promise of food or income.

Each spring, the chicken flock had to be regenerated by hatching a new brood on the farm or, in later years, buying day-old chicks from the local hatchery or even ordering them through the Sears Roebuck catalog with Parcel Post delivery.

For ages, chickens were hatched "nature's way" with a setting-hen brooding (incubating) her own clutch of eggs. Small chicken coops sheltering a single brood hen were common in earlier days, but gave way to incubators as farm flock size increased. Amusingly, about every spring, one old hen would sneak off and hide her clutch of eggs, in the barn or under the corncrib. Then on a warm day in late May, she would come out of hiding, marching proudly across the yard clucking to her new brood of eight to ten young chicks.

Getting Modern

Hatching our own chicks in an incubator was an elaborate project. For several weeks prior to incubation, we gathered and took special care of fertilized eggs from the laying flock. Fertilized eggs meant having a proportionate number of roosters to mate with the egg-laying hens. Again, by simple observation we got some "natural" sex education. Roosters would scratch vigorously and—having uncovered some good food tidbits—would (with a low croaking cluck) gather a harem of hens around to share his find. Invariably, one or more hens would respond to his mating ritual and crouch down, inviting the rooster to mate.

Special care meant storing the eggs in a cool area, which wasn't difficult in farm houses during the winter months! As incubation days approached, the eggs were candled to be sure they contained a live embryo. Candling was done in a dark room by holding each egg up to a small spot of light to view its contents. (Originally, a candle was set in a one-gallon tin can with a one-inch, light-emitting hole cut in the side, thus "candling.") In looking at the contents of the egg, we were seeing the miracle of life. If the yolk was clear, we knew the egg had not been fertilized. If we saw a pinhead sized red spot (the embryo) we knew the egg was fertilized when the hen and rooster mated before the egg was laid. The live embryo remained dormant at room temperature or cooler.

The next stage was setting up incubators, square or rectangular wooden boxes standing on four legs. There were racks inside on which to lay the eggs. A kerosene-burning, lamp-like heater was an integral part of the incubator box. It maintained a constant ninety-nine degree temperature during the twenty-one-day incubation period before hatching started. The incubators were checked daily and the eggs turned

Figure 21.2: Baby chicks in brooder house.

every couple of days. There was plenty of intrigue as we kids helped with the work, anticipating arrival of the new chicks.

At our house, two incubators were set up in a large upstairs bedroom. We took the smelly kerosene fumes in stride, but an occasional rotten egg sent us scattering, holding our noses!

After twenty days we started watching and listening for the "peck, peck" noise of little chicks responding to primordial instincts in breaking their way out of the egg (womb). By day twenty-one the crescendo amplified and within a few hours dozens of wet, ugly chicks emerged. In a few minutes they turned into cute fuzz-balls, ogling their new world and leaving a clutter of empty eggshells. The chicks revealed momentary panic when we grabbed each one, dipped their beak in a water dish, teaching them to drink—taking their first oral nourishment. This first cycle of entry into the world came to an end when, at two days old, they were moved to an awaiting brooder house.

By early March my folks wanted to have 500-day-old chicks, whether hatched on the farm or bought from the local hatchery. The chicks were safely housed in the newly-scrubbed brooder house with waterers and feeders carefully arranged around the brooder stove. A brooder stove was a specially-designed, low-profile kerosene burner covered over by an umbrella shaped "hover." Heat that concentrated under the hover provided a warm, sheltered area for the chicks. We kids carefully tended the chicks morning and night. Playing with the cuddly little fuzz-balls was amusing. But filling the feeders, the waterers, and checking the heat and kerosene supply was a continuing chore. Good care was important to avoid any catastrophe, such as heat loss if the brooder stove ran out of fuel. If that happened, the cold chicks would crowd together, pile up, and suffocate.

Figure 21.3: A red fox.

Food For The Family Table

Fried chicken was our main summer meat supply. In fact, we often bought a second brood of chicks in late May both for more eating and for a larger egg-laying flock.

The 500 chicks were about half roosters (males) and half pullets (females). The pullets were grown into mature laying hens by fall. But what about the 250 roosters? Well, at about twelve weeks of age, sporting a new red comb and weighing one-and-a-half pounds, those fryers were about the best thing you could touch your taste buds to! With our family of eight hungry kids smelling the aroma of fried chicken, only one "dinner's ready" call from Mom was needed to bring us hurrying to the dinner table. Three fryers disappeared rapidly!

During the chicks' growing phase, we had to be on the lookout for threatening varmints. If a weasel got into the brooder house, it would bite young chickens by the neck and suck out blood, but strangely would not eat the chicken. It was disheartening to find a dozen dead chickens. Civet cats were a threat, but their smell often gave them away and they would be hunted down and shot. As the growing birds ranged farther out around the farmstead they could be taken by a red fox. My Dad and older brothers knew of a fox den in the field and set up an ambush for the invading culprit. My brother Ken got up at 4:30 A.M., took the double-barreled, 12-gauge shotgun and lay hidden near a field gate, hoping to ambush the fox as it approached the farmstead. Sure enough, the culprit came for his quarry. There was a lot of excitement as Ken brought the trophy, the dead fox, to the farmyard.

The growing flock ranged to feed in the open grassy farmyard when a few weeks old, until big enough for the frying pan. Roosters were caught by the leg with a long wire hook. As they got older and wilder it became more difficult. That led to a "*Ripley's Believe It or Not*" solution to catching some roosters for the dinner table. We used our .22 caliber rifle, but shells were very hard to come by in those Depression years. My brother, Art, or I would lie on our stomachs in the yard among the flock, taking aim

Figure 21.4: Horned owl.

until we could align two roosters and shoot them through the head with one bullet! Most of the roosters became victims of the frying pan.

It seems primitive now, looking back, how we had to kill and bleed the roosters in preparation for frying. When the birds were quite young we could ring their necks, but when they got older we cut their heads off with a hatchet and chopping block. Although accepted as quite natural, it was strangely discomforting when the headless rooster's death spasms caused it to jump wildly about for several seconds before it succumbed. We quickly dipped the rooster into an awaiting pail of scalding hot water so the feathers could be removed easily. In the house, Mom lit a small role of newspapers and singed the bird's damp skin to burn off excess hair. I clearly remember the distinct acrid odor from the burnt hair. The fryers were now ready for butchering in preparation for the frying pan.

Chicken Thieves Take Wing

Often these growing birds, probably by instinct, preferred roosting in nearby trees rather than in the chicken house. One summer morning at breakfast, Dad said there was something taking chickens out of the trees during the night. One night he even got a glance at what looked like a large hawk. Understanding that hawks never hunted at night, we were perplexed at what was going on.

When I was about fifteen years old, I was permitted to range rather freely with a .22 caliber rifle, looking for varmints or just target shooting. My brother Art and I walked less than a quarter-mile over to neighbor Jim Little's very large evergreen grove where we were surprised to find two large horned owls. In daytime they would not leave the cover or safety of the grove but, instead, flew from one end to the other as we pursued them. With one of us remaining at each end of the grove, we shot both owls and proudly brought them home. Their wingspan measured over four feet! Trophy birds. Looking back now, and at the time not realizing these were "chicken thief owls," we farm boys were a little quick on the trigger in shooting harmless wildlife.

But this story has not quite ended. Within a few days after shooting the owls, oats threshing was scheduled on the Little farm. Bundle-haulers, coming in from the large field just south of the evergreen grove, told of finding chicken bones on the top of many oats shocks. Gee whiz! Problem solved! The giant owl plucked a young chicken out of our tree, carried it a quarter-mile, landed on an oats shock and enjoyed a hearty moonlight meal.

Two-Legged Thieves

Evidence of just how hard up rural people were was found in ongoing reports of "chicken thieves." Though the threat was possibly exaggerated, it did happen. One strategy the thieves used was to watch for families making their weekly evening shopping trip to town. They would then drive up to the hen house hauling a chicken crate, load up and make a fast and clean get away. My brother Howard, age sixteen or seventeen, was teased about imagining an impending theft. If a car drove by slowly, Howard knew they were casing the place! If our parents happened to be away for the evening he would insist that we turn out the lights, and sit and wait for any would-be culprits. One night he was sure a driver, going by slowly, was using a spotlight to locate roosting chickens. At these times, Howard kept the 12-gauge shotgun handy. He meant business!

One night, while on "watch," Howard was sure he saw a would-be chicken thief drive into the farmyard. He grabbed the 12-gauge and started to sneak out of the house. Sister, Dorothy, half curious and half scared, decided to sneak downstairs to reinforce her older brother. Being younger (ten and twelve) Art and I were spooked out of our wits!

Then Dorothy kicked a pair of shoes someone carelessly left on the stair steps and they came tumbling down. Howard, stationed on the back porch, was ready to draw a bead on the thieves' car. Supposedly, hearing the ruckus the thieves panicked, and wheeled their car around and took off!

Howard never quite forgave Dorothy for ruining his apprehension of the thieves. The rest of us never quite accepted the reality of a robbery in progress.

Roundup Time

In October around corn-picking time, when the lively leghorn pullets were roosting in the trees, Dad would call for a "roundup." It was time to catch the pullets for confinement in the newly cleaned and bedded laying house. We employed a number of schemes to catch them, but invariably, one of us boys was "out on a limb" as we climbed the old maple trees to grab roosting birds.

In the laying house, the pullets—with good care and laying-mash rations—would soon start laying eggs for "home consumption" with plenty leftover to sell. Egg cases filled with fresh eggs were taken to Rystad's grocery store in Rembrandt where they were bartered for groceries. If there were a few dollars cash leftover it was usually spent for clothing, gasoline for the car, or on other family needs.

Mom supervised egg gathering. As a small boy, I often had to crouch down and retrieve "stray" eggs laid back under the chicken roosts. Imaginary or not, I always felt mites crawling on my skin afterwards. After finding an occasional soft-shelled egg, I understood why we always kept coarsely ground oyster shells in one feeder. The calcium-rich oyster shells provided the mineral needed to harden the outer eggshells.

After eight or ten months, egg production would taper off sharply, but the hens were not done producing yet! Another less venturesome roundup took place when the old hens were taken from the laying house, placed in wooden chicken crates, loaded in a two-wheeled trailer and pulled behind the family car to the local produce market. They eventually ended up in a can of store-bought chicken soup the city folks relished. But it didn't match the chicken and dumpling stew my mom made!

Like many chores on the farm, caring for the chickens was work, but we made a game out of it. Might just as well—we had to do it anyway! Now, sixty-five years later, we enjoy Kentucky Fried Chicken. But I sure long for one of those young, tasty, no fat, leghorn roosters fried the way Mom did: each piece salted lightly, rolled in flour, spiced, then fried in sizzling lard and butter in a cast-iron frying pan over the wood-burning kitchen stove! Yummie! WOW!

During the Great Depression a well cared for laying flock was an important and integral part of every family farm.

CHAPTER 22
THE COW HERD

A herd of cows was found on nearly every farm and ranch before, during, and for quite a few years after the Great Depression. In pioneer days, it may have been one or two cows just to provide milk for drinking and cream for butter and cottage cheese. A cow had a calf once a year that was grown and fed out for butchering. If a heifer, it was often added to the cow herd.

By the 1920s, as farm acreage and farm families became larger, there was a profusion of large gambrel-roofed hay and livestock barns. Most were attractively painted red with white trim. The ever-present cow herd grew from a typical half-dozen cows to herds often ranging up to fifteen or more.

Cow herds were right at home grazing in farm pastures. Only seventy years before this time, millions of buffalo roamed and grazed on native grasses of the prairie. Up until and including the Great Depression most farms had fields of native grass on hilly or poorly-drained soils. A cow herd was the best way to utilize these pasture areas. By the mid-1950s, many pastures succumbed to larger tractors, better plows, and new tile drainage machines, turning them into row crop fields.

A Typical Farm Herd

Often herds were "dual purpose." Shorthorns, for example, were valued for their meat as well as milk. Feeding out calves and selling them for slaughter was an important income source. Many farmers would match their ten homegrown calves by purchasing a dozen or more "feeders" raised on western ranches and sold to farmers each fall. This made up a feedlot of cattle to fatten and sell on the butcher market. However, as the milk and milk products (such as ice cream and cottage cheese) market grew, dairy breeds of Jerseys, Guernseys, and especially Holsteins became more popular.

The bellicose behavior of the herd bull kept us kids on the alert when bringing the cows in for milking. Neighboring bulls separated only by the public road or by a fence line, sent chills up our spines when they bellowed and pawed the ground! While we later learned this was largely "territorial bluffing," we thought a ferocious fight was going to break out any time. We felt safer riding our pony Dixie to bring cows in from the pasture. We envied a few farmers who trained their dog to "get the cows" on command. With the enticement of being fed, cows could be trained to come in from the pastures when called. In the quiet evening, an echoing of "Come boss, come boss," was heard around the neighborhood.

Steady cash income from selling cream and marketing calves fed out for slaughter made cow herds important economically. During the Great Depression any cash income was critical. But beef slaughter cattle selling for $4.35 per hundred weight in 1933 added little to the bank account; recovery during the 1930s is evidenced by beef prices almost doubling to $8.44 by 1939. Notably, the post-WWII boom pushed beef prices to $24.80 in 1948.

Figure 22.1: A few cows would stand patiently in the barnyard for milking as brother, Ken, was doing here. In summertime this was much cooler than in the barn. (circa 1928)

Because they had to be milked every morning and night, the herd demanded time, attention, and considerable labor by the family. As milking machines were not yet in general use, milking was done by hand. We boys had to start milking at the age of seven or eight. It was one of the first "demanding" jobs we were given. Cows were named and identified as individuals and each of us kids knew our two or three cows would be stanchioned in the barn for us to milk.

Cowboys, But Not the Movie Version

Except in the dead of winter when cows were kept in the barn overnight, the first job every morning was to round up and bring the cow herd in from the pasture. This meant putting the bridle on Dixie, jumping on bareback and galloping, maybe a half-mile, to where the cows were feeding or resting. This was repeated late every afternoon. Though a riding saddle hung by the pony's stall, to save time we seldom used it. We boys were pretty good bareback riders! Occasionally, we got thrown off when Dixie, a spirited pony, shied from being surprised by a small animal or other unfamiliar object.

In addition to producing considerable income, the cow herd provided other benefits. From our work with the herd we learned to take responsibility. It enhanced a regular work ethic, and taught us about taking care of animals and sexual reproduction. A cow would only produce milk (lactation) when, after nine months of pregnancy (gestation), she gave birth to a new calf, which naturally needed its mother's milk to stay alive. But getting the cows pregnant required a male, a herd bull, to mate with the cow at the appropriate time, when she was receptive or "in estrous." Bulls became very possessive and aggressive when a cow was "in heat." Mating time caused some commotion in the cattle lot when an 1800-pound bull mounted the cow to accomplish the act of breeding. Seeing how baby calves were conceived, it didn't take much imagination to translate this to how other mammals managed it.

Figure 22-2: When cows grazed in pastures or when gleaning the harvested cornfields, we rode Dixie to round up the herd for milking. (circa 1930)

So This is Animal Husbandry!

Nine months after breeding, a newborn calf arrived. There was much concern about keeping the calf alive and giving it a good start. This started by letting the calf suckle the now "fresh" mother to get a feeding of rich colostrum (first milk). We learned the colostrum was loaded with antibodies, giving the calf essential nourishment and resistance to sickness. However, a cruel fact of life soon came into play. The calf was weaned when one or two days old! We wanted to milk the cow to use her surplus milk. This resulted in a mooing mother cow, a bawling calf, and an immediate need to teach the calf to drink milk from a bucket. This was no small task and required a special technique. Responding to the calf's instinct to suck, we placed a small amount of fresh warm milk in a small bucket, a "calf pail." Then straddling the calf and wetting our fingers with milk, we coaxed the calf to suck our fingers and milk from the pail. This went against the calf's instinct of wanting to suck, with its head up, from the cow's warm teat, instead of from the bottom of a hard pail. After a few feedings, the calf got the hang of it and didn't need to suck fingers to drink milk from the pail. The greatest threat during the next few weeks was the calf getting scours (diarrhea) and possibly dying. The standard treatment was to break a couple of eggs in the milk feeding pail. This usually cured the problem.

Now we had another "fresh" cow to add to the milking herd. Dad liked to keep a minimum of nine cows milking—that's how many stanchions were in the barn! After about three months of milking, the cow would be receptive for breeding, which was willingly and ably taken care of by the herd bull. Thus, the reproduction cycle started

Figure 22.3: A calf weaned from its mother drank from a pail.

over again. After being bred, following nature's evolution, the cow's milk production slowly began to decrease during her gestation and she would "dry up" in six to eight months preparing for another newborn calf to feed.

Domesticated Doesn't Mean Harmless

The herd bull, particularly in some dairy breeds, was often quick-tempered and dangerous. At times it would attack, sometimes killing a man. With those breeds, the herdsman always had to be alert. Tragically, this happened to a well-known neighboring farmer. He was attempting to separate a bull and cow while in a barn pen when the bull swiftly turned and butted and gored the farmer, killing him instantly. We were shocked and in awe, realizing the massiveness and strength of an 1800-pound animal compared to the frailness of a 180-pound man.

The dominant nature of the large, mature herd bull was always a concern when handling the cow herd. This fright was amplified by their antics of arching their massive necks, pawing up clouds of dust, thereby displaying their aggressive demeanor. Proof that this left lasting impressions on a young farm kid were my dreams—really nightmares—of a bull chasing me and my split-second escape over a fence or the barn door. I even had visions of the bull angrily looking up at me as I escaped up the haymow ladder! These dreams reoccurred for years after I was full grown.

Milking was an experience. For some reason, Dad was a slow "stripper" milker and he was glad to leave the job to us boys. There were usually three or four of us in the barn to help. Milking had to be done rain or shine, no matter how hot or how cold. However, in winter with the barn filled with livestock it was a warm place to work—much better than in summer when inside the barn seemed hotter than outside temperatures.

The farm scene often generates some earthy humor. In every group of farm animals there is one animal more contrary than the others. In our cow herd this label fell to Wippet. She was last to come in from the pasture, most stubborn about going into the barn, and most likely to kick while being milked. The latter resulted in an angry—if not injured —farm boy and hobbles (leg restraints) for Wippet! The cows liked to browse around the huge straw stack that was always in close proximity to the barn. Art, frustrated by Wippet's orneriness, expressed some minor obscenity. This brought Dad to the scene of the conflict! Art—facing discipline and in complete frustration—said, "Wippet can run around the straw stack so fast she can crap in her face!" Visualizing the incredulity of such a scene—to our amazement—Dad began to laugh. Even Wippet was startled as she ran straight for the barn door! Later, though mentioned guardedly and with laughter suppressed, we never forgot the humor of the spectacle.

Cows were stanchioned side by side and, except during the lush summer grass season, were fed grain and hay. We called the cows by individual names: Roany, Red, Wippet, Big Spot, and others. We sat beside the cow on a one-legged "T-style" milking stool, and held the milk pail between our legs, partially under the cow's udder. We soon learned the technique of squeezing the cow's teats to get the maximum milk flow. The first squirts zinging the bottom of the pail soon formed foam. The milk made a soft "shush, shush" sound as the pail filled up.

It wasn't always so serene, however. In summer, common houseflies took over the cow barn. Even though we tried all kinds of fly spray, the cow's natural defense, her tail, was a formidable weapon. Inevitably, the milker would get a hard "swack" across the face by an (often dirty) cow's tail. We tried different schemes to stop the tail switching, such as holding her tail between our knee and the cow's leg or clipping it to an overhead tie. Unable to switch the pestering flies she would involuntarily kick at them, spilling milk and bruising the milker. There were always one or two cows that were more ornery than the others and were treated with caution.

Boys Will Be Boys

While the cows were milked, our ever-present cats (mouse catchers) would meow by the tin pan waiting to be fed. Often an older, mother cat learned to sit on her hind legs and drink milk as we, somewhat mischievously, squirted milk into the cat's mouth!

When finished with milking, we carried pails of milk to the house and ran it through the cream separator located on the back porch. The cream was valued for household needs and for selling to the town creamery. We saved skim milk for cooking and drinking. Any surplus went to feed growing farm animals.

In late summer when pastures would often turn brown from hot, dry weather, we used our pony Dixie to herd the cows along road ditches near our farm. The hungry cattle voraciously consumed the green forage, weeds and all. We had to guard field gates to prevent the cows from getting into the neighbor's cornfield. It seemed there was always a neighboring herd bull wanting to challenge any strange cattle trespassing his territory. His pawing and bellowing, though mostly bluff, scared us kids!

Bloating Cattle

During the dry summers of the mid-1930s it was tempting to turn hungry cattle from dried-up native grass pastures in to graze on lush clover or alfalfa fields. Occasionally, cattle would break through the fence to help themselves. In either instance, there was a real danger of cattle bloating from feeding too rapidly on the green legumes. Bloating resulted when their rumen (large stomach) filled with digestive gases. The enlarged rumen exerted pressure on the heart until it stopped beating. The critter would stagger, then fall over. If not treated within a minute or two, it would die. Treatment meant using a knife to pierce the bulging rumen to allow gas, with a "swoosh" to escape. My Dad had a trocar, a knife-sheath tool. The sheath (tube) provided for better gas escape.

Our good neighbor Reuben Braunschwieg was rather excitable and had a speech stutter. One time our phone rang with his wife, Etta, in a frenzy, asking: "Could Art come over right away? Cattle are bloating." Dad grabbed his trocar, jumped in the car, and raced a half-mile to help Reuben. As typical their milk cows were named: Blacky, Spot, Bluie (a roan), and some other common names. Arriving at the farmyard, Dad trotted out to where Reuben was hollering and waiving his arms—trying to drive the critters out of the alfalfa hay field. Upon seeing Dad, Reuben hollered, "B-B-B-Blackie's down! Stick-kha! Stick-kha!" As Dad drove the trocar in, the rumen collapsed, and Blackie (greatly relieved) ran off with her tail in the air! Next "Aht! Aht! B-B-Bluie's s-s-s-staggas!" Again Dad used the trocar. Swoosh, Bluie's relieved. This waving and stuttering went on for several minutes as three more were stuck before Reuben and his boys got them into a barnyard. They only lost one young heifer.

Reuben, recovering from near panic, thanked Dad and offered the obligatory, "What do I owe you?" Dad's response was familiar, "Oh, that's okay; maybe you can help me sometime."

This story obviously was not funny at the time but, while driving home, the hilarity of the wild stuttering scene struck my Dad and he humorously related it to the rest of us over supper.

4-H Projects

For several years, we selected our best calf (or two) and entered them in our 4-H Club baby beef project. We won a few blue ribbons while showing them at the county fairs, but never won a championship. But again, it was a good experience. Keeping feed and weight records taught us something about economics. 4-H clubs were not only learning experiences, but also social events.

Figure 22.4: For my 4-H baby beef project I bought this steer we had raised, from Dad. (circa 1941)

Small cow herds began to disappear during WWII because of the labor shortage. After the war, they didn't make a comeback because the small herds were not economically efficient. Fewer, but larger, herds replaced them. Farmers became less diversified and more efficient by concentrating on fewer enterprises such as hogs only, feeding cattle, or straight grain farming with no livestock.

Farmers willingly adapted to buying milk and butter from the supermarket as their city "cousins" had been doing for years. This was one more event in a succession of changes during the last half of the twentieth century that quickened the demise of the family farm.

Figure 23.1: Butter churn.

Figure 23.2: Ice cream freezer.

CHAPTER 23
BUTTER AND ICE CREAM
VALUE ADDED: A NEW NAME FOR AN OLD PRACTICE

Churning Butter

"Value added" became a buzzword in the last half of the twentieth century. It simply means turning a raw material into a more valuable product. During the first half of the 1900s, converting raw products into a more usable form right on the farm was a common practice. For example: bluegrass was fed to cows which resulted in the production of cow's milk; milk was separated into skim milk and cream; cream was churned into butter—all that was a common value-adding process. The ultimate in "value added," according to the taste bud test, was homemade ice cream!

After the cows were milked both morning and evening, we carried the fresh milk in pails to the house to be separated. Separating was accomplished by running the whole milk through the "separator"; a spinning "bowl" separated the lighter rich cream from the heavier skim milk by centrifugal force. We each had to take our turn at cranking the DeLavel separator. After family needs were satisfied, surplus skim milk was fed to farm animals. Cream, being of value, was accumulated in five- and ten-gallon cream cans and sold at the cream buying station in town. This cash income was "traded" at the store for the week's supply of food and cooking items taken from Mom's carefully prepared grocery list.

Part of the cream was served with meals and part was churned into another bowl of butter about every ten days. We had a barrel churn, an improvement over the earlier plunger-type "log cabin" churns, but it preceded the mechanical gear-driven paddle models mounted on a square two-gallon glass jar. Our five-gallon wooden barrel churn had a tight clamp-down lid; two axle pins cradled it in a wooden stand. We turned it by using a crank attached to the axle. The churn was filled about one-third full with cream, then cranked to assure ample agitation. We were reminded not to crank too fast or slow to assure the right amount of churning.

We kids disliked the monotonous job of churning and never knew how long it would take to make butter—varying from five to twenty minutes. The cow's feed and the cream temperature had an effect. It was exhilarating to call out, "Mom, I got butter!" With a wooden butter paddle Mom would place the butter in a large crock bowl. There she would knead and press out excess buttermilk, add just the right amount of salt and mold the butter into a nice loaf. In winter, we stored it in the unheated back porch; in summer it was kept in the icebox. Butter was used in baking and other food preparation aside from being served on the table with every meal.

Mm-mm, that was real butter!

Making Ice Cream

On the farm ice cream was only made for special occasions: birthdays, having dinner guests, a picnic, family gatherings, or whenever we could talk our parents into it! The primary limitation was that selling cream was an important income source, and it took a lot of cream to make farm-rich ice cream! Getting ice for freezing in winter was no problem. We simply cut it from a nearby creek or from the livestock watering tank where, in spite of the wood-burning tank heater, a band of ice would accumulate around the inside wall of the round, wooden tank. In summer, it took precious cash to buy a block of ice from the local iceman.

Mom had her own recipe for ice cream, which never got a murmur of complaint. Cream, two eggs, sugar, and vanilla flavoring (always plain—vanilla!) were mixed and heated on the stove and then placed in a six-quart, cylindrical metal container with the ladle, a stirring device, inside the container.

While Mom was preparing the mixture, we boys were busy getting ice. Small chunks cut from the water tank were placed in a burlap bag and pounded gently with a sledge hammer or the flat side of an axe until we had a bag of small pieces to easily pack around the ice cream container. We got a coffee can full of salt from the granary where bags of rock salt (for livestock) were stored. With salt, the ice and water solution could be reduced to below freezing temperature (below thirty-two degrees) to freeze the ice cream.

Now we were ready to make ice cream!

The ice cream container placed inside the wooden barrel was turned around by a metal gear-and-crank mechanism that fit on top of the barrel. A fixed restraint kept the ladle from turning, thus "stirring" the ice cream solution as the container rotated. We slowly added layers of ice and a little salt as we continued to crank the freezer. In a matter of a few minutes, it began to crank harder. In ten or twelve minutes we could no longer turn the crank. We had frozen ice cream! Now the first of highly anticipated rewards took place: we had to remove the ladle so the ice cream could be easily spooned out for later serving—of course, some ice cream clung to the ladle! We drew straws to see who got the first lick of the ladle! There was no delay as the ladle was shared and, in two or three minutes, was licked clean!

Then the container lid was corked and sealed with wax paper before packing with ice. This caused the ice cream to harden—preserving it until the awaited dessert was served!

In later years we, as did most people, shifted to the convenience of "boughten" manufactured ice cream. After a time of eating the more bland and soft store-bought ice cream, I chanced to attend a homemade ice cream social. It was after taking a big spoon full of homemade ice cream and feeling sharp sinus pains from the ice-cold delicacy I realized how different ice cream had become. In the change to "boughten" ice cream, we lost a "good old days" experience. Real homemade ice cream was something to be enjoyed slowly!

CHAPTER 24
HOGS: THE MORTGAGE LIFTERS

Hog production on farms expanded as it gained a reputation for generating income with relatively little cash risk. In the 1920s and 1930s, nearly every farmer raised hogs. Those who did it well seemed to be the more successful—they made more money. With this reputation, economists and animal husbandry professors at Iowa State College dubbed hogs "mortgage lifters," a dependable means of paying off bank loans and farm mortgages.

Before concrete feeding floors or self-feeders, ear corn was scooped from the wagon and scattered on the ground for awaiting hungry hogs. Responding to the competition, a hog would bite into an ear of corn and run to the perimeter of the herd to eat unmolested—maybe!

The advantages of raising hogs were ample and obvious. Hogs were hardy and adapted to various growing conditions. Nearly all feed, bedding, and other needs could be both produced and consumed on the farm without expensive processing. Hogs were thrifty grazers of legume pastures and gleaners of corn left in the field following harvest. There was little to buy outright except low-cost minerals and, at times, protein supplement, such as soybean oil meal or tankage. Other than a hog house for early spring farrowing, shelter could be minimal: a low profile shed or in summer a grove of trees. Of course, water had to be provided, usually by a float-controlled waterer attached to a water tank.

In the cold of winter when ice accumulated around the waterer, it was no fun to get down on hands and knees to refill water heater lamps with kerosene or relight wick-style burners. A few minutes after removing mittens to attend the heaters, my entire body was shivering. Heat loss from bare hands was rapid. Removing a cap and earflaps had the same—but quicker—effect. It confirmed my parent's caution to dress warmly in severely cold weather.

"Independent as a pig on ice." When first hearing this expression I was curious that it didn't seem to fit the analogy intended. Zero temperatures froze hard slick ice around the water fountain or on a concrete feeding floor which proved a real hazard for hogs. They lose footing, fall spraddle-legged and cannot get up. They become very dependent, panic-stricken. I presume the word "independent" comes from their squealing and fear if you try to help them get up or try to drag them off the ice to safe footing. Once on solid ground they calm down and recover quickly.

Hogs required "hog tight," woven-wire fencing to keep them confined on the farm. This meant we boys got plenty of experience in building fence. Hogs evolved in the jungle and savannas (grasslands), rooting up tubers for food. With this trait stamped in their genes eons ago, they could root up and ruin a good alfalfa field in a few days unless they were "rung." It was a challenge to hold a 200-pound hog by the snout with a wire snare and pierce its nose while attaching a wire hog ring! After that when they tried to root, the pain put a stop to it. It was cruel, but it worked.

Figure 24.1: "Low technology" hog feeding. (circa 1934)

Production Starts With Reproduction

Farm swine production started with a breeding herd of ten to twenty brood sows—females bred to raise a litter of pigs. Popular breeds were Hampshire, Poland China, Duroc, Chester White, and a few other breeds. We had spotted Poland Chinas. A farmer would usually save back gilts (young female swine) selected from his own herd and would occasionally buy a new bloodline to improve his herd. With a gestation period of 115 days, the herd sire (boar) would be turned in with the gilts for breeding about four months before the desired farrowing date. To take advantage of the oncoming warmer weather, farrowing was usually scheduled for springtime— March or April. Many farmers also had a fall farrowing.

Farrowing was a tenuous time when every effort was made to save as many newborn pigs as possible. This often meant staying up with a farrowing sow well into the night.

Hopefully every sow would raise a minimum of six pigs, but a litter of eight or nine was ideal. Instinctively, each pig would seek out a teat to nurse, a few minutes after birth. The farmer "midwifing" helped the young pig find a "dinner plate" (nipple) as soon as possible. He also prevented injury to the first-born pigs while the nervous sow strained and kicked, giving birth to the remainder of her litter.

A sow seemed to sense when all of her litter was born and when they were all nursing "their" nipple. "Theirs" because once claimed, that nipple—that location— belonged to that pig until weaned. A little pig would fight immediately and fiercely to protect its territory. It was music to the farmer's ears to hear the sow's *ruh, ruh* in rhythm with the vigorous motion of her nursing litter. Then we knew the birthing was over, the sow was contented, and the pigs found their places at the "dinner table." This rhythmic *ruh, ruh*, a call probably as ancient as the swine species, was repeated several times a day all through the sow's lactation time—six weeks or more. It soon developed that several sows would instinctively nurse in unison, adding drama to the ruckus. And it always gave us assurance that the litters were coming along fine.

Handling livestock always had a certain physical challenge and some danger— whether it was being bucked off the pony, kicked by a horse, or butted or kicked by a cow. We always had to be alert for a charge by a mad sow protecting her litter or because we were holding one of her offspring for medical treatment. Testimony to the pig's wild side were contests at the county fair where a sizable prize was offered to the young boy who was first to catch a greased pig!

Health, Pests, and Disease

All farm endeavors carried on for gain and profit entailed risks and setbacks. So it was with the swineherd. Though hardy, hogs were subject to some afflictions. Cholera, a quick-spreading infectious disease, could kill a whole herd unless they were vaccinated. Vaccination meant catching and holding each scrappy, month-old pig while the veterinarian gave it shots of vaccine. Somehow, this job was always done on Saturday when we boys were home from school!

At four weeks of age, all male pigs were castrated to eliminate a rank taste in the meat, apparent in older male hogs (boars). Castrating was a simple but invasive surgical procedure. It took two workers: one to hold the "victim" on a small table while the other slit the scrotum and rapidly—but carefully—removed the testicles, then dabbed the incision with a disinfectant. When Dad's eyesight began to deteriorate, he taught me the procedure at age fourteen. Though intricate in nature and essential to raising butcher hogs for market, no special notice was offered or expected for learning how to perform the surgery. I did it because it was necessary and part of the responsibility of a farm kid's growing up.

The growing pigs, called "shoats," had to be sprayed for mange mites, a tough little crab-like insect that lived in the folds of a pig's skin. They sucked blood and caused a painful skin mange.

In the 1930s, a new death-causing disease called erysipelas appeared. Though contagious, infection between hog herds was sporadic. Symptoms were reddish (fever) skin lesions and crippling due to swollen leg cartilage. Dad was depressed after losing several market-weight butcher hogs. It was a blow to the already meager farm income. In a few years a medical treatment was developed, reducing the threat.

Oddities

We read and heard about "freaks of nature," such as a two-headed calf or pig. In 1938 when weaning the six-week-old nursing pigs, we noticed one having an awkward time getting around. On closer examination, we discovered the pig was born without his left front leg. Knowing a pig with only three legs would have quite a struggle in the herd, we kids decided to make it a pet and built a pen connected to a small shelter. In Swedish the word three is spelled "tre" and is pronounced "tray"—and that became the name of the pig. Tre was quite a playful, amiable pet that we fed and cared for every day during the summer. Before long, Tre was let out of his pen and would hang around the back porch awaiting food and wanting attention in the way of a corncob scratching his ears. By fall, when Tre was approaching 175 pounds in weight, my parents posed the question about his future. The local hog buyer didn't want him fearing he would be injured or killed while being transported to a distant meat-packing plant.

Figure 24.2: Nels with prize 4-H sows. Note these fat, lardy hogs. (circa 1920s)

Often in farm life, especially when dealing with animals, there was not a lot of allowance for emotions, and the practical took over. Thus we kids reluctantly accepted the idea that Tre would be butchered—for our own dinner table! There was something different, even a little eerie, when a slice of pork roast from Tre was placed on my dinner plate!

I accepted it as pure coincidence, but the very next year we discovered a five-legged pig in our herd. A small half-leg grew out from the left shoulder! The deformity proved no hardship, so he was left with the herd and eventually sold along with others making up a load for market.

Finishing for Market

Young shoats were usually fed a ground oat mash soaked in water to form a "slop," or soaked whole oats—both meant to aid digestion. When around 125 pounds, the main feed for the hogs shifted to corn. It was usually shelled off the cob, or carried in a metal bushel basket or in pails to wooden troughs in the hog lot. In the later 1930s, self-feeders were developed, holding twenty to thirty bushels and providing feed for several days. Often in the fall, new corn crop—whole ears—were spread on the ground and eaten off the cob without wasting any.

Hogs are credited with being smart animals. Suffice it to say they would come in from the pasture in a hurry when called for feeding time. At supper time, the hog calling sound: *poo-aay, poo-aay* would echo around the neighborhood. Hog-calling contests were a popular event at county fairs!

In the 1930s, agricultural colleges urged farmers to add protein (tankage, soybean meal, linseed meal) to swine rations and to feed minerals. This brought on a surge of feed salesmen! They had yeast feeds, minerals, various "supplements," and a little "snake oil." In fact, feed salesmen became a nuisance. A joke about hog feed salesmen expressed some irony of the times, "Oh, ya, he used to farm. Went broke raising hogs!"

Historically, fat lard-type hogs were produced in the U.S. for their rendering lard, a favorite for cooking. Lard was in high demand during WWII when lard derivatives were used for explosives and lubricants. After the war, surplus lard drove the price of hogs down and agricultural scientists and farmers rushed to produce more "meat-type" hogs. Several meatier breeds such as Yorkshire, Landrace, Tamworth, and others were shipped in from Europe—primarily Denmark—which rapidly changed the type and conformation of American breeds. It also brought leaner cuts of pork that weight-conscious Americans enjoyed.

At six to seven months of age and weighing 220 pounds the fat butchers were marketed and it was finally the farmers' payday. And it was true—often the money went to the bank to help "lift" a mortgage off the books.

Figure 25.1. Note the Shepherd dog that skillfully rounded up this nice farm flock.

CHAPTER 25
SHEEP

Farmers Either Wanted Them or Wanted Nothing to do with Them!

Several Agricultural Colleges encouraged farmers to diversify and to consider a "farm flock" of sheep to accomplish that end.

Through the 1920s and through the Great Depression, horses, cows, hogs, and chickens were family farm necessities. For a number of reasons this was not so with sheep. There were more risks to handling sheep. I attended an Extension Education meeting on livestock production where Rex Beresford, Animal Husbandry Professor from Iowa State College, was fielding questions. A young farmer, saying he had no experience but an interest in raising sheep, asked Beresford what equipment he would need. Without hesitation Beresford said with complete candor, "You'll probably need a skinning knife."

A few farmers had successful farm flocks of thirty to fifty sheep but it was generally believed that raising sheep had more risks. Sheep were pretty good foragers and scavengers, but a sheep will die for no apparent reason much more often than other farm animals. When housed in open sheds in severe cold weather, they can die from overcrowding. In pastures, there is a danger of attack and death from coyotes or roving bands of domestic dogs. Marketing wool involves shearing and limited market outlets.

There were a few farmers who specialized in feeding out a large flock (in the hundreds) of western-grown lambs every fall. They had the proper sheds, feed bunks and fencing—and they understood sheep.

When I was a small boy, a neighbor gave us kids an orphan baby lamb that we bottle-fed cow's milk. The lamb became a delightful pet, but also a nuisance—which we readily overlooked. Strangely I don't know what became of him. I suspect he went to market one day when we kids were in school.

A New Venture through Our 4-H Club

Sometimes a little luck helps. When I was a 4-H Club member, our county agricultural agent convinced me the western lamb feeding project was worthwhile. My dad didn't raise sheep and was a little skeptical. He made it clear it was my project! I borrowed money from the Production Credit Association and bought two pens (sixteen each) of western lambs. Signing a promissory note for the loan at age fifteen, was—in itself—a worthwhile experience. I built a low, shed-type shelter, remodeled some wood hog troughs for feeding bunks, relocated a small watering tank, and fixed the feedlot fence. I was excited, but a little awed, on October 1, 1940, when the truckload of lambs arrived at the farm.

I had been carefully studying the care and daily feeding rations for lambs, which called for a mixture of corn and oats. Starting with two-thirds oats and one-third corn, the corn was to be gradually increased during the 115-day feeding period. Protein pellets were fed with the grain. Fresh alfalfa hay was provided in a homemade manger. There was always a salt lick.

Sheep were fed grain in an elevated trough or bunk. Interestingly, they chewed like people, holding their lips tightly pursed and never dropping a kernel or grain of feed. They were neater than other farm animals.

The infamous Armistice Day blizzard struck on November 11. Although my sheep shed was only 150 feet from the house, I had my hands full in caring for the sheep during the day-long blizzard. I had to shovel through snowdrifts to be sure they were properly fed and sheltered. Fortunately all the sheep survived.

In early December, the county agent stopped to see how my project was coming. My sheep looked good. He became alarmed at how much I was feeding them. "My gosh, you're going kill those lambs from overfeeding!" I was a little unnerved, but knew my lambs were feeling good and doing well. He cautioned me to observe the lambs carefully every day. I was concerned, but kept on with the feed level. My concern turned to worry when—about two weeks later—I found a nice, fat lamb dead. No symptoms or cause was evident. A neighboring sheep feeder advised me, "That will happen." I eased back on the feed a little.

The third week in January, we 4-H Club members took our fat lambs to the Clay county fairgrounds in Spencer, Iowa. There were about 200 pens (3200) of sheep and—co-incidentally—Professor Rex Beresford from Iowa State (still smoking his curved-stem, "grandpa" pipe) was there to judge them. It was prearranged that buyers would pay the going market price or better for our lambs at the end of the show.

Beresford rapidly moved from one pen to the next, judging each pen. After the pens were judged, we could each select one lamb and enter it into the individual champion contest. He sized up each lamb and adroitly measured the backfat over the lamb's spine by placing his hand firmly on the sheep's back to measure its backfat or "covering."

Beresford pulled my lamb out and placed it at the top! I pretended not to be in a state of shock. But the strength of my feeding program and my unbelievably good luck were confirmed when he named one of my two pens best in the show! My other pen won third. And the individual lamb I selected was grand champion of the show!

At the closing banquet that night, I was a little embarrassed making trips to the front speaker's rostrum to get my prizes. But I was pretty proud upon getting home and spreading fifteen silver dollars in prize money out on the kitchen table. Happily I made a nice profit on the lamb-feeding project.

My parents were somewhat amused, and proud too.

Part Four

The Mechanization of Farming
From Horses to Tractors

Oiling the Windmill
Arne Waldstein

Crazy sentry standing there
Ugly, yet proud of your mission.
Unheralded by man, the benefactor
Challenging each wind
Wherever on the compass
Greeting its waves with compulsive response.
Jerking water deep from Earth's bosom
For man to eagerly suckle from your flow.

Untiring servant
Giving much
Demanding little.
A complaint now and then.
Metal on metal pierces the ear!
I'll acknowledge your call,
With an oiler.

A brave hand ascends the bottom rung.
Fright overtakes me three-quarters way up
I freeze momentarily.
Grasping the iron rail!
Like a child to his mother.
From below: "Come on, afraid?"
How much no one will know.
"Don't look down!"
Inch upward—on the platform!
Steady now.
The oil reservoir is filled.
I feel the strained metal relieved,
And so am I.

Coming down is easy.
She's running free again!
Softly.
Gung—gong, gung—gong
Gung—gong————

Windmills were one of man's earliest efforts to harness nature's energy with a mechanically-driven
machine. It benefited human sustenance and took some drudgery out of daily life.

CHAPTER 26
FROM HORSES TO TRACTORS

The Great Depression Started with Horses and Kerosene Lanterns: Ended with Tractors and Electric Lights

Optimism Overcomes Despair

The transition from horsepower to tractor-power ushered in the most dramatic changes in the history of farming. Simultaneously there were truly revolutionary advancements. The list is illuminating:

- Horsepower gave way to tractor power—much greater production capacity with less labor.
- Kerosene lamps to electricity—incandescent bulbs turned dark into light; electric motors worked quietly, around the clock.
- Man's muscles to hydraulic cylinders—machines took the heavy lifting and much of the hard labor out of farming.
- Inadequate grease cups to pressure-powered grease guns—reliable lubrication kept new machines running longer and more smoothly.
- Steel-lugged wheels to rubber tires—more economical traction, better fuel efficiency, smoother riding, and greater operator comfort.
- Open pollinated corn to hybrids—this achievement alone increased yields 50 percent.

It seems an anomaly that it happened during the Great Depression—most within a short span of six or seven years! (From 1935 to 1941.)

No doubt, these many developments were motivated by the urgency to improve things. They speak volumes about American ingenuity, innovation, ambition, and willingness to change and take risks. Americans can be down—yet not out!

Tractors were the dominant change agent. Farms were getting larger, kids were leaving the farm for more attractive city careers, and labor costs were increasing. Horses were costly to feed and had limited work capacity. A quip often heard was, "You don't have to feed the tractor when it isn't working." With gasoline at eleven cents a gallon and distillate (fuel oil) at eight cents, tractors were quite economical to operate. And, there was the genuine excitement of engines and machines!

The Prelude

The industrial revolution following the Civil War adapted engines to power factories and spurred invention and the ensuing manufacture of automobiles. The success of cars and trucks and the imagination of farmers and small machine shop mechanics soon translated into the development of and market for farm tractors. Even before the 1920s, men were busy trying to convert engine power to traction power for tillage. Most of those early tractors, of which the steam engine tractor was

Figure 26.1: Brother, Art, is on the left, a neighbor kid is behind him, and I am on the right in a white stocking cap, peering over the tractor fender. (circa 1927) Curiosity and excitement about machinery started at an early age.

the forerunner, were clumsy hulks often referred to as "clunkers." They never caught on with the typical family farmer.

Improved 1920s Models Catch On

By the 1920s, efforts were flourishing to design smaller, more maneuverable and efficient "plow" tractors. Farmers, seeing the advantages over horses, began buying them. Dozens of different makes of tractors were being built. Those that didn't quickly improve design and engineering dropped out of the picture. Today, many of those early tractors, relics of the past, are sought after by antique collectors. They became relatively rare after many of these outmoded machines were victims of scrap iron drives during WWII.

McCormick-Deering (later International Harvester, marketed under the name of Farmall) was one of the more successful tractors built during the mid-1920s. John Deere's roots go back to 1837 when a blacksmith named John Deere in Grand Detour, near Dixon in northwestern Illinois, invented the steel plow. Deere used a hardened-steel saw blade to shape and polish a steel moldboard plow that would "scour clean" when plowing the heavy black clay soils of the Corn Belt. It revolutionized primary tillage. The John Deere company tractors started with the Waterloo Gasoline Engine Company's Waterloo Boy built in 1912. It became John Deere in 1918, and in 1923 their popular two-cylinder Model D, a three-bottom plow tractor, was introduced. It remained in production for thirty years, until 1953—a probable record.

Other well-known and successful makes were Fordson (a brainchild of Henry Ford and produced by the Ford Motor Company), Oliver (an outgrowth of the older Hart-Parr from Charles City, Iowa), Case (Racine, Wisconsin), Allis-Chalmers

(Milwaukee), Twin Cities (later Minneapolis-Moline), and Massey-Harris (later Massey-Ferguson). There were many others. Most didn't withstand the rigors of engineering and competition.

All these early models had their shortcomings, such as not starting in cold weather. I remember Dad and my older brothers lighting a cob fire under the oil pan of the Fordson to heat up the engine oil. Even then, a team of horses occasionally had to pull the tractor to start it, as hand-cranking became too exhausting. Shortcomings could turn into complete frustration. Once a neighborhood farmer actually took out his 12-gauge shotgun and shot his tractor!

The Sounds of Farming Change

From about 1925 until 1932 we had a Fordson tractor. As tractors were run long hours into the evening, I remember hearing the noise of different tractors echo through the neighborhood. There would be the steady roar of the poorly muffled standard four-cylinder engines. When the machine turned on the end rows, it quieted down as the governor or hand throttle slowed the lugging engine. The *pop-pop, huff-huff* rhythm of a lugging, two-cylinder John Deere had the most distinct identity. The Fordson, with a worm-gear rear main drive, had a distinctive, constant howl of its own. Doing late evening chores, Dad was content to hear the howl of the Fordson. He knew the plowing was getting done.

Hard Times

These early efforts to replace horses with tractors came to a halt with the onset of the Great Depression in 1930. At its depth, in 1931–1933, bank foreclosures and loan redemption caused many farmers to lose their tractors. Tractors were more reliable mortgage chattel than horses and didn't have to be fed after being repossessed! I recall at four years of age, in 1929, the thrill of sitting on my older brother's lap for a chugging ride around the barnyard as steel lugs bumped along over the hard ground. I don't know the circumstances, but in 1932 our Fordson tractor disappeared from the farm. It was probably repossessed to settle a debt—delinquent because of the difficult economic times during the Depression.

Row Crop Tractors Emerge

While these standard-tread, plow tractors served tillage purposes quite well, they lacked the high clearance needed for row crop farming. Similarly, they did not meet the rapidly increasing demand for machines that could plant, cultivate, and harvest corn—the predominant and expanding crop. Thus, in the late 1920s, row crop—tricycle-type tractors—were successfully designed and manufactured. They were popular with farmers. An early arrival on the scene was the two-row designed Farmall Regular (later named F-20). In 1928, a John Deere GP three-row arrived. It was converted into a two-row tricycle model in 1929. Most of the dozen major manufacturers had row crop models by the early 1930s.

As we moved through the Depression years, more efficient, better-designed tractors, planters, mounted cultivators, and corn pickers were designed. The John

Figure 26.2: John Deere Model GP. (circa 1930)

Deere Model A (1934) was representative and its design was soon paralleled by other makes. We welcomed improvement in weed control and in tillage with the new two-row tractor-mounted cultivators.

As farm size began to expand, even slightly, farmers quickly felt the extra burden put on horses. This, in addition to losing horses to sleeping sickness, hurried the anxiety of farmers wanting to buy tractors.

Tractors Get a Reprieve

After farming the early years of the Depression solely with horses, there was enough financial recovery so my Dad could buy a used John Deere GP in April 1936. I remember the day when the implement dealer delivered it to the farm on a flatbed truck. This tractor cost $350.00. What excitement! My older brothers were always ready to take the GP with various tillage machines to the field—much preferred to harnessing up four horses. With the tractor engine idling, the downward-directed exhaust pipe shot out perfect smoke rings. Fifteen feet from the tractor, they were two feet in diameter. Of course, little kids playfully jumped through them!

The John Deere GP was the first tractor I was to drive, at twelve years of age. With Dad riding on the grain binder operating the controls, he would holler at me if I didn't drive right. That tractor served us well as it took over heavy plowing and tillage from our aging horses.

Sensing farmer demand for tractors and industry's slowness in responding, some blacksmith shops built "homemade" tractors. A successful one was the Thieman, built by the Thieman Brothers at Albert City, Iowa. Thieman's built the frame and tricycle wheel arrangement, then added a Model A Ford or other car engine, drive shaft and rear axle with chain reduction drives to the rear tractor wheels. These tractors were too light for extensive, heavy plowing, but worked very well for cultivating and other light farm work.

Inventing a Better Wheel

The earliest wheel designs used diagonally-mounted angle-iron lugs. These were followed by spade lugs, which had more traction as the lugs remained clean from

Photo 26.3: A 1998 photo of Wayne Thieman with his vintage Thieman Tractor built by his father and uncles starting in the mid-1930s. WWII material shortages curbed production.

compacted soil. Around 1935, in response to tractors getting stuck in wet potholes, a new steel "skeleton" wheel was designed that helped solve the problem.

During this time major tire companies, including Firestone, Goodyear, Goodrich, and others, were experimenting with rubber tires and looking at farm tractors to greatly expand the tire market.

The large, heavy, steel wheels required extra power just to move through the soft soils in the field. Having enough traction to pull heavy loads was always a challenge. Factors such as soil compaction, soil clinging to the iron wheel lugs, smoothness of ride and reducing vibration all favored the new rubber tires.

At first farmers were quite skeptical about rubber tires holding up and having ample traction. Allis-Chalmers was one of the first to equip their new tractors with rubber tires in about 1937. Characteristically, farmers were curious. Surprisingly, these tires improved field traction and stood up very well. The anticipated flat tire problem seldom happened. Rubber tires improved efficiency and saved gasoline. And the bonus of a remarkably smoother ride made believers out of even the most skeptical. Rubber tires swept the tractor market within just two years.

Innovation Plus a Little Genius

It was interesting how farmers and mechanics developed a genius for maintaining and repairing tractors. When pulling a moldboard plow, wheels on one side of the tractor ran in the six- to seven-inch-deep furrow, tilting the tractor to one side. We were unaware that lubricating oil in the higher or "land side" of the tractor drive train was gradually transferred to the lower opposite side. As a result, the high side on our GP ran out of oil causing the rear wheel bearing to fail, which resulted in a crack in the main cast-iron wheel housing. It presented a crisis to buy a new casting and to find the necessary mechanical skills to make the repair. I'm not sure what prompted Dad to call Chris Olson, a highly skilled blacksmith in nearby Alta. Chris said he would come to the farm and "take a look."

A couple of days later, Chris arrived in his service truck to check the damage. He asked Dad if we had an iron ring, six inches in diameter. Fortunately, and by coincidence, we kids had an iron bearing ring (a race) leftover from a Fordson repair years before. In playing we used a flat stick to roll the ring, racing around the farmyard. Chris, in his Scandinavian accent said, "Dat looks okay." As we jacked the tractor up to remove the rear wheel Chris told us to build a cob fire. With the wheel off, we could readily see a crack in the cone-shaped housing. The damaged bearing was removed. The steel ring was heated until red hot in the intense fire. Using iron tongs, Chris positioned the hot steel ring, like a collar, around the cone casting. We watched in amazement as Chris, a large muscular man, made long, arching swings with a heavy sledge, striking a steel punch and driving the steel ring in place, compressing the fracture. As the ring cooled it shrunk, squeezing the crack even tighter. A new wheel bearing was installed, and the tractor ran for years with no problem. We guessed his repair bill was a tenth the cost of a new housing!

The Village Blacksmith

The town blacksmith shop has been an intriguing place as commemorated by Longfellow's poem, "The Village Blacksmith." Chris Olson was characteristic of the best of the "Smithies"—magicians at firing the forge, deftly shaping red-hot iron into plow lathes or modifying and repairing machinery. Sparks flew, like Fourth of July sparklers, from his electric arc welder. With oxyacetylene torch molten, bronze flowed to bond broken cast-iron gears. When time allowed we boys slipped over and stood near the large doorway, at a safe distance, peering in at the working blacksmith. Blacksmiths played a big role in keeping the many new farm machines working.

Buying the John Deere Model A

We had misgivings when Dad talked about trading in the faithful old GP, but were thrilled when a new 1939 John Deere Model A row crop tractor arrived—streamlined and with rubber tires! This new tractor cost $950.00. By that time, we were down to four draft horses. The tractor, and we younger generations of engine lovers, took over. With the two-plow Model A, we farmed a half-section—320 acres. As the tractor didn't need an overnight rest like horses, we boys thought it made sense to run the tractor "around the clock." We rigged the tractor with lights to accommodate our ambitious plans. When working after dark we noticed the tractor ran better and had more power. Later, we learned additional moisture in the air improved engine fuel

Figure 26.4: Our 1939 John Deere Model A. Home on army furlough I was glad to help cultivate corn. (circa 1944)

combustion. But when working at night, time seemed to drag on very slowly. We couldn't take in the usual surrounding daylight attractions: seeing a circling hawk, surprising a reclusive red fox, waving across the fence at a neighbor or evaluating our own progress. I wasn't surprised that nighttime fieldwork didn't catch on. Later, even with comfortable tractor cabs, it was done only when fieldwork became urgent. The Model A was poppin' along in good rhythm when I enlisted in the army in late 1943, and it ran for years afterward. Through diligent work, engineers and manufacturers put out a long line of dependable and economical "work horses"—tractors—that surely changed life on the farm.

No Genius Just Common Sense

With the increasing use of tractors and machines, our learning curve benefited from many common sense solutions. My brother Art was the "chief operator" of the John Deere Model A. Dad hardly ever drove a tractor, happy to leave it up to us ever-willing boys. Once, Art became concerned about some endplay and a related noise in the tractor crankshaft. We were a little skeptical when the local "shade tree" auto mechanic said the tractor needed new main bearings. As that would be of considerable expense and not characteristic of the John Deere, Dad decided to consult with Herb the John Deere Dealer Mechanic at the place where we bought the tractor. He said, "I'm coming out your way. I'll stop and look, in a day or two".

After a quick look Herb loosened the flywheel bolts and asked Art to apply pressure against the opposite, pulley end of the crankshaft with a fence post. Herb then firmly struck the flywheel hub with a five-pound sledgehammer. He retightened

Figure 26.5: Ken's feed grinder. Art in cab and me at the rear of the grinder try to figure out how this truck mounted hammer mill really worked.

the bolts and said, "That's it." There was no more unusual engine noise, it ran fine. No new bearings were needed! When asked if there was any charge. Herb said, "No, that's okay."

When we had no money, goodwill and trust became a common coin—the medium of exchange.

Rhythm of Machines

Interestingly, the variety of farm machines had their own distinct sound and rhythm: the *pop, pop, huh, huh* of the one- and two-cylinder engines; the steady chug and cackle of the four-cylinders; the *humm* and *ker-chunck* of the grain binder; or a rattling protest from gears and chains on the corn picker. Any change or disruption of this rhythm caught the farmer's ear instantly, warning of needed adjustment or a quick stop for inspection to avoid time-consuming and costly breakdowns. An eardrum-piercing squeak called for the grease gun or oil can.

Machines Replace Muscle

Some of the hardest work—real drudgeries—of farming, came at the handles of pitchforks or scoop shovels. There were hay and straw to gather, stack, and store. Every winter day, hay and straw were carried or loaded—via pitchfork—for hauling to feed and bed livestock. Much of this eventually resulted in tons of manure that, come spring, had to be pitched onto the manure spreader and hauled to the fields. Similarly, after the oats had been harvested and stored, they were scooped out of the granary for feeding livestock or for hauling to market. Corn was scooped from cribs to the corn sheller or feed grinder. It was likely shoveled again when fed to livestock. Some days the scoop shovel or pitchfork was a constant companion of the farmer. It is little wonder that the invention of the hydraulic cylinder, its adaptation to tractor-

Figure 26.6: This Wincharger includes a small tower for mounting on the house. Ours was mounted by means of clamping a twenty-foot wooden four-by-six to protrude above a box elder tree near the house. It is visible in the house photo at the beginning of Chapter 3.

mounted manure loaders and many other uses, was so keenly welcomed during the push to farm mechanization.

Adapting machines to multiple uses during the mechanical revolution was evident by a variety of innovations. Agricultural college experts encouraged farmers to grind grain for more palatable and nutritious livestock rations, but many farmers couldn't justify owning a burr mill or a hammer mill feed grinder. One example of fulfilling a need was my brother Ken's on-farm feed grinding service, started in 1938.

Kerosene Lanterns to Electric Lights

For centuries, night light was limited to a bonfire. My generation grew up coping with dim kerosene lanterns. I remember one day dad came from the field at suppertime and needed to shave off a days whiskers before going to a School Board meeting. A curious kid, I watched as he shaved at the kitchen sink, above which hung a small medicine cabinet and mirror. Using a brush, dad lathered his face generously with hot suds from a shaving mug. The razor was like a straightedge but had a double-edged, changable blade. His weakening eyesight prompted the use of a six-inch, round magnifying mirror. Complaining about the poor light, he told me to hold the kerosene lamp up by his face. The lamp, having to be held carefully, suddenly became unbelievably heavy. I never complained but was approaching agony by the time he said, "That's good enough." No wonder bright electric lights were a sensation! Few inventions made such a sudden, significant difference in farm life.

A brightly shining kerosene lamp and—more so—the white-light Aladdin lamps made home life quite pleasant. However, carrying a dim lantern around the dark barnyard and into coal-black buildings doubled the work of doing chores. Often the hand carrying the lantern was also needed to carry a bushel basket of feed, to pitch hay, or to do numerous other tasks. Of course, in the barn we could hang the lantern on a nail while milking the cows or harnessing horses. We were always mindful that a lantern could cause a fire, reminiscent of Mrs. O' Leary and "the great Chicago fire."

Ironically, all during my youth an electric highline ran by our farm, but we couldn't afford to bring service to the farmstead. The electric companies weren't interested—overlooking a great, untapped farm electricity market. In desperation, my Dad bought a six-volt wind-driven "Wincharger" (wind charger) in 1935. It charged a battery to run the radio and one illuminating lightbulb hung from the kitchen ceiling!

In the latter part of the 1930s, the Roosevelt administration's Rural Electrification Administration (REA) began to rapidly extend electrical lines and provide service to farms all over the U.S. We got electricity in 1940. The demand and market spread rapidly as farmers soon learned the benefit of using electric motors to wash clothes, pump water, and run machines. Electric lines were extended around the farmstead, the bright electric lights making a dramatic difference in the dim farm buildings. Farmers were always thinking up new ways to use this "magical" new power source.

Interestingly, electric power soon translated into other benefits making farm life more enjoyable. Electric motors that pumped water did away with watching over the gasoline engine. A twenty-gallon steel pressure tank equipped with an automatic switch enabled us to pipe a steady flow of water to livestock and of course to the house. An electric water heater in the basement finally gave us instant hot water—a taste of luxury! But farm families were just getting started! Clothes closets were converted into full bathrooms. Water pressure allowed an "indoor" flushing toilet while septic tanks and leach fields solved the sewage disposal problem. We were no longer limited to the Saturday night bath! Farm people had finally "arrived"!

The Great Depression was often referred to as the "dark days." Though many forces helped overcome those dire economic times, nothing helped brighten the outlook and living of farm people more than electricity.

Part
Five

The Aftermath
Heirs of the Great Depression Inherit a War

The Aftermath
Heirs of the Great Depression Inherit a War

The farm family's struggles during the Great Depression didn't end in concert with overcoming that adversity. In fact, we were thrust headlong—without reprieve—into the other major historical event of the twentieth century, WWII. It affected the life of every Great Depression family.

It can be argued that worldwide discontent and suffering during the Great Depression planted seeds that gave rise to well-known tyrant leaders who mesmerized the world, and led inexorably to WWII.

It is appropriate here to tell about the lives, deeds, and experiences of these farm kids as we took part in this historic period.

The stories told here are not necessarily, or are by any means exclusively, my experiences, but were encountered by millions of young, Great Depression-era Americans who responded to the gigantic WWII effort.

CHAPTER 27
WORLD WAR II ENGULFS AMERICA

From Rumblings of War to the Real Thing

By 1939, ominous signs of war were creeping into the lives of families all over the nation. But with the battles in far-off Europe, most Americans were complacent.

Signs of war became more evident from shocking daily news reports—enactments of the military draft and the Japanese attack on Pearl Harbor, December 7, 1941, which led to the declaration of war. The war brought on shortages, rationing, sacrifice, and innovation.

As this drama unfolded, it seemed to be more pervasive to rural farm families. There was no large business or corporate entity insulating the family farm—a home and a business when a key component, a son, was taken away by war.

One Family Takes Measure in a World at War

Ours was a typical, wholesome family gathering in November 1940 for Thanksgiving Day. Aromas from a huge roasting turkey, potatoes, yams, cranberries, fresh pies, and all the other "fixin's" verified Mom's kitchen skills. We were in a festive mood, but there was a cloud of worry over most families, ours included, about the broadening war in Europe.

Dad, being an immigrant from Sweden, was more sensitive to friction and hostility between European nations than were most of our neighbors. Having served the required year of military service in Sweden, he had more awareness. Over dinner, Dad was speculating with my older brothers about their prospects for being drafted into military service. It was a friendly, sociable discussion, but I could tell from Dad's demeanor and the uncommon urgency in his voice that he had foreboding about what lay ahead. My older brothers made comments about what they may have read or heard. But their attitude was cavalier—"What comes, will come." They expressed no qualms about having to go to war. Without explicitly intending to, they summarized the outlook: Nels was thirty-two, married with two daughters—probably would not be drafted; Ken, twenty-six, married and a baby girl—probably not. Howard, twenty-two, single—would most likely have to go; Art, seventeen, would have to go "only if the war dragged on." At fifteen, I strangely felt left out when told—with a knowing chuckle—"not to worry."

The above scene is evidence that we underestimated Hitler's war machine—and later Japan's—while being overly optimistic about American military superiority. Germany's "blitzkrieg" (lightning war) invasion of Poland in September 1939 should have left little doubt about Hitler's threat to world peace.

In the later part of the 1930s, while farm families were still struggling to lift themselves out of the Great Depression, they couldn't help but notice reports of political struggles around the world. My parents followed, both by radio and daily newspaper, the reporting of world news, especially that of Europe. We often discussed it over supper. Frequent reports about military maneuvers and preparations added to

Figure 27.1: War clouds cast a shadow as family gathers on the farm for Thanksgiving Dinner in 1940: (From left to right) Kenneth, Astrid, Mom (Anna), Howard, Dad (Arthur), Dorothy, Lois, Arne (me), Nels, and Art.

the unease. The Great Depression was, in fact, worldwide, causing discontent worldwide with people and nations seeking a better way. When economic failures (depressions) were blamed on the capitalist system, socialism, communism, and fascism gained acceptance. This led to conflict between economic and social groups and gave opportunity for tyrants and dictators to emerge from those power struggles. Prime examples were Adolph Hitler in Germany (an insane genius), Mussolini in Italy (a strutting buffoon), Joseph Stalin in Communist Russia (a ruthless tyrant), Mao and communist cohorts in China (cruel but authentic revolutionaries), and Premier Tojo of Japan (a military expansionist).

Following WWI, Veterans were looked upon with respect. In our community, they were given special recognition on Memorial Day and Fourth of July celebrations. Because most communities lost service men in that war, they were now reluctant to become involved in another war, only twenty years later. Isolationist and "America First" feelings were pervasive.

A Military Draft—Conscription

President Roosevelt had trouble getting war preparation measures through Congress. However, a military conscription (the draft) was started in the fall of 1940. My older brothers along with their counterparts nationwide had to register. Thereafter, upon reaching age twenty, all men had to register. Tellingly, the draft age was later lowered to eighteen.

By late 1940, a scattering of young men were plucked up by military draft notices from every community. Within six months, it was common to see soldiers home on furlough. They were minor celebrities. Anticipating the inevitable draft call, my brother Howard (on whom Dad depended for farm work) enlisted in the Army Air Corps in the fall of 1942. In the process Dad told Art and me we would have to fill the gap in getting the farm work done. We didn't need to be told. A work ethic was a part of family farm life. After a year at Luther College, Decorah, Iowa, on a basketball scholarship, Art stayed home to help on the farm. I was in high school.

Pearl Harbor

There are some events in life we remember down to the exact time, where we were and what we were doing. The Japanese attack on Pearl Harbor was such an event.

On a cloudy Sunday afternoon, December 7, 1941, my brother, Art, and I were out in the farmyard playing catch, honing our baseball skills. My sister, Dorothy, came out of the house excitedly exclaiming, "Japan has bombed Pearl Harbor!" After asking, "Where's Pearl Harbor?" we hurried to the house where Dad and Mom were listening intently to the radio while news commentator H.V. Kaltenborn gave up-to-the-minute reports. Getting out the atlas, we soon located Pearl Harbor in Hawaii. It was the beginning of a long, ongoing education in geography as warfare and military battles engulfed the world. With the surprise of the attack, and difficulty in getting facts, a state of shock—then dread—hung over the country.

We didn't have to be told we had a war on our hands, though President Franklin Roosevelt confirmed it through news releases to radio and newspapers. Following President Roosevelt's nationwide radio broadcast, Congress declared war on Japan on Monday, December 8, 1941.

Our somewhat isolated, peaceful family and farm were immediately thrust into and became part of the major wartime effort. Talk of isolation stopped—Americans were mad! On Monday, men across the nation lined up at army recruitment centers. World War II had suddenly become full-blown, and Americans were determined to do whatever was needed and make any sacrifice to "win!"

Before Pearl Harbor, shortages in supplies began to appear, but after the attack, rationing was accepted, broadened, and fully supported even though most items were dearly needed on the farm. Gasoline, tires, repair parts, new machinery, and food—particularly sugar, coffee, and canned foods—immediately took on a new appreciation. Though ration books and stamps were a nuisance, people abided by the rules.

When all our armed forces were immediately mobilized and rapidly expanded, the people were ready to dig in for a long war.

In retrospect, nothing demonstrates American's resiliency, innovation, and daring more than the bombing raid on Tokyo, Japan. Recalling the devastating U.S. defeat at Pearl Harbor on December 7, 1941, the disbelief and shock hung over America for weeks. It was near miraculous when in just a little over four months, on April 18, 1942, that the U.S. carried out the spectacular bombing raid on Tokyo. No one ever seriously considered launching B-25 "Billy Mitchell" twin-engine, medium bombers off an aircraft carrier. Even with the short training time, Lt. Col. James H.

Doolittle did just that! He led a fleet of sixteen B-25s off the carrier U.S.S. Hornet to strike Tokyo with primarily incendiary (fire) bombs. Though the bombs caused numerous fires in Tokyo, the greatest benefit was the Japanese civilian population learning they were not superior or invincible. I recall the feeling of pride and the "we'll show 'em" presumption greatly bolstered America's confidence in its struggling war effort.

A Wartime Mode Settles In

With the reality of war, the strength and battle successes of our adversaries began to sink in. Our farm community changed. People were grim, even fearful, as numerous sons and hired men who worked on farms enlisted or were drafted into the military. Slogans such as "Food for Peace" and "Feed our Fighting Men" promptly translated into farmers and their families willingly doing their share. Unnecessary use of gasoline was avoided. Tires and inner tubes were patched and re-patched. We drove cars more slowly after a federal directive limited speed to thirty-five miles per hour. Farm supplies were used sparingly. Because of rationing and shortages, food was carefully conserved. Honey replaced sugar; oleo margarine replaced butter. Coffee grounds were stretched to brew more than one pot. Housewives used substitutes to create wartime menus. People "made-do" or went without, but never veered from the effort to produce as much as possible to support the war effort. Large banners and signs were posted in public buildings, admonishing people to "Help our Fighting Men!"

The war expanded as Hitler attacked and occupied neighboring countries, one after another, with his blitzkrieg warfare proving all too effective. Interestingly, Dad's Thanksgiving Day evaluation of our family's involvement was a little optimistic—which I presume held true for many American families. Of five boys, Nels was in the Navy Sea Bees, South Pacific. Ken, because his arm broken from a fall off a pony didn't heal straight, was declared 4-F. Howard served over three years in the Army Air Corps. Art was given a C-2 agriculture deferment to produce "Food for Peace." On November 1, 1943, I went to Omaha and enlisted in the Army Air Corps.

By the summer of 1943, millions of young Americans were in military camps all over the U.S. and in foreign countries. That summer, we went to the movies as much to see the newsreels as the featured show. The news in general—but especially the newsreels—glamorized the war effort. Officials and celebrities were filmed christening victory ships, collecting scrap metal, and displaying rationing cards. The newsreels frequently featured clips of military training activities.

Well-deserved recognition was belatedly given to people on the "homefront," those who stayed home but diligently supported the war effort. My brother, Art, wanted to go into the military but Dad, in his late fifties, needed help to continue farming.

My oldest sister, Astrid, extended her nursing career and came out of retirement to work at a local hospital in Boise City, Oklahoma. There was a shortage of nurses because many joined the army and navy Nursing Corps. Lois, trained and working as an office secretary, kept working after marrying Bill Hubley, a medically discharged

Marine. Dorothy quit her clerical job to work in the New Brighton, Minnesota, munitions plant, making artillery shells.

During the war, extensive paper and scrap-metal drives were organized. Paper was needed for recycling. Iron was needed to build Jeeps, trucks, tanks, and artillery. Nearly every farm had an accumulation of worn-out farm machines, and obsolete horse-drawn plows and cultivators. A few farm families had abandoned small gasoline engines or an old car. These were hauled to collection centers for rail shipment to smelters and processing centers. Farm folks were positioned to get involved and they did with enthusiasm. For the first time since WWI, daylight saving time was adopted to stretch out the workday, for more production of war material.

People living on farms and in small towns, isolated from factories and repair shops, had to be innovators. Because of shortages in labor, supplies, gasoline, and spare machinery parts, we learned to hone our work efforts to save time and to make repairs or changes on short notice. These skills became habitual. We heard time and again during the war how American GIs were innovative; they didn't need orders from above to solve logistic or field problems. This was different from the more regimented German or Japanese chain of command. American boys saw the problem, then took initiative to solve it.

Valuing the inherent freedoms of living in a democracy and steeled by the Great Depression, Americans developed inner strength, responsibility and intuitiveness that prevailed in our war effort and certainly contributed to the ultimate victory.

Figure 28.1: Basic Training at Amarillo, Texas, many GIs had a picture taken to send folks back home: this is mine.

CHAPTER 28
FARM FIELDS TO AIRFIELDS

During my senior year in high school, when it appeared likely I would be caught up in the draft, I became preoccupied with joining the Army Air Corps cadet pilot training program. With the future uncertain, we young men became somewhat cavalier about the present. I became lax with school studies and regretted it years later when in college and in a business career. When I graduated from high school in May 1943, I was raring to enlist in the Air Corps.

Because the county draft board had more than filled its draft quota and because of the serious farm labor shortage, the Chairman of the Board suggested I stay home during the summer and help local farmers produce a crop, "Food for Peace." With some reluctance, I agreed.

Corn harvest was completed the end of October, and on November 1, a friend and I drove to Omaha to enlist. Though anxious about passing all the tests, I was accepted and went home to await my call for active duty, expected in the next few days. As it was a slack time for farm work, time dragged on and I became restless. At Dad's urging, because of the labor shortage, I hired on at the Kingan meat packing plant in Storm Lake. In contrast to the open fields and fresh air on the farm, I hated the stench and work at the plant. As a new and knowingly temporary employee, I got shuffled around daily to the most repugnant jobs. When moved from the hot, kill floor (butchering area) to the freezing hide shed, time was docked while I changed clothes. That made me appreciate the labor union—an empathy I retained the rest of my life. I was happy when my notice to report came in early 1944, and that translated into a positive attitude when entering the army.

Leaving Home, Awkward Goodbyes

The memory of my departure by bus from Storm Lake to Army Camp Dodge in Des Moines, to be sworn in, stands out for an odd reason. While waiting around before departure, I felt a tightness in my chest because of an endearing feeling toward my mother. Because of my stoic and aloof Swedish upbringing, I could not and did not put my arm around her and express that inherent love. That troubled me as I got on the bus and it never vanished from my heart or mind. Of course a quick handshake, the man thing, was ample for Dad. I'm thankful now that even those of us with northern European roots are a little more expressive. I feel good that my grown kids can freely give me an affectionate hug and that I can reciprocate with no embarrassment.

At Camp Dodge, I was given "busy work" for a few days while awaiting shipping orders to the Amarillo, Texas, Army Air Base. At Camp Dodge I had another emotional—though minor—experience. I had occasionally heard of kids getting homesick even while staying overnight with family acquaintances. My brother Art told of Luther College freshmen sobbing in the dorm room. I didn't recognize it immediately, but while assigned to scrub out an empty barracks alone, I had a brief but distressing spell of homesickness—a lump in my throat and a very lonely feeling. Luckily, I soon figured it out, got over it, and laughed about it. That experience benefited me when I was much farther removed from home. I never got homesick again, but I saw a few young soldiers overcome with it.

Go West, Young Man!

The troop train to Amarillo, Texas, for Basic Training was my first train ride. Basic Training toughened us up. The Army taught us discipline and responsibility, and we learned what army "orders" really meant. In six weeks, when Basic Training ended, I was ordered to the Western Flight Training Command at Stockton, California, and rode by troop train through the Rocky Mountains. This farm kid got a stiff neck gawking at the first view of mountains and peering from the train car windows up the 1,000-foot vertical walls of the Royal Gorge in Colorado. The railroad tracks ran beside the narrow Arkansas River as it snaked along, forming the bottom of the Gorge. It was breathtaking and pure adventure!

At Stockton, our cadet flight training was put on hold, because the Army Air Corps had too many pilots. We were given a temporary designation of "on the line trainees" (OLT). I was assigned to the flight line, attending and servicing the training airplanes. Being around engines and machines, like driving farm tractors, was exciting.

Though disappointed that our flight training was on hold, I purposely assessed the situation: I was happy serving my country and was certainly provided the necessities of life, if not any frills. I made good friends, "buddies." The army barracks was a melting pot for young men from different backgrounds, religions, nationalities, and races. During WWII, "Negroes" were segregated. One Chinese bunkmate, Robert Woo, and I became good friends. Woo was a great guy. He had an infectious smile. At about five-feet-five, he was nearly ten inches shorter than I. Sometimes we GIs would engage in some "horse play" to create a little levity in the barracks. Woo and I would square off, ready to duke it out. Then, one of us would give a ludicrous reason to call off the fight. This day-to-day living experience broadened my perspective about people who were different.

When growing up, I hardly ever heard the word "queer" (meaning a homosexual person). The surreptitious nature of the comment implied sex and something bad or despicable. This aroused my curiosity and sent me consulting the dictionary. I learned new words but little else. Of course with exposure to "barracks lawyers" I got, at maximum, a rudimentary education of what "queers" were about. An effeminate male was a sure sign—mimicked by barracks clowns. I accepted that this lifestyle was a choice. None of my reading or inquiry provided a definitive answer as to the cause. Through the USO (social-gathering place for servicemen), a buddy and I became friendly with some girls. Rather strangely a young man seemed to hang out with them. He was a very effeminate male. This observation proved correct when he made a guarded overture to me. I didn't contain my rage and that was over. Some months later, while standing at a USO dance hall urinal, I sensed an unnecessary touching by a man next to me. With obvious displeasure I turned to see a heavy bearded, normally masculine man, who retreated. That blew the effeminate theory. I came to realize that we (society) didn't know much about homosexuality. And that it seemed to be genetic. I questioned the justification for my hatred and decided it should be abated until we learned more about a very complex human behavioral condition. Similarly it seems that American society has been and is, sixty years after my first encounters, still struggling with the ambiguity of sexual identity.

We could now get more frequent passes to get off the Army base, which were rare when in Basic Training. We visited San Francisco and many other interesting sights in central California. Once, four of us cadets volunteered to help load out supplies from an Oakland military depot to Pacific war zones. Railroad cars hauled material a few miles to the ship loading docks. A large Farmall W-9 tractor was used for spotting railroad cars at the loading points. One Sunday, there was no one who knew how to drive it. That was one of the few times when volunteering looked like the right move. I did so immediately and enjoyed driving the tractor around all day while my buddies helped with the stevedore work. Sometimes being a farm kid had its advantages!

Watching History (and Tragedy) Happen

While I was at Stockton, the full weight of the war struck all Americans when on D day, June 6, 1944, Allied troops crossed the English Channel to invade Normandy. A cloud of anxiety fell over the nation and persisted for days, as we anxiously awaited developments of the invasion. Pictures of our boys fighting—and dying—to establish beachheads were grim.

We knew an invasion was coming, but the finality of that colossal event struck all Americans. Even though we had been through the African campaign, defeating German General Rommel (the desert fox), had made landings in Italy, and had started Pacific-island-hopping to drive out the "Japs" (politically correct then!). D day brought war home in a vivid way.

Following D day, I went to the newsroom at base headquarters and read bulletins being posted on a large wall-sized bulletin board. I was startled when the mechanical Teletype machine started cackling like a machine gun. The news bulletins and murmured conversations referred to "rough seas," landing craft stranded on beaches, infantrymen with heavy packs not making it to shore. The ingrained glamour of war began to fade as the casualties, the ugly part of war, began to strike home

The real grimness of war struck me again when a B-24 bomber from an area Army air base came in with an engine fire trailing back to the tail rudder. Apparently, an officer panicked and ordered the crew to bail out at too-low altitude. Two airmen were killed before our eyes, as their parachutes couldn't open. The "unfortunate" of war.

Again the pumped-up glamour of war was subdued with sad, real-life experiences. A young soldier friend in our barracks, having shown no signs of stress, shockingly took his own life by hanging himself in the barracks latrine.

In the fall of 1944, I was transferred to Castle Air Base, Merced, California, for similar flight line duty. Cadets in their final stage of flight training, before graduating

Figure 28.2: Army buddy, Warren Ward, and I stand by an AT-6 Advanced Trainer: Castle Field, Merced, California, 1944.

and getting their wings, were at Castle. We had AT-6 Advanced single-engine Training planes, just one step below the main WWII army fighter planes, P-40s, P-47s, and P-51s. We OLTs, myself included, were envious of the cadets on the verge of accomplishing their goal while we were stuck in a holding pattern.

Castle was a good base and Merced a very nice, hospitable, smaller town. There was a contingent of German prisoners of war quartered in the vicinity. I got to observe and visit with a couple of English-speaking German prisoners. I learned they considered themselves very lucky to be prisoners of the U.S. and were not anxious to go home.

In conjunction with the training of Cadets and working in base operations there was quite a group of permanently assigned officers on the base. In order to qualify for their extra flight pay they had to log four hours of pilot time per month. Coming out to the flight line, where a few of us OLTs were working, they occasionally asked if one of us wanted to ride along. I got to see a birds-eye view of Yosemite National Park and many other western Rocky Mountain sights. One time a Captain Ferguson invited me to ride along, but didn't tell me he had to log some acrobatics time. The scenery was a collage of upside-down and swirling panoramas! The only satisfaction I got out of that flight was from not having to use the upchuck bag or clean up my own vomit (an unwritten rule) in a messed-up cockpit!

While at Castle, I volunteered for temporary assignment to an air base at Portland, Oregon. We were recruited to help move jammed-up Army post office (APO) Christmas mail and parcels going overseas. It was interesting but mundane work. Most exciting were the beautiful sights of the Pacific Northwest: Mt. Shasta, Mt. Hood, Mt. Rainer, tall growth timber, and the Pacific Ocean. It was in sharp contrast to the Midwest and was another rewarding adventure.

At Castle Army Air Base on a usual morning, after the training planes were in the air, I went to the base library to read up on war action around the world. When walking to the library, it struck me as a little unusual when the base loud speaker system came on. An abrupt matter-of-fact voice pronounced: "President Franklin Roosevelt is dead. I repeat: The President died yesterday, on April 12, 1945, in Warm Springs, Georgia." Then silence. I was stunned. My parents, like many Depression farmers practically worshiped President Roosevelt. After being under Roosevelt's leadership for three terms and three months into his fourth term, Americans couldn't comprehend the country without him. People were fearful, agonizing, "What now?" The public was not prepared for a change in leadership. Fortunately, by then the Allies were beginning to win the war with a succession of important victories.

Little known Vice President Harry Truman was sworn in on April 13, 1945. Truman proved to be a very practical, level-headed leader. Truman had to face some very serious world political and diplomatic problems: Soviet Russia's deceitfulness, its tyrannical Premier Joseph Stalin, America's dropping the atomic bomb on Japan, and later during the Korean conflict, removing General Douglas MacArthur from his command position. Truman faced all of these and many other challenges with boldness and credibility.

In April 1945, army buddy George Prescott of Texas and I got passes to go to San Francisco and observe the first international meeting for organizing the United Nations. We were impressed by the formality and gathering of such prestigious leaders. Again, I could feel history in the making.

Moving On

In May 1945, I was transferred from Castle to Luke Field west of Phoenix, Arizona. Luke was a good training base. The sights and terrain of the Sun Valley were in striking contrast to central California. With the Mexican influence in Arizona, the people were different. Because of these contrasts to an Iowa farm, I again learned more about America and its people.

In the meantime, there was some grousing among us cadets about delaying our training while pushing a squadron of Chinese nationals through their Advanced Training. Again the glamour of flying was brought to reality in seeing a Chinese pilot killed when his P-51 crashed while doing a practice landing. Oddly, when ordered to abort his landing, the Chinese student pilot abruptly advanced to full throttle. The powerful torque from the 2,000 horsepower engine flipped the plane over, landing it on the cockpit canopy, and killing the pilot. There was little comfort in knowing that an American farm kid, with experience in revving up the tractor engine, was unlikely to make such an error.

While on the flight line at Luke, I watched the Army's first jet fighter plane, the P-59 by Bell Aircraft, come in for a landing. It had a small jet engine under each wing. It was strange when this quiet jet plane flew over after hearing the roar of airplane propellers and combustion engines day after day. We knew it was something special when the plane was parked at an isolated ramp and immediately cordoned off by military police (MP). Though bursting with curiosity, we couldn't get within 200 feet of the aircraft.

I served at Luke Field until November 1945 when I was shipped to the Sioux Falls, South Dakota, Army Separation Center to be discharged from the Army.

Because of my young age and other factors beyond my control, my war experience wasn't what I had dreamt about—becoming an Army Air Corps pilot. I never had any regrets or complaints, though. Just the opposite, I always felt a patriotic emotion when "Old Glory" was lowered for the evening retreat or other occasions. I learned what a great country this is in terms of resources, geography, and people. And I witnessed how a people under freedom can harness their resources to defeat even the strongest dictatorships and tyrants.

World War II was probably our last "good" war. We have since had an indelible lesson about fighting a war that people "believe in" as contrasted to one they did not—Vietnam.

CHAPTER 29
RETURNING: SOLDIERS TO CIVILIANS

Veterans Use the GI Bill

As a farm kid, I never envied town kids, though they had closer access to the grocery store candy counter, movie theater and playmates. Though I reflected on becoming a farmer, such thinking was on the back burner when I entered the Army Air Corps. Though I remembered the WWI lyrics, "How you gonna keep 'em down on the farm after they've seen Par-*ee*," the possibility of farming still lingered.

One of the most significant pieces of legislation resulting from WWII was the Veterans Readjustment Act of 1944 (the GI Bill). It opened possibilities for higher education that was previously out of reach of the vast majority of returning war Veterans. It was proved, during the decades following the war, that the GI Bill was one of the best investments the government ever made. Best because it greatly improved the capability of over seven million returning WWII service men and women who took advantage of it. That translated rapidly into improving our nation's productivity.

Two unrelated occurrences set me on a path different from farming. In November 1945, while traveling from Luke Army Air Corp base in Arizona to the army separation center in Sioux Falls, South Dakota, I stopped to visit my sister Astrid and her husband Don Carson at Boise City (in the Panhandle of western Oklahoma). Astrid was a registered nurse, a very practical person, with whom I always had a good rapport—although she was fourteen years my senior. Astrid had read about the new GI Bill passed by Congress offering returning GIs financial aid for continuing their education. To most GIs, this meant college studies, although the Bill had other Veteran benefits too.

I had read about the GI Bill, but hadn't zeroed in on how best to use it. Astrid was quite adamant that I go to college. Although I scored comparatively high on the Army Air Corps General Classification Tests, she had more confidence in my academic ability than I did.

The second factor that set me on a path different from farming was my having two older brothers: Art had already staked out a farming career and Howard, arriving home from the service shortly after me, wanted to farm. There wasn't enough available land for me to be involved. There was no room at the Inn! Then I, along with many other returning farm boys, began looking beyond the farm fence line boundaries for our future.

College Bound

Assessing the situation I concluded that college was my best option and, in January 1946, enrolled at Buena Vista College in Storm Lake, Iowa—along with about 130 other returning GIs. The older and mature Veterans made up about a third of the college enrollment. These mostly men and a few women, with extensive travel and experience, had no time for freshmen antics. They changed the nature and environment of college campuses for years to come.

Figure 29.1: A proud Dad with his five grown sons. Three recently discharged from WWII military service. (1946)

There are incidental episodes in our lives that—in hindsight—were quite insightful and have, in fact, significantly changed our lives. When entering Buena Vista College in January 1946 I had some foreboding about college-level studies, but privately pledged that I would give it my best shot—I would study. I was one of forty-five students taking American Government under Dr. George Reynolds. About twenty of us were newly discharged military Veterans.

There were dire, I'm sure exaggerated, comments about Dr. Reynolds' tough mid-semester exams. Reynolds distributed foreboding "blue books" and listed six essay questions on the blackboard. Each student was to answer five. I wrote for the allowed fifty minutes. The following week Dr. Reynolds handed back our blue books and started writing numbers on the blackboard: 1 (student) 98 (grade); 2, 96; 4, 93; and so on until two students with a grade of under 75 failed. I cautiously opened my blue book and saw the number 98! Oddly, feeling somehow awkward, I closed my book. However students furtively compared grades, but didn't hide their curiosity over who got the 98.

Sitting beside me, friend and classmate, Marvin Quinlan, foresaw my quandary and laughingly reported, "Here is number one!" I wasn't prepared for the immediate designation of "brain." Though I tried to respond with an "aw shucks" demeanor, inside I was elated. Thereafter, feeling the urge to live up to my new status, I have wondered how that one event gave direction and momentum to my college career. I shouldn't imply that I was a perpetual honor student—I wasn't. However, my grades were entirely satisfactory.

When Veterans returned home from the war, no cars were available. Most of us were desperate to get some wheels! My search led to a 1929 Chevy, abandoned in a nearby farmer's grove. Though it wouldn't run, it looked salvageable. We towed it

Figure 29.2: My 1929 Chevrolet sedan.

home and with the help of my brother Howard (a veteran Army motor pool mechanic) got it running quite well. With some body patchwork, a paint job, and scrounged used tires, I drove it until out of college. In a take-off from status cars (limousines) my two nieces jokingly dubbed it the "lemon-zeen."

A casual event while at Buena Vista made me more aware of my roots. I became friends with a young woman, Lee, who had been in the Navy WAVES (Woman Accepted for Volunteer Emergency Service) during the war. I asked her to accompany me on a Sunday afternoon visit to the farm. We had a good time visiting, and my Mom served a light snack. While driving back to Storm Lake, I was quite surprised when Lee said, "I hope I didn't embarrass you." I responded "Of course not, why?" She said she had difficulty understanding everything my folks said! It was only then, at twenty-two years of age, that I fully realized what a distinct Swedish accent my folks had!

In the fall of 1947, with farm roots still intact, I transferred to Iowa State College at Ames, enrolling in Farm Operations with major studies in Agronomy and Economics. The Iowa State campus was populated with several hundred Veterans. A great many who couldn't be kept "down on the farm," opted for off-farm careers.

One time when home visiting my folks on the farm, I confronted a lingering point of view held by a few country people. While working in the field, I met a neighboring farmer in one of those familiar "friendly fence line encounters." I hadn't seen Soren for sometime and when he inquired, I explained that I would soon be graduating from Iowa State. Soren, by no means a progressive farmer and with little education, promptly informed me, "You can't learn to farm from a book!"

Figure 29.3: Uncle Charlie gave me an enjoyable tour of Rio Grande, New Jersey, in his Ford Model T delivery truck. It ran like a top! (1946)

While visiting home on Memorial Day 1948, I was up early and shocked to see contrasting green rows of four-inch high corn showing up distinctly above an inch of newly-fallen white snow! Never having seen this before, we feared it would damage or destroy the young plants. With a bright sun, the snow melted rapidly, causing no serious damage.

In 1949, we were reminded that farming always had new challenges and risks begging for solutions. That summer European corn borers, that had escaped detection in imported broomcorn, hit Corn Belt cornfields like a plague. That fall farmers were dismayed to discover ten to fifteen bushels of corn on the ground lost from ear droppage when corn borers riddled corn stalks and ear shanks. Though only a half generation away from handpicking the entire crop of standing corn, no one now had an appetite for picking a small part of the crop from off the ground. Grabbing for the most available "cure," the infamous (as proven later) insecticide DDT was sprayed on cornfields for the next few years with abandon. Its use was stopped after the insecticide was found to be devastating to native birds, including the beloved American eagle population in North America.

Summer Jobs

With no regular classes during the summer months, a part of the college life was finding summer employment—any means to earn some money. Still wanting some adventure and with a little wanderlust in my veins, I chose jobs accordingly. In 1946, I worked for a railroad construction gang in Pennsylvania and New York state. I saw some new country and learned something about railroading. As a bonus, upon quitting in late August to return to college, I saw the sights of New York City and then visited my mother's brother, Uncle Charlie, whom I'd never met, in Rio Grande, New Jersey. I spent three days with Uncle Charlie before returning home. His years spent as a merchant seaman were evidenced in a green privet hedge around his house that was

Figure 29.4: I was pleased when Lois and husband Bill (Fairmont, Minnesota) picked up Dad at Sioux Rapids, Iowa, and came down to Iowa State College (Ames) for my graduation in December 1949.

neatly trimmed in the shape of ships. Our visit was an enjoyable and rewarding time for both of us.

In 1947, I worked for farmers Fran & Mary Morgan near Storm Lake. I had two entirely different motives for wanting to work there: one, to get farm experience and two, to be nearer a nice girlfriend living in Storm Lake. In 1948, I went out west to harvest wheat. Starting at Boise City, in western Oklahoma, where my sister Astrid and husband Don Carson lived. I worked some in southwest Kansas but then returned to Boise City to work for Millard Fowler, a large wheat farmer, until college started again in September.

In 1949, while Dad took a two-month trip to Sweden, I stayed home with Mom and helped on the farm. I enjoyed the opportunity to spend time with my mother after living away from home for seven years. Regrettably, I never asked her more about her youth and life in Sweden. When young we have a carefree perspective of life—thinking it will go on and on. My mother's death, less than a year later in March 1950, taught me a poignant lesson: you can't ask your parents about anything after they're gone. And my Dad's death one year later compounded my miscalculation. Both my parents are buried at the Little Sioux Valley Lutheran cemetery, next to the church site, where as a youth, I pondered these eventualities.

Although I never had to struggle academically at Iowa State, I studied diligently and developed an enthusiasm for learning when outstanding professors taught subjects of curiosity and interest. In December 1949, I graduated with a B.S. degree that helped prepare me for a career in agribusiness.

In my job-seeking effort I learned another lesson. That first job isn't, after all, a life or death decision. It does provide a place and time to find out what you really want to do. A majority of college graduates change jobs within the first five years after graduation.

The March of Time

In a sense we have come full circle. Starting as a farm boy around 1930, secured by the strength of a farm family and assuming work responsibility, we as all farmers at that time—indeed as all Americans—had no inkling of the financial impoverishment that lay just ahead in the Great Depression. Nor were we able to foresee the coming of World War II and the trauma it dealt our nation. It was a trauma felt by every American family. It affected every farm family, down to farm kids such as myself, whose remote rural security was forever changed by the climactic chain of events.

After soldiering in that war, I came back to where my memories began. Experience and education helped prepare me for my niche in getting on with this nation's work. At the conclusion of the Depression, the war, and the inevitable post-war transformation: life didn't stop.

Being the youngest of five boys, I wasn't brought into family discussions very much. After getting my college degree I found it interesting when, in a roundabout way, one or the other brother would ask for my opinion. I was pleased, but after a few years adopted a credo: "Be cautious in giving family members advice; if it turns out right they will never remember: if it turns our wrong they will never forget."

The following epilogue brings closure to another period by telling how our lives fared during the last half of the twentieth century.

Part 6
Epilogue

Figure 30.1: Fiancée, Marianne Aust. (1951)

CHAPTER 30
TIME OF TRANSFORMATION

In spite of the saying. "You can't go home again," the majority of WWII servicemen—having lost two to four years out of their private lives—were anxious to get home, to get on with their civilian lives and careers. Most assumed marriage was a part of their future; raising a family was ingrained in their upbringing.

For many returning servicemen, fond memories and nostalgic longings for home were destined to be a letdown. Being away, making new friends, and having other encounters, most high school sweetheart flames had waned. Veterans, farm boys, were exposed to thinking outside "the box," different from their counterparts who never left the farm.

Marriage

A year out of college and with job responsibilities, I was charting my life ahead. This paralleled my meeting a lively young schoolteacher, Marianne Aust, who was to become my wife. Like me, she was a first-generation American. Her parents immigrated to the U.S. from Germany following WWI. Otto Aust had served in the German army for five years during WWI, was wounded, and taken prisoner. His wife, Marie, epitomized family support and loyalty. They adopted their new country enthusiastically, and became citizens and spirited patriots of the United States. They became farmers. The Aust family arrived in America a dozen years later than my parents, but in many ways, their lives were parallel to one another's.

Marianne has proved to be a great helpmate and partner in our marriage and careers. Her ambition has been demonstrated by pursuing her own education and teaching career. Marianne never lacked for a sense of humor and easy laughter. Interesting how this can make the journey through married life a lot smoother.

Family

We were married in June 1951, before birth control pills simplified family planning! We had son, Fredric, in July 1952, Arne Paul in August 1953, Elizabeth in December 1954, and Mark in June 1957. I received friendly kidding by our company's office staff about such a rapidly growing family. Hazel Carey, a secretary, chided me about birth control. She was a devout Catholic and advocate of the rhythm method. I got one-up on Hazel and some hearty laughter when I told her the trouble with the rhythm method was that "You had a house full of kids before you learned the tune"!

Our thriving, happy family seemed normal. Like many young families we were preoccupied with meeting our needs, leaving no money for "wants" or luxuries. We didn't mind. Our kids did the normal and expected: Sunday school, public school, homework, Little League ball, and other sports and community activities. Hand-me-down family clothes were a way of life. A wholesome diet, Merthiolate for scratches, Vick's Vapo-Rub at the first sign of sniffles, and regular reading of favorite stories kept us pretty healthy. Dr. Spock's book was our child-nurturing bible. I presume we were a typical rural American family.

Figure 30.2: A growing family is happy in anticipation of Christmas (1961). Children, clockwise and by age: Fred, Arne Paul, Elizabeth, and Mark.

Parents with young children in the first half of the 1950s lived under the dread of their child getting polio (poliomyelitis). From 50 to 75 percent of victims coming down with the virus suffered permanent paralyses. Though polio had persisted around the world for centuries, it wasn't until the early 1950s that it approached epidemic proportions in the U.S. Hearing daily reports of new cases during the warmer months was frightening. In 1949, scientists at Harvard isolated the poliovirus. In 1954, Dr. Jonas E. Salk developed a successful vaccine. It was soon approved and we—along with millions of other young parents—rushed to get our kids vaccinated against the disease. Within a couple of years, a vaccine pill became available. With vaccines, the affliction was pretty well eradicated. It was a great medical success story and we were most thankful.

It is interesting how humor, especially the homespun variety, can not only defuse a family quandary, but can also result in hearty laughter at family gatherings years later. When our kids were half grown, Sunday breakfast gave us a chance to slow the pace, expand the menu beyond cereal, and enjoy some family conversation. For one such Sunday, our main course was to be eggs, bacon, and waffles. But a minor crises arose when Mom discovered there were only five eggs—for six of us! For some reason, I was inspired to seize the moment and stated that I would solve the egg problem. Despite some unspoken curiosity I diverted their concern by being inordinately upbeat. As soon as the bacon was done I quickly broke the five eggs in the skillet, stirred them all together with the spatula and divided them into six "eggs." Then I ceremoniously served each one an "egg." Finally, one of the kids offered that these eggs were "kind of flat." Another chimed in, these were "Dad's flats." I quickly acknowledged the new recipe. Everyone joined in, taking the ploy in good humor. To this day, some thirty-five years later, the mention "Dad's flats" brings some knowing, hearty laughter.

The benefits of the GI Bill surfaced again when we built a house in Storm Lake in 1958. GI loan guarantee provisions provided for a low down payment and a low interest rate (4.5 percent). This made it possible for hundreds of thousands of Veterans to buy their own homes, build equity, and have a stake in their community. Thankfully, that is the way it worked for us.

Community Service

I'm not sure how our attitude toward community involvement developed. It may have been a combination of factors. My dad served as president of the Highview Consolidated School board in the mid-1930s, was a loyal Roosevelt Democrat, and served as a township committeeman under the AAA farm program. My father-in-law, Otto Aust, was actively involved in a farm organization and CROP (a refugee food assistance program). He was an adamant Republican. I concluded that community service was one way to pay back for the benefits of living in a progressive community in a free society. The term "participatory democracy" is relevant in terms of maintaining an effective representative government. Participating in your community is "grass roots" government at work.

I served in civic, church, and political activities. After observing that a few acquaintances became "over-volunteered," I learned to limit voluntary activities at any one time. During this time my wife, Marianne, kept active in family and community affairs while continuing her education, earning a bachelors degree in 1968—twenty years after getting her two year teaching certificate. Her teaching career was interrupted when our small children needed her care. As she truly loved teaching, especially seeing first and second graders achieve reading skills, she reentered her teaching career when our children became older.

Racial Prejudice Persists At Home

How, in my early teens, I developed empathy for African Americans and other minorities is obscure. It extends beyond early school studies and discussions about slavery and other hardships but that surely aroused my compassion. My early reading of *Uncle Tom's Cabin* and later *An American Dilemma* by Gunnar Myrdal and *Black Like Me* by John Griffin, in addition to learning about the Civil War and President Lincoln's compelling statements had a lasting effect on me. When our church sponsored the "Friendly Town" program, Marianne and I decided it would be a good experience for our kids. In this program, minority and poor kids from the inner city stay a week with farm and small-town families. Chuck Conner, a cheerful nine-year-old African American kid from Des Moines, stayed with us. The first day, none of our kids' usual playmates came over. We heard through the grapevine that parents didn't want their kids to play with "a Black." The second day, two neighbor kids came over. The next day, three or four more. After that, when neighbor kids learned Chuck could talk, joke, laugh, or be sad just like them, it didn't seem to bother them that he looked different from them.

Rewards

These experiences remind me how fortunate and lucky a person is to be an American. It means being able to contribute to the process of building and sustaining world leadership. It is only in America where a farm kid, who struggled through the Great Depression and served in WWII, could move on to benefit from so many opportunities and share in the good life.

CHAPTER 31
CAREERS

A Full Life Will Embody a Rewarding Career

Now, at the turn of the twentieth (and twenty-first) centuries, we can see in hindsight what great strides this nation made during the last half of the century (1950–2000). This was in part a result of deferred goals, pent up ambition, and the character of WWII Veterans. The crucible, in which this character was molded, goes back to the Great Depression, which steeled tenacity and a never-give-up attitude. Then we believed—on faith alone—that better times lay ahead.

To this same crucible, having no time to cool down, was added the cauldron of WWII: a surge of patriotism, personal sacrifice and a broader view of our nation cast in the roll of world leadership.

During my entire working career I saw Veterans rise to the challenge time and again: in community leadership, business ventures, politics, and in steadfastness of purpose.

That First Job

In January 1950, following graduation from Iowa State College, I lived and worked in Fort Dodge, Iowa. Joining a Toast Masters Club, each week I stood in front of twenty or more convivial members and gave a speech, varying from two to five minutes in length. In listening to these men, nearly all Veterans, I observed how much their military experiences had become a part of them. They didn't dwell on war experiences but reflected a confidence, and they had well-defined goals. The willingness of Veterans to speak out contradicted Mark Twain's satirical advice: "It is better to keep your mouth shut and appear stupid than to open it and remove all doubt." Recalling an 'old saw' recited by an astute college professor, "If you don't keep learning after graduation in five years you'll be ignorant." I took this dictum to heart and made continuing education and self-improvement a continuing process.

Changing Jobs

I enjoyed the challenge of evaluating farms for loan security while with the Equitable of Iowa Insurance Company's Farm loan department. However wanting to become more involved in production agriculture, after a year and a half (in 1951) I joined the new Albany, Georgia, office of Opekasit Farm Management Inc., of Lebanon, Ohio. Of course, being newly married added to the joy and adventure for both Marianne and me.

Most of my Opekasit associates were WWII Veterans. An example of steadfast determination was an associate who—through field promotions—rose to the rank of colonel while serving in Europe under General George Patton. At Opekasit Farm Management Inc., we were at the cutting edge of change in southern agriculture: from sharecroppers (usually "Negroes") to commercial farms; from mules to tractors. I relived the transition that had overtaken Midwest farming fifteen years earlier.

Figure 31.1: Georgia peanut farmers.

Without realizing it, while in Georgia I witnessed the beginning of the end of Southern racial segregation. Raised in rural Iowa, where there were no Blacks, I was discomforted by the deep-seated prejudice against "Negroes." I observed that middle- and upper-class whites did not treat "Negroes" as harshly as the poorer Whites, and I concluded that prejudice was driven—in no small part—by economic (job) competition as much as by color. Some days when my Farm Management work took me as far as Selma, Alabama (235 miles away) Marianne worried about my safety. "What if you had car trouble and some Negroes came along?" I told her "Not to worry if it was Negroes, but I might be concerned if it was likkered up, White, red-necks.

While working in Georgia I came to realize how innocent and naive we upper Midwesterners were about the deep-seated prejudice and hatred in the segregated South. Through a Dr. Peterson who had Iowa State conections, I was invited to Tuskegee Institute, a Negro college, to speak to his class about what I, a northerner, foresaw in southern agriculture. Though I never pushed it as a "cause", I did want to help Negroes better realize their potential. At Tuskegee I spoke before an assembly of over 40 black male college students. Having tried to avoid holding racial prejudice, I hoped to establish a rapport with the class. They listened curiously when I suggested opportunities in farming lay ahead. Suddenly I felt unnerved – there was no real communication. They didn't believe me! From their sullen stare I saw prejudice cutting both ways. Yes, I was naive. Centuries of legal slavery and then second class citizens had left deep scars. Dr. Peterson assured me that my message was encouraging. He was being kind.

Pursuing an objective to be an owner-businessman, in 1954 I joined H.E. "Buck" Stalcup, Storm Lake (northwest Iowa) in the Farm Management and Land Appraisal business. Stalcup was widely recognized as a leader in developing rural appraisal techniques as well as being an accomplished teacher of the subject. My farmer roots still intact, an agreeable condition in our arrangement was for me to operate a quarter section farm—160 acres—until business growth developed for me to be needed full-time.

Figure 31.2: This peanut combine is evidence of the surge of mechanization in the 1950s and after.

Operating the farm fulfilled a longtime dream, and it was indeed a helpful experience to walk in the farmer's shoes.

In 1957, I quit the farm operation to go full-time with Stalcup Agricultural Service (incorporated in 1969) and worked there for forty-five years. To me, it was the best of both worlds: having ample opportunity to apply my education in technical agriculture almost daily, and using decision making skills while working with the land and with farmers.

While serving as President of Stalcup Agricultural Service Inc., I learned the importance of harnessing employees' strengths to the best advantage of the business and certainly to the greatest benefit and satisfaction for the individual employee.

During my working career, an axiom proved true time and again: "Working smart is more important than working hard." This became apparent in observing different farmers carrying out their farming operations. Planning work—hours or days ahead—and then working at a steady pace gets results. However, racing to the field at full throttle and with little planning does not.

Though I was Stalcup's first associate in 1954, when I retired on June 30, 1999, we had seven associate partners.

In Good Soil Roots Grow Deep

A common thread clings to farm kids. Particularly those whose careers keep them close to farming. That weave of thread more than nurtures a desire to own some farmland: to walk on your own "dirt," smelling the aroma of freshly worked soil. Some of that desire was inherited from our parents who struggled during the Great Depression—who wanted the security of owning their own farm; but that was often out of reach.

So it was with my business associate, Dwight Young, and myself when an opportunity arose for us to buy a half section (320 acres) farm in the fall of 1969. For two or three years our Saturday recreation was spent working on our farm. For us, it wasn't work, but fun—recapturing the nostalgia of our youth. We took out unneeded fence, repaired buildings, and planned multiple land improvement and conservation projects. This included two center-pivot irrigation systems—the first of only a handful in northwest Iowa. Fortunately, over time we were able to add to that acreage, which has proven to be a sound—but just as important to us—a much-enjoyed investment.

Becoming Professional

In the early part of the twentieth century, farmers were sometimes referred to as "rubes" by city folks and were the butt of "country hick" jokes. This changed during WWII, when the self-reliant farm boys stood out both in training and under battle conditions. I saw business leaders hire young men with a farm background because their strong work ethic was widely recognized.

In 1951, I joined the 1200-member American Society of Farm Managers and Rural Appraisers (ASFMRA) and its counterpart, the Iowa Society. Because of these organizations, I was able to attend seminars and associate with men of similar interests and expertise. Later, in Farm Management schools, I taught young professional managers how to hone their skills. It was challenging work. In the meantime, the ASFMRA grew to over 3500 members and I made lifelong friends from around the U.S.

While teaching management schools, I observed that it was difficult to teach a student how to be a manager. It became apparent that successful managers inherently had these skills. At best, we could help teach them stratagems and devices to use to become better managers. In the process, while I couldn't find a clear definition of management, I created one that the students seemed to grasp quickly.

Management in the most succinct terms is: "Using resources to the best long term economic advantage." This is applicable to any enterprise whether producing a crop, manufacturing goods, or providing a service. The concept is the keystone of capitalism and the free market system. In these organizations I was continually rubbing shoulders with men raised on farms during the Great Depression, who served in WWII, got an education through the GI Bill, and went on to professional careers in agriculture. They were part of the workforce that helped accelerate the application of technology that drove the great advancements in modern, scientific farming; that happened during the last half of the nineteenth century.

Working in Turkey

Adventurism certainly prompted me when, once again, I found myself back on a stage set in large part by WWII. We can't seem to get away from the influences of that historic event. An ironic outgrowth occurred when the U.S. (being the winners of that war) did an historically uncharacteristic thing by providing aid and assistance to the losers! This not only included many nations directly devastated by the war but also the economically and socially downtrodden of the world. The U.S. Marshall Plan for Europe, implemented in 1948, was the most striking example of U.S. programs for war recovery. Our assistance and recovery programs in the defeated and occupied Japan started an economic boom in their economy, which lasted for decades. The United States Agency for International Development (USAID) spawned food and technology

Figure 31.3: Topraksu in Turkey is equivalent to the U.S. Soil Conservation Service. The farmer on the left and the three technical engineers showed me this structure to control runoff and conserve water from an irrigation project. (1974)

programs around the world to assist the downtrodden.

In 1974, the USAID circulated a request for an agricultural consultant to serve in Turkey. Intrigued, I immediately applied and was hired. Starting in late May, I traveled to Turkey and got my first of several "culture shocks" when de-planing in Istanbul. Twenty military guards had cordoned off the walkway to the customs area, with sub-machine guns held at ready.

After centuries of Ottoman rule, the Republic of Turkey was set up in 1923 and Kemal Ataturk was elected Premier; he served until 1938. Ataturk ousted inflexible Moslem cleric domination and turned Turkey "to the West"—adopting European civil, social, and business practices. While traveling through the country, we occasionally saw an old man—while in the field or herding livestock—kneel down facing Mecca and offer required Moslem prayers. When I indicated curiosity my Turkish traveling companions shrugged their shoulders—"That's for old men."

At Ankara I met with my USAID supervisor and was briefed on the assignment. I was provided with an interpreter and guide named Saher, a driver and car (a Chevrolet Suburban), and usually one or two agricultural "engineers." Saher and other advisers had all attended college in the U.S., most at Utah State. We spent six weeks traveling throughout Turkey. I insisted on getting off the beaten path, out into the farming country. Folks in one remote village said I was the first American they had met.

My job was to bring new production technology to Turkish farmers. I took the work seriously and insisted we get out on the farms and talk to "real farmers." I had this intent even before hearing complaints that previous "armchair consultants" had spent their time with government bureaucrats.

After traveling for a couple of weeks and thirsting for a good cool glass of fresh milk, I was delighted when an old, gnarled-handed farmer had his daughter serve a glass to me while we sat in a small farm shed. In anticipation I took a generous swallow and came very close to choking when it turned out to be a very sour yogurt. Of course, having no refrigeration, that's what they could serve!

I soon concluded that bringing new technology was not as important as getting known technology off the bureaucratic shelves and into the hands of farmers! Turkish farmers were poor. Centuries of farming had depleted their soils and they were not using fertilizer effectively. In many ways American and Turkish farmers think alike: how to produce a good crop and how best to handle and market it profitably.

In remote eastern Turkey I got an introduction to "Third World" toilet facilities; a square, flat piece of concrete or stone raised about three inches above the floor with footprints showing you where to squat over a five-inch, round hole in the center. There was no toilet paper or flushing mechanism. Instead, there was a pail of water and small skillet-like pan for you to use for your sanitary needs!

Though by no means wealthy, the typical Turk was fairly well-dressed and had meaningful work and plenty of food. From time to time I did experience culture shock. When entering the town of Kars in extreme eastern Turkey we were caught in a traffic jam as herdsmen (mostly women, children, and a few old men) brought the one hundred or so co-mingled cows in from the open range to the individual owner's pen. Each family milked and took care of their one to three cows. I noticed a plainly dressed woman, following the herd and carrying a pail, hurry over to where an animal defecated. She picked up the runny manure with her bare hands and placed it in the pail. My Turkish companions, uncomfortable at the display of such stark poverty, said she would dry the manure for burning fuel. There were few trees to provide firewood in the open grasslands of eastern Turkey. Consequently, nearly every sheep paddock had a slat panel fence for drying manure, for fuel.

While traveling, my Turkish companions and I became well acquainted and our conversations ranged freely. The pending impeachment trial of President Nixon and his eventual resignation baffled them. I never figured out their undercurrent of chauvinist-sexist comments and attitudes. A clue to a different mindset was their reluctance to geld horses as is customary in western countries.

Food was fresh, wholesome, and well-prepared. I soon accepted the Turkish custom of inviting foreign customers to walk through the restaurant kitchen to see the different hot dishes cooking on large cast-iron stoves. I relished breakfast: a loaf of fresh baked, course-textured, golden brown bread, fresh honey, white cheese, and fruit juice.

My Turkish traveling hosts were considerate in stopping at many historical landmarks. At Ephesus in western Turkey, we visited the (supposedly) last home and burial place of Mary, mother of Jesus. North of Izmir at Bergama I found the ancient ruins and stone amphitheater intriguing. In the extreme east, snow-capped Mt.

Ararat, supposedly conceals clues of Noah's ark. In southeastern Turkey a large earthen dam and hydroelectric generators, similar to those on the Missouri River, were being built on the Euphrates River.

While at the southeastern Turkish border, my colleagues suggested we make an excursion into bordering Iran. I was delighted, although somewhat apprehensive, about not having a passport visa to enter Iran. I placed my destiny in the hands of my companions! Entering near the town of Khovy, we spent about three hours driving through the countryside and another village. At that time, the Shah of Iran was a close ally—some would say puppet—of the United States. Plain statues of the Shah stood in the town square.

I was stunned at the starkness pervading the villages—raggedly dressed people were very subdued as they moved about: most were walking, a few were riding donkeys or occasionally a small horse-drawn wagon. Although it was very interesting, I was relieved when Iranian border guards—recognizing my Turkish companions— waved us through to Turkey where I had the necessary legal documents to travel.

The Turkish people were hospitable and appreciative of U.S. efforts to help them. I often wondered how one piece of succinct advice in my report was taken: "Close the coffee houses during the day. Make the men go to the fields and help the women"— who with hand tools were doing all the fieldwork! Most farm families lived in small, scattered villages. They had a few, co-operatively owned, small, modern tractors. But they were used most often as "taxis" to haul women to the fields on flat racks! Though Turkey has made tremendous advances, the old Muslim cultures in neighboring Arab countries treat women as chattel property. It presents a roadblock to Western thought, to applying current economics (using resources most effectively), and to societal efforts for improving their standard of living.

Working in an entirely different environment, coping with language barriers, and adjusting to native customs was challenging. But it certainly gave me a new appreciation and understanding of the developing nations' struggles to harness new technology.

Extending Public Service

Self-employment can allow for more flexibility to get involved in community service, such as politics. I got more involved than anticipated after serving on several boards and committees, including serving as Chairman of the County Republican Central Committee. Meantime, Governor Bob Ray (a political friend, whom I admired) appointed me to the Iowa Agriculture Promotion Board. Governor Ray's encouragement was instrumental in my deciding to run for the Iowa Senate in 1978.

While individual politicians—and therefore politics—are ridiculed, we must understand that only through personal involvement will democracy work. Politics in its best form is free discussion and persuading others of particular ideas. Getting involved means politics, and politics is the lifeblood of representative government.

After formally announcing my candidacy, I learned some stark things about human nature. When I made the announcement ("declared"), a few people started looking at me a little askance—even some long time acquaintances! An example was

Figure 31.4: Serving in the Iowa Senate. (1979–1986)

overhearing an off-hand and ill-informed comment: "He may not be rich now, but he'll have plenty when he's through." In truth, I sacrificed income every year I served!

Following a hard campaign, I won a seat in the Iowa Senate in 1978 and was re-elected in 1982 for a second term. One reward of serving is meeting many good people—good citizens—often knowledgeable on issues. A candidate struggling to get elected is indebted to people who offer their support. Any public office holder should benefit from dialogue with the public.

Though I never considered myself a politician, nor did I enjoy the "politics" of it—excessive blather and posturing over irrelevant matters—I got satisfaction from crafting the best legislation possible to resolve a problem or solve a public issue.

The political arena vividly reflects a wide spectrum of human character. Sometimes the best and occasionally the worst. It takes a fairly strong ego to run for election. But an ego can get out of hand—such as politicians starting to believe their own press releases! At the other end of the spectrum are many smart, hard-working and civic-minded politicians who daily contribute to the political process and help author reasonable legislation.

Serving in the state Senate confirmed my belief that political labels are very misleading. Believing that politicians and government have an insatiable appetite for

Figure 31.5: Our consultation work was conducted primarily out on the farms where we could see and solve problems first-hand.

spending, I was a fiscal conservative. And believing you really can't legislate morals, I took the moderate view that government should generally keep its nose out of peoples' private lives. No body of politicians has demonstrated the character—nor has any group of bureaucrats demonstrated the judgement—to qualify as our moral guardians! In the final analysis, democracy has to rely on the common sense of a reasonable, educated, and moral public.

While chairing the Senate side of the Budget Appropriations subcommittee, I learned some peculiarities about the bureaucratic mindset. After doing a survey of eighteen county directors to learn about the real problems they faced out in the counties, I concluded that most social service employees in the state office did not understand the needs or know the solutions to problems at the local level. This condition is endemic to "big government." Another example of this peculiar mindset: In the 1930s and before, we had County Poor Farms, where poor and needy people could find food and shelter. It was understood that, if able, they would share in farm and garden work. Milking the cows or hoeing weeds in the fields and working daily in a large vegetable garden was great therapy for them and helped sustain the County Home. This same scenario applies to state prison farms from which social engineers insisted on selling the dairy herds and farming operations to be replaced by motel-like quarters equipped with televisions, and billiard and weight-lifting rooms. Of course any productive work (therapy) was out of the question. Before this, it was decided that "Poor Farm" had a bad connotation. The name was changed to "County Home" until that too had a bad connotation; then, the term "Welfare" came into vogue. The cycle continued as we changed the name to "Social Services" and in 1982 we changed to a less demeaning name: "Human Services." We spent $100,000 to change letterheads!

31.6: Here, Iowa State University and private Iowa farm management teams work to identify and solve problems in Slovakia. (Circa 1993)

Not much else changed.

At the end of my second term in 1986, I chose not to run again. Demands of business and family deserved more of my time. I consider my time serving in the Senate to have been a very worthwhile experience. That kind of experience can be gained only by doing it.

Helping Czechoslovakia Recover

Again in 1990 we had to deal with the remnants and fallout of WWII.

Tearing down the Berlin wall was quickened in November 1989 when Eastern Europe satellite countries were rapidly breaking away from Soviet control. The Soviet Union—communist Russia's empire—was collapsing, imploding from within. The seventy-four-year experiment in communism, started in November 1917, ended in August 1991 as a failure.

In January 1990, I joined a delegation of agriculturists appointed by Iowa Governor Terry Branstad to visit the Soviet satellite countries to see what assistance Iowa might offer to aid in their transition from communism back to a free market economy. We visited Hungary, Czechoslovakia, Poland, and East Germany. One of my conditions in joining the delegation was that it not be a "chamber of commerce" tour, but that we get out on the farms—mostly collectives—and talk to the people in the forefront of the change. I had fears of being escorted from one communist bureaucrat to another, having to listen to the now defunct party line. Fortunately, that was pretty much avoided.

We looked and listened. I pondered. They had rich soil, an adequate growing season, surplus machinery, surplus labor, and ample technology. Technology? The Russians had ready access to our latest agricultural technology! We gave it to them.

Figure 31.7: Nov. 12, 1994: Receiving D. Howard Doane Award. Joe Durant,
Chairman of the National Awards Committee presents the highest award offered by the ASFMRA.
Award is for: "Outstanding Contributions in the Field of Agriculture."

Then what was the problem? An obvious one was that the system didn't reward individual initiative or efficiency. While flying back across the Atlantic, I kept thinking about it—trying to bring the problem into focus. Finally it struck me: they lacked management (in its simplest meaning): "using available resources to the best economic advantage." They weren't even close.

After returning home, I talked to Dave Topel, Dean of the College of Agriculture, Iowa State. When Dave said they were looking into assistance programs for Eastern European countries, I emphasized that those countries lacked good farm management skills. Iowa State's faculty and Iowa's group of working Professional Farm Managers had what the Eastern European countries needed most—good farm management skills: identifying priorities, setting goals, and decision-making. Though Iowa State had been talking to USAID about providing assistance programs, they had not designed one.

In July 1992, I was teamed with five Midwest agricultural specialists to visit Czechoslovakia. Bob Jolly, a very able economist from Iowa State University (ISU), headed the delegation. Michael Duffy, ISU economist, assisted. Our job was to do a "needs assessment" and then design a program to fulfill those needs. When hearing our design was hands-on, basic farm management, Jolly asked, "What vehicle will deliver it?" He facetiously exhorted us to "Design the truck!" Our vehicle was comprised of teams of consultants, drawn from working private farm managers and university agriculture experts. It was fine-tuned, fired up, and it worked. The Czechs and Slovaks were good students, and our consulting teams were practical teachers.

Paralleling the Farm Management program, ISU conducted several agricultural-related programs. The Farm Management program included research and consultancies in Czechoslovakia from 1992 through 1994. It was staffed co-operatively by ISU specialists, eighteen private sector professional farm managers, land appraisers, and three co-operative elevator managers from Iowa. All served in a consulting-teaching role.

The collective farms had been under a communist "command driven" regime since 1948: over forty years and two generations away from making their own decisions. A telling remark came from one of the collective farm directors while trying to get a grip on a free market economy and on-site decision making: "We don't know what we don't know!" And from another seminar participant: "We lack the courage [I interpreted to mean confidence] to make decisions."

Having been involved in the design and implementation of this U.S. assistance project, I was pleased (in the face of many foreign aid program shortcomings) that USAID graded the Iowa State University project as one of the best, of more than 120 then carried out in that region. It feels good to be a part of a winning team!

Free Market Capitalism: Getting It Right

After completing a September 1993 consulting assignment in Czechoslovakia, Marianne and I took the train from Vienna, Austria, to Sorrento on the west coast of southern Italy. There we joined twenty other "students," mostly from the U.S., in a two-week Elderhostel. We learned about the early history and culture of that area including the remains of ancient Pompeii, a city buried in 79 A.D. when Mt. Vesuvius erupted. On leaving by train from nearby Naples, we traveled to Rome and Florence. An experience in Rome dramatized, once more, the uniqueness of our U.S. economic system. We stayed for four days at a modest hostel (pension) near the center of the city, just a block off the famous Republican thoroughfare. Eating out, getting a taste of Italy, presented the usual tourist's dilemma. I had found it annoying when friends returned from a European trip and complained that they couldn't buy a "good ol' American hamburger." To get the best feel of our host country, we related to the dictum: "When in Rome, do as the Romans do."

When moving about Rome, we didn't find the typical Italian restaurants especially friendly or inviting, and they were never crowded. Across the narrow street from our hostel, an Italian proprietor stood in front of his restaurant, casually waving a white dishtowel and by his mannerism pleading with people to come in. Thinking it would be nice to patronize this very Italian man's family restaurant, we stopped in for a lunch. While his restaurant was clean and could comfortably seat forty people, it seemed strange that we were his only customers. When our two sandwiches and two beers came to over eighteen dollars we understood why. Only four or five blocks away there was an attractive American McDonald's. But we purists wouldn't consider eating there! Noticing that younger natives were flocking to McDonald's, we decided to give it a try. The food was excellent, the service fine and the prices about half of what the Italian restaurant charged!

Italy ostensibly practices a free market and private enterprise economic system.

Although most scholars understand capitalism is an imperfect system and needs statutory regulation, they agree that the key element—marketing—must not be overlooked. If the restaurateurs of Rome were paying attention, McDonald's was dramatically showing how marketing is done! Thereafter, we had no qualms about eating at McDonald's in Rome.

My Cup Overflows

These stories—from birth in 1925, to youth spent as a farm kid, to years spent in the Great Depression, to service in World War II, to going through college, to getting married and having a family, to a work career—frame a chronology of experiences. My chosen and realized career in agriculture had many highs and very few lows. One "high" toward the end of my work career was receiving the D. Howard Doane Award from professional colleagues.

The Ages of Aquarius

Though a different application than draining water from farmland, this photo exemplifies the threads of progress that ran through rural America during much of the twentieth century. Taken in 1978, while I was in Laurens, Iowa, campaigning for election to the Iowa Senate, it reflects endeavors, woven indivisibly into the fabric of rural America and prominent throughout the western Corn Belt. These towns with their stores, supplies, blacksmith shops, "picture shows" (movies), and dependable people were indispensable to the surrounding farmers. And the farmers were indispensable to them. These water towers epitomize the transition of mechanics from a different but parallel perspective. The oldest, smallest, and least refined water tower was built in the late 1920s when new farm tools and machines were—at best—crude. The second tower was built in mid-1930s when more sophisticated farm tractors and machinery began to appear. The newest and largest tower, built in 1972, shows the ongoing drive to improve things mechanical. That, too, is very apparent in farm machines designed during these times.

What! Another Career?

Frequently in my life I have taken up the challenge to voice opinions on events and public policy issues. This includes open-forum opinion articles and editorial page essays. I was responsible for an in-house business newsletter from 1981 to 1994. After partial retirement in 1992, I had time to write a regular monthly column entitled "Philosophies" for the Storm Lake Pilot Tribune newspaper, until fully retiring in July 1999. A journalist I respect once said a "writer has to write." Maybe that's my paradox!

Risk and Reward

Similar to my own parents' lives, I wonder how many thousands of times the great migration to America disrupted and sometimes fractured individual lives. There are thousands of stories out there and many more have vanished with the passing of time. Some stories have had sad endings, but for the vast majority—including my own—the American experience worked out exceptionally well.

CHAPTER 32
TAKING MEASURE OF THE AMERICAN FRONTIER

The Atlantic seaboard states, being the first settled, needed the earliest property surveys and legal descriptions. The New England states, the earliest settled, were surveyed and measured by a rather rudimentary system of "metes and bounds," using either existing or designated land marks such as a rock (which may be moved) or a tree (that could be destroyed). Further south the more rural areas were surveyed using (measured out) land lots. As the level survey method was used, the curvature of the earth was not taken into consideration. The rectangular system corrected these shortcomings.

The Rectangular Survey

The rectangular survey system lays out boundaries and provides a legal description for farms and other parcels of land. This ingenious yet simple system is based on principles used by early ocean navigators who, by using a sextant, determined their location and direction of movement by surveying off Polaris (the North Star) and other stars. The system was devised primarily in the 1790s and Principle Meridians (PM) were established at certain fixed land points. After 1796, township and baselines emanated from the PMs. The system was broadly implemented by the early 1800s. President Thomas Jefferson was a leading advocate of the rectangular survey system. Lewis and Clark, to accurately plot land points along their expedition route, used the sextant and compasses to draw quite precise maps. The Federal government pressed to implement the rectangular survey for systematically laying out unsettled Government lands and territories.

The system has had profound impact on the economics and geography of the U.S. It defines how central and western states look today, how they were settled, subdivided, and deeded by the government, or sold privately to a land-hungry, expanding population. The system's surveys includes practically all land west of a north-south line including Alabama and Ohio or five-sixths of the lower forty-eight states. Most state and the U.S.-Canada boundaries were established by the rectangular survey. Where applicable, rivers (such as the Mississippi and numerous smaller ones) define farm, county, and state boundaries.

Nearly all the land in the upper Midwest is surveyed from the fifth Principle Meridian located in east central Arkansas.

The drawings and exhibits on the following pages graphically show how the rectangular survey worked and applied to describe farmland. It is the starting point for platting town and urban subdivisions to this day.

The starting point is a geographically designated point, a Principal Meridian (PM) from which all rectangular survey lines emanate. There are over twenty PMs in the U.S. The western Corn Belt is measured from the fifth PM located in east central Arkansas near Blackton.

A granite monument marking the exact point of the fifth Principal Meridian is located in the small (37.5 acres) Louisiana Purchase Historic State Park about three miles southeast of Blackton.

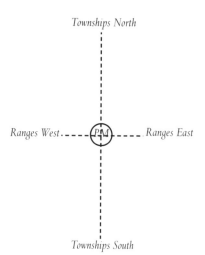

Townships North

Ranges West ----- PM ----- *Ranges East*

Townships South

Buena Vista: A typical Midwest county.

24 miles

6 miles

Brooke	Barnes	Lee	Poland	T-93N
Elk	Scott	Lincoln	Fairfield	T-92N
Nokomis	Washington	Grant	Coon	T-91N
Maple Valley	Hays	Providence	Newell	T-90N
R-38W	R-37W	R-36W	R-35W	

Brooke: A typical township.
Section numbering method shown.

6 miles

6	5	4	3	2	1
7					12
18		Brooke			13
19		Township			24
30			27		25
31					36

Township 93 North

Range 38 West

The plat below shows how a typical farm is laid out and legally described. This example is the farm my parents rented from 1923 to 1940. A section of land is one mile square, containing 640 acres. At the section line (boundary) each landowner gave the county a perpetual easement to a thirty-three feet (two rods) wide strip of land. This provides a sixty-six-foot "right of way" for public roads. The farm we lived on, shown on this page (in heavy outline), is legally described as: The southeast one-fourth (SE1/4) and the east one-half of the southwest one-fourth (E 1/2 SW 1/4) of Section 27, Township 93 North, Range 38 West of the fifth PM, Brooke Township, Buena Vista County, Iowa, and containing 240 acres more or less.

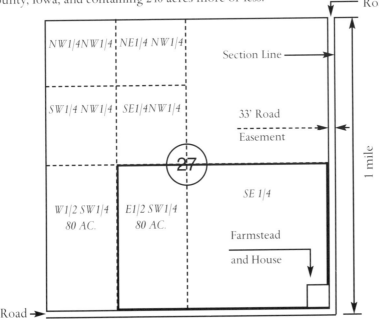

Because straight lines on a round earth eventually converge, "correction lines" are established. Imagine starting at the centerline (equator) of a basketball and pasting one-inch paper squares to cover the ball. As the north and south longitudinal lines come together at the earth's poles, these lines (or paper squares) will converge in surveying and need to be corrected in platting. The east-west latitude lines remain parallel to the equator. Correction lines are fixed about every sixty miles south to north in the Midwest. The town of Correctionville, Iowa is so named because it lies on a correction line, evidenced by a jog in Main Street.

Looking Closer to Home

The two aerial photos on the following pages show the same farm as the preceding plats, outlined with a dashed line. The photos (one taken in 1939 and the other in 1990) show in detail how the landscape was changed in the half-century. Changes were driven by farmers improving the land to increase the amount of tillable cropland, which meant less hay land, pasture, and wildlife habitat. This was accomplished largely by drainage (tiling) of wet land, plowing up native grassland and . clearing trees and native brush.

1939: Before

Looking at the two photos carefully reveals significant change. Starting at the northwest corner of the farm, the diagonal lying wet slew has been tiled and shaped into a seeded waterway. Moving clockwise (east) five gullies encroaching from the north have been tiled and leveled. Two small native prairie grass fields were plowed up and are now being row-cropped. When the gravel road along the east was graded and paved (circa 1965) the 500-foot string of 80-foot-tall cottonwood trees was destroyed. A small wet area just north of the farmstead has been tiled. The orchard north of the grove is gone; the grove is smaller, as is the farmstead area.

The south-bordering dirt road has been graded and graveled. Note the cow pasture creek has been tiled (drained) and the pastureland is now all in row crop. Trees along the road, maples by the pasture and tall cottonwoods further west, have all been removed. The large grove of trees, remaining from an abandoned farmstead, on what we called "the west eighty" (eighty acres) has been bulldozed (cleared). The 600-foot string of black walnut trees northwest of the grove has been removed, as have the willow trees to the north. The narrow native grass hay field has been tiled and now row cropped. The straight dotted lines (1990 photo) in two areas are terraces, installed for erosion control.

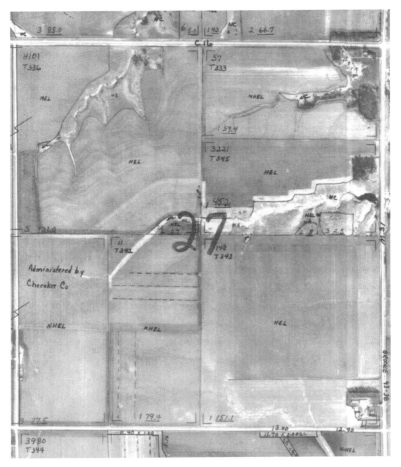

1990: After

Note the 200-foot-long wild plum brush toward the east center, along the field divide, has been cleared. The white oval spot to the south is a straw pile, blown by the grain separator at threshing time. By 1990 many fence lines have been removed, there are fewer fields but they are much larger.

The aerial photos clearly show the land use and cropping systems changed—although gradually—on this one farm. When you add highway construction, urban expansion (sprawl), and other land conversions to the equation, we will see how dramatically the nation's landscape has changed over the last fifty years.

Though a part of human nature fears change, it is the most constant event of life. That analogy is certainly applicable to twentieth century farming in the United States.

CREDITS

Figure 2.2: Dirt roads were a challenge for cars. Courtesy of Hank Zaletel and the Iowa Department of Transportation.

Figure 2.5: Smaller barns like this one were more typical. Courtesy of Arnie Hicks.

Figure 5.3: This photo of men scooping out the snowplow appeared in the Storm Lake *Pilot Tribune* newspaper February 10, 1936. Courtesy of the Storm Lake *Pilot Tribune*.

Figure 5.5: Severe hail damage to corn. Courtesy of Farmer's Mutual Hail.

Figure 6.1: Hen pheasant. Original illustration courtesy of Arne Paul Waldstein.

Figure 6.2: Red-tailed hawk. Courtesy of U.S. Fish & Wildlife Service.

Figure 6.3: White robin. Courtesy of Mary Hoefing.

Figure 6.4: Bull snake. Original illustration courtesy of Arne Paul Waldstein.

Figure 7.6: Two boys playing marbles. Courtesy of The Center for Western Studies, from *Boy Off the Farm*, 1982.

Figure 9.1: Little Sioux Valley Church. Courtesy of Little Sioux Valley Church.

Figure 15.1: Mower. Courtesy of Farm Progress Companies.

Figure 17.1: Primary tillage. Courtesy of J.C. Allen & Son.

Figure 17.2: Planting corn. Note check wire. Courtesy of Iowa State Press.

Figure 20.1: Scalding a hog. Careful and quick work prepared the hog for butchering. (circa 1933) Courtesy of Farm Progress Companies.

Figure 21.2: Baby chicks in brooder house. Courtesy of Farm Progress Companies.

Figure 21.3: A red fox. Courtesy of Roger A. Hill.

Figure 21.4: Horned owl. Original illustration courtesy of Arne Paul Waldstein.

Figure 22.3: A calf weaned from its mother drank from a pail. Courtesy of Farm Progress Companies.

"Philosophies" columns: Courtesy of the Storm Lake *Pilot Tribune*.